Clans and Castles

Book 1
in the Checkmate Series

CLANS AND CASTLES
Book I of the CHECKMATE Series
by p.m.terrell

Published by
Drake Valley Press
USA

ISBN 978-1-935970-41-5 (eBook)
ISBN 978-1-935970-40-8 (Trade Paperback)

Author's website: www.pmterrell.com

What Reviewers Say About p.m.terrell's Historical Books:

"Terrell's writing is impeccable, the subject well researched, the fiction well developed and innovative, but most of all, it is a 'can-not-put-down' read!" — Syndicated Reviewer Simon Barrett

"Author p.m.terrell transported me to another time and place as she drew me in...This is a book for readers of historical fiction and those who enjoy suspense, action and romance. Terrell's writing is strong, her research impeccable. The dialog helps the reader get into the story." —*Midwest Book Review*

"p.m.terrell weaves a great story of the Neely's and their journey during one of the most fascinating periods in Tennessee history. The work is well written and has a sharp eye for detail. A rich and inspiring story!" —Ken Feith, Nashville Government Metropolitan Archives, regarding *River Passage*

"With an amazing attention to detail, internationally acclaimed author p.m. terrell brings a new level of excellence to historical fiction." —Richard R. Blake, *Vine Voice*

"Needless to say, with terrell's love of Ireland and her intense action sequences we are gifted with yet another interesting history lesson" —Reviewer Donna Coomer, *Between the Lines*

SPECIAL THANKS

To Dr. Tyrone Bowes Ph.D. of Galway, Ireland and Company CEO of Irish Origenes, whose map, *The Clan Territories of Ireland*, is the most complete clan map I have encountered. The full color map and additional information is at www.irishorigenes.com.

To Anthony Christie for sharing his knowledge of castles, knights, swords and battles.

To Dr. Jonathan Eric Nance for the inspiration to write a new series.

And very special thanks to my father, John William Neelley, Sr., who always made sure we knew about our Neely/Neelley heritage.

MAP OF IRELAND'S CLANS

The Clan Territories of Ireland

www.irishorigenes.com

MAP OF INISHOWEN PENINSULA

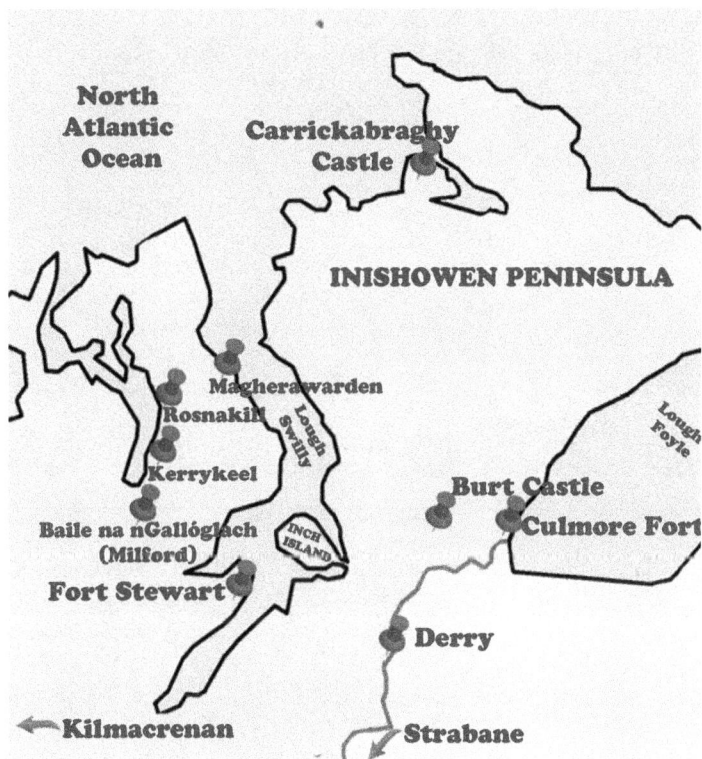

North
Atlantic
Ocean

Carrickabraghy
Castle

INISHOWEN PENINSULA

Lough
Foyle

Magherawarden

Rosnakill

Lough
Swilly

Kerrykeel

Baile na nGallóglách
(Milford)

INCH
ISLAND

Burt Castle

Culmore Fort

Fort Stewart

Derry

Kilmacrenan

Strabane

FOREWORD

Before the 12th century, Ireland had been divided into a number of kingdoms. Each kingdom had existed for centuries, sometimes warring with neighboring kingdoms and at other times becoming their allies. All of that was to change when the Normans invaded Ireland in the late 12th century, setting off centuries of conflict between Ireland and England, their neighbor to the east.

In 1588, Philip II of Spain dispatched 130 ships in a failed effort to invade England. Having been defeated at the Battle of Gravelines, the Spanish ships attempted to return home by taking a route around western Ireland when they were caught by a massive storm, blown off course and onto Ireland's western coast. Queen Elizabeth I believed the Spaniards were attempting to occupy Ireland and she sent a substantial force to stop the invasion. With rumors that Spain was sending additional troops to assist Ulster's Hugh O'Neill in driving out the English, Queen Elizabeth declared Ireland as an English colony.

Although a peace treaty was signed between England and Spain in 1604, England—now ruled by King James I—instituted a policy in which Scottish Lowlanders and English citizens were granted lands seized from the native Irish. Although this had been done in some instances dating back to the 12th century, the idea was to populate the island with Protestants loyal to the English Crown by establishing Plantations and displacing Irish citizens. Scottish Highlanders were forbidden from participating because they had caused as many problems for England as the Irish.

When I began this series, I planned to write about my Neely ancestors. However, my odyssey would take me into a pivotal era that transformed Ireland. By 1608 when William Neely, only 18 years old, joined Sir William Stewart of Wigtownshire to immigrate to Ulster, an uneasy peace had settled over Ireland; within months it would erupt into O'Doherty's Rebellion, led by the last Gaelic Irish King of Ireland, Cahir O'Doherty. I could not tell the story of William Neely without also telling the stories of Cahir O'Doherty, Mary Preston O'Doherty, Niall Garbh O'Donnell, Phelim MacDavitt, Sir George Paulet, Sir Henry Hart, Frances Hart, Sir William Stewart and many others that would change the course of Irish history, for their lives were to intersect into deadly confrontation in the spring and summer of 1608.

In many ways, the story of William Neely is the story of every ancestor to those of Scot-Irish descent, for they all traveled the same path from the Lowlands of Scotland to the Ulster province of Ireland, most between 1606 and 1652. If you are of Scot-Irish descent, this is part of your story…

1

1608, Wigtownshire, Scotland

The winds were fervent across the Irish Sea, pushing the waves into the shoreline with uncharacteristic intensity, stopped only by the jagged rock below before misting William Neely. He stood alone atop the cliff, his feet spread wide to withstand the gusts, his black hair caught as though a woman's fingers caressed them. He listened to the wail of the winds like so many sirens purring their song, their voices in unison, cajoling, luring, beguiling.

The final remnants of the sunset lingered on the water's surface, the horizon meeting in a blaze of orange that left him wondering where the sky ended and the sea began.

He heard tales of a land across the sea from his native Scotland; a land, though only twenty miles from where he stood, that was far different from the desolation that formed Wigtownshire. It was a land of a thousand shades of green, or so they said, of more grass than livestock could graze, a place where a man's eyes rested on beauty. On the rare clear day, he could barely make out a series of lumps on the distant horizon but try though he might, he could never quite make out the details, details that other men spoke about with awe and admiration.

He could not imagine such a place but surely the men he had encountered over the course of his eighteen years could not have fabricated a land that varied so little in the finest details, for men set years apart held the same tale. Someday, he would traverse those waters so his own hazel eyes could behold the splendor of which they spoke, though he didn't know how he would manage such a journey for surely it was nearly as impossible as reaching for the moon.

Wills thought he spotted the tall masts of a seafaring ship, but one couldn't be sure in the waning light. The vessels never ventured to this part of Scotland; though the land jutted out a fair distance from the rest of the country, it was said the serrated rocks below the water could split a ship in two and then finely chew the remains. No; they sailed a bit farther south to England, which was not far, or they ventured northward to a more hospitable part of Wigtownshire. For the most part, they visited the Lowlands where the land was flat and one could see for miles around, staying well away from the warring and suspicious Highlanders.

He shifted his feet as a particularly vicious gust seemed determined to set him on his seat. The ships were not the only thing that remained clear of this slice of his homeland. The rains did as well. Ah, he could see the storm clouds brewing over the sea, the white tuffs beginning to seethe with gray and black until the entire sky was dotted. And on occasion he could even see the torrents well out from shore like a wall of water falling where there was plenty of water to be had already. Then the clouds appeared to separate, some moving northward and some southward but always skirting around this peninsula as if warned away by some invisible force.

"Do you not hear me, boy?"

The voice jarred him out of his thoughts, forcing his gaze from the waning splendor to the starkness that lay behind him. Almost by instinct, he reached behind him to touch the pommel of the sword that rested against his back. As his father approached, he relaxed his grip but his body remained tensed.

"Are you dreaming again?" His father shouted to be heard above the rising winds. As he drew near, he reached out with a long, thin arm as if to box Wills' ear but his son's feet were swift and his hand sliced through the air instead. "The sun is gone and we've no time to waste," he continued in their native Gaelic, undaunted. "We've far to travel."

Wills grunted in reply and fell in line as they made their way along the shoreline, moving inward as the darkness swept in. Ahead of them, he could barely make out the silhouettes of his two brothers.

The four traveled silently, not wasting their collective energy on idle talk. Their attention was needed to maintain their balance across the rugged land. It seemed to transform beneath their feet like a living, breathing creature; the rocks that extended above the soil like fingers intent on tripping them up while the moss and the bog between the stone worked to suck them under.

Ah, to be sure the bog had lost a good bit of its power as the drought had dragged on year after year, but there it was, belching at his feet as if it was seething and writhing just beneath his worn boots. Perhaps it sensed in his slender body some semblance of moisture and it sought to drag him under and rob him of it, requiring it to stay alive.

The beautiful sunset upon which he had gazed was now but a memory, and the moon had not yet been able to escape the grasp of the clouds that extinguished whatever light the crescent might have offered. When he could, he glanced upward and tried to locate the stars that would guide them northeastward, eventually leaving the sea—but not his dreams—behind.

With a muted sun's warmth gone, the chill set into his bones. Like his father and brothers, he wore a threadbare shirt that had already been thinned with use by the time he had received it. His breeches were not much better and a good bit of skin was left exposed before his tatty leather boots warmed his calves. He could feel the ground through the wafer-thin soles and now as the skies grew darker he relied more on his feet to tell him whether he walked on rock or bog, dried-out grass or cushiony moss.

The land was laid out around them flat and barren, which was why they traveled at night under the protection of the darkness. One could travel for a day without encountering another soul, whether human or animal, and yet one could also see to the horizon in daylight, easily spotting someone's approach. The elders, of which were scant, told of a day in which Wigtownshire had been filled with forests, but when pressed, they would not or could not say whether they themselves had seen them or if they had only been told a myth with no connection at all to reality. Oh, and for certain there was wood furniture; the tiny home in which they lived had a table and chairs, and the house itself had a bit of wood holding together the mud and stone, but surely a forest would have had more wood than that. He didn't know since he had never seen one.

It was said that the soil was thin in these parts. His mother and sisters grew some herbs and if they managed to survive, they were used more for medicinal purposes than for food. Crops were impossible; complaints abounded that the land was too wet, too parched, too boggy or too rocky. They subsisted primarily on lamb. The creatures provided nearly everything they needed to survive, from their clothing to their blankets to every meal they devoured. And it was the lamb that had brought them into the darkness and on a journey that would last through the night; if they were lucky, they would spot their home at the end of their return as the sun rose the next morning.

Wills' thoughts eventually faded with the kind of numbness that sets in on a lengthy trek, enveloped in total silence for even the birds had fled to more hospitable terrain. The hours dragged on, marked only by the occasional grunt as a brother stubbed a toe on a particularly loathsome outcropping or another became bogged down in the muck. Eventually, their blankets came out; so thin the grime was part of the fabric holding it all together, but enough to wrap about their shoulders and torso, dropping downward in an anemic attempt to shield their legs from the bitter cold.

They moved with precision toward a distant neighbor until at last Wills' older brother James held up his hand. He stopped in his tracks, along with his brother Rory, while his father stealthily moved up beside James. Wills tried to follow the direction in which James pointed, narrowing his eyes in an attempt to focus more acutely on the landscape. And there in the distance, he spotted them: tiny, almost imperceptible figures moving. He might have missed it, had the land not been so bleak, so flat and so devoid of life. But now as he watched them, it was as if a paternal instinct rose within him.

Thus would begin the most dangerous moments of their mission. Like the others, he withdrew his sword from the tattered sheath and they each spread apart as they made their final approach. Unlike their hike, they traveled close to the ground, sprinting one moment and kneeling the next; there was not even the semblance of a bush behind which to hide.

An occasional bleat carried over the winds, echoing in the silence, but most of the sheep appeared to be sleeping or grazing. There were no dogs guarding them; there wasn't much point to it, since the bear and the fox had died out long before Wills had arrived on this earth; perhaps they too were only a myth like the tales of forests. Besides, dogs had to be fed and there was only occasionally enough sustenance for humans. The sheep were endured because the sheep kept them all alive.

They converged a short distance from the herd. They lay flat on their stomachs, their swords at the ready beside them.

"How many did they steal from us?" Wills' father Thomas asked.

Rory pointed to a small flock off to their left. "About that many."

Thomas turned to Wills. "You can count, boy; how many?"

"They stole ten."

"And many are there?" he asked, nodding his head toward the flock.

Wills narrowed his eyes further as he sought out the dingy white sheep in the gloom. "Sixteen."

"Then leave six. We came for what they stole and nothing more."

Ignoring the larger herd to their right and in front of them, they moved off to the left. They remained low to the ground until James gave the signal that there were no shepherds about. They drew themselves upright as they got nearer, fanning out once again to move beside and behind the flock.

Wills watched their behavior with an expert eye; he had been shepherding lambs from the time he could walk. They had acute hearing and were easily startled, which could cause them to bolt. They also had better eyesight than a man's, or so it was said, though they preferred to remain away from the shadows. But they were also easily led. It took identifying one of the flock's leaders, approaching them with the surety of a shepherd, and leading that one in the direction in which they needed to go. The others would follow. To be sure, it was easier with a dog, especially when the herd was large but this one was manageable with only two or three for each. The four of them had been needed more for the fight, should the thieves be about.

James gave the signal for them all to stop and they complied without hesitation. He kept his hand raised in the air as still as a statue, his head cocked. Wills instinctively bent his own head as if it would help focus his hearing. Somewhere in the distance, he heard the faint sounds of a man's voice.

His sword was still held at the ready; though James had signaled the absence of shepherds, it wouldn't be the first time they had been surprised. This back-and-forth had gone on for generations. The neighbors stole their sheep and they retrieved them. Then the neighbors stole them back plus a few more if they could find them, and so it went. With jobs as scarce as a tree, this was the way they eked out their living.

As he scanned the horizon, he thought at first that his eyes were playing tricks on him; for there, rising just off shore were three tall masts rising like spires. As the clouds shifted, the crescent moon peeked through with pinpoint precision, illuminating the ship as men toiled to bring down the sails. The occasional shouts had awakened distant neighbors and now the four men watched as the thieves left their small home and made their way away from them and toward the shoreline.

James signaled; now was the time. He moved in first and as the sheep began to panic, the others surrounded them, herding them into a smaller, tighter group preventing their escape. Every second counted now; one glance in their direction would bring the thieves with swords drawn and it would not end until blood was shed and one side retreated.

As the shouts from the ship grew louder, the herd was driven southward, the men running beside them with their torsos parallel to the ground, keeping their bodies no taller than the sheep, until they were out of sight.

2

Dawn was peeking over the distant horizon, the Lowland delta shrouded in heavy mists by the time the sheep were herded into a small open plain. It appeared otherworldly, Wills thought as he counted the sheep once more, their dingy white wool blending in so seamlessly with the mists that they appeared more like apparitions than living creatures. He caught his father out the corner of his eye, stooped and exhausted, trudging slowly in the direction of their tiny home. No doubt Wills' mother would be there awaiting his return with a bucket of water boiling over the hot heather they used as kindling in the fire pit, and a scoop of herbs with which to make a tea.

"Wills, you watch the herd and I'll relieve you midday," Rory said. He was slightly taller than Wills and his hair was lighter; his mother's shade of deep brunette. His eyes were sharp and his jaw squared.

"I will not be staying," Wills declared.

"Is it on account of the ship?" Rory asked, rolling his eyes.

"It is. I'll be going back."

"You would be going back all that way to take a second look at a ship." The statement was said with more than a little disdain.

"I am."

"Did you happen to notice the flag she flew?" One eyebrow shot up.

"I did. It would be an English ship, she is."

"I do not understand you, William Neely. I wish for once you would plant your feet on the ground and take your head out of the clouds."

"And what does it matter whose ship she is?" Wills asked calmly. He waved his hand toward the south. "Not a half days' journey is all of England. Isn't it why we speak English as well as Gaelic?"

Rory spat. "You cannot trust them. They would just as soon take all we have and leave us to die as long as our wretched, filthy bodies are not left on their doorstep."

"Take all we have? And what is that, precisely?"

Rory pointed toward the sheep. "The herd, for one. Our home for another."

Wills snorted. "Who knows whose sheep they are? I do not see any bearing our name. And as for the house, it does not belong to us. We are tenants there and any day the laird can order us gone, just as they have moved our neighbors in the past."

"Ah, and who would that have been but the English? High and mighty, they are, in their fine, fancy carriages. They look at us as though we were muck, something less than human. If they hate us so, why is it that they don't leave us alone?"

"You know the answer to that. Men have fought for power and ownership for as long as they have walked the face of this earth as if he who owns the most will alone acquire the keys to the Gates of Heaven." Wills spotted someone moving through the mist just past his brother's shoulder. As Rory continued lambasting the English, he narrowed his eyes until his sister Elizabeth came into view. His tensed muscles relaxed as he watched her. Beth was a tiny thing, barely fifteen years old, a mere slip of a girl with long, straight brunette hair and vivid blue eyes. When she smiled, which she did frequently, her entire face lit from within. Now she carried a basket over her arm, no doubt looking for heather or perhaps a truffle or two, which on rare occasions lay hidden in the boggy soil amongst the withered remains of ancient roots.

"And who will watch the sheep?" Rory was asking, exasperated.

"You know as well as I, no one will take them in the daylight. They will come in the night, as they always do."

"Where are you going?" Beth asked as she joined them.

"We saw an English ship just north of here," Rory said before Wills had a chance to reply. "And now this dreamer thinks he can walk back there and take a look at it."

"Oh, Rory," Beth said in a soft, lilting voice, "what harm can there be in that?"

"Father has warned him against it. He is to stay clear of the English—and clear of the Highlanders. And they will not be far from that ship, I guarantee it. And what if they conscript him into the King's service?"

Wills chortled. "You do not like the Highlanders, either?"

"You know I do not. *We* do not. They are heathens, barbarians."

He turned away and began walking northward along the same path he had taken through the night. He waved his hand in the air and called over his shoulder, "Tell Mother I will be back by dusk."

"Oh, let me walk with you," Beth said, hurrying to catch up with him. "Just for a little way."

He didn't respond but he didn't object to her presence, either. Truth was, she was a calming influence; on him and on the whole family.

"Tell me about the ship, Wills," she begged, pulling her plaid about her shoulders in an effort to fight the chill. "Is it like all the others?"

"I don't know," he answered. "It was dark and I did not get a good look at it."

"Is it English, as Rory says?"

"Perhaps. Most likely." He stole a look at her out the corner of his eye. She was watching her steps, hopping from one moss to the next in order to avoid slipping into the softer bog. "There are English troops in the Highlands," he went on, "and the ships bring supplies to them."

"And what are they doing in the Highlands?" Beth asked.

Wills smiled. It was a conversation they had again and again, like a fairytale told to a child who knew the story by heart. "Well," he started, "it has been six years since the death of Queen Elizabeth of England. And Elizabeth's cousin Mary, Queen of Scots, had a son named James, who became the King of Scotland when he was just a wee lad of thirteen months."

"Yes," Beth said, "James is the great-great-grandson of King Henry VII."

"Very good," Wills commended. "Which is why, upon Elizabeth's death, James ascended to the throne of England. So now he is King of both Scotland and England, though the two have not been united. Insurrection has seen to that."

"And," she added, "he is also the King of Ireland."

"He is at that."

"So why do the Highlanders continue to fight the English, if their king is also king of England? Aren't they happy?"

"They want total independence from Britain," Wills said thoughtfully. "The hatreds run deep, most especially in the Highlands." They grew silent, each with their own thoughts. The winds rolled in from the sea, sweeping the mist more thickly about them and causing Beth to shudder in the cold. His thoughts turned to the Highlanders and the centuries-old tales of warfare, failed and bitter quests to rid their lands of English influence.

"I do not know why our brothers hate the Highlanders so," Wills said. "They are Scots, after all."

"Ah, but every people needs someone who is more lowly than they are, 'eh?" Her voice was soft. "I suppose it is that way everywhere. Each people pick another people that they can point at and say, 'Ah, but we are better than them over there.' Otherwise, if they are the same as us, then there is no one lower, which would make us equal to the lowest of the low." She stopped to pick some heather along the path.

Wills continued walking and after a few moments he heard her rushing up behind him to catch up. When she was once again beside him, he said, "I met a Highlander once."

"No."

"I did. I just kept walking one day until the ground was no longer flat; it was rolling. And in the distance, I could see the Highlands."

"What do they look like?"

"Very tall. Very formidable."

"And did you go there, to their village?"

He shook his head. "It is said they war among themselves and in order to venture onto their lands, you must obtain permission first."

"But how do you obtain permission, if you cannot go there to ask for it?"

He laughed. "I don't know."

"What was the Highlander like?"

"He was very kind, actually. Friendly, in fact. He was in the rolling hills, as was I, and each of us asked the other if that was his land."

"So you spoke the same language?"

"Of course we did. We are Scots. Though," he added, "he did have a thicker accent. I thought we were very different from the English until I met him. Now I see how the English have influenced us in the Lowlands, influenced our speech and way of life."

"What did he look like?"

"Very tall. Much taller than I. And his arms looked to be twice as long."

"No."

"'Tis true."

"So you came away thinking what? That we are more like the Highlanders or more like the English?"

He walked in silence for a moment as he considered her question. "Neither one," he said. "We are crammed in between the two. On the one hand, we have the Highlanders—large, rugged, warring. It is said they are influenced by the lands to the northeast of them, on the other side of the North Sea, where the men are twice the size of the English."

"Giants."

"Ah," he chuckled, "giants indeed... And on our other side, there are the English. Very proper, very orderly. Even when they are not."

Beth laughed. Her laughter sounded like tiny bells. "And there we are, right in the middle."

"Neither Highlander nor English." He paused and then mused, "I wonder why our family dislikes the English so?"

"Why, because they have more than we do," Beth answered. "Every people must have someone they begrudge, someone they can blame when their lot in Life is not what they believe it should be, don't you think?"

He grunted but as they continued on in silence, he considered her words. Only fifteen and yet her soul seemed so much older, so much wiser. Of course it was true, what she said. Everyone needed to point to someone with power and blame them for their sorry lot in life, and everyone needed someone else to point to and declare they are better than that group over there. So the Lowlanders had the English they despised for having power and finer things, and the Highlanders they despised for being lower than they.

"And what of the Irish?" Wills said as once again Beth hurried to catch up with him after stopping to gather more heather.

"The Irish." She spoke the words in a hushed voice. "It is said they are very, very small, barely as tall as my waist."

He laughed. "Surely not."

"Oh, but it is true. They practice magic and spells. The men are hunched over like gnomes. The women do not look like women at all. And they smell."

His laughter continued. "Why do they smell?"

"I do not know, but they do."

They reached the edge of a dried-up lough and Wills stopped. "You had best turn back now," he said. "You mustn't get too far from home."

"I know." She sighed. "I wish I could come with you, Wills. I wish I could see the ship, too."

"One day, Beth. One day."

"Will you tell me all about it when you get back?"

"Of course I will."

"I will want to know everything."

"I will tell you everything."

"Every last detail."

"Every last detail. I promise." He bent to kiss her on the forehead. "Now, off with you. If anyone asks about me—"

"I will not tell them anything," she interjected.

"Ah." For a fleeting moment, a memory rose in his mind's eye; a thrashing the likes of which he had never had before nor since, meant to be a lesson not to venture far from home without an elder's permission. Then just as quickly, it faded. No doubt Rory had already told their father, if he was not sleeping off the night's work, and the thrashing was awaiting him no matter how far he walked nor what he ventured to see. "Thank you, Beth."

She looked down at her basket. "I'll go back toward home," she said reluctantly. "The heather is harder to come by these days, and we need it to fuel the fire…" Her voice faded.

As she remained there, he began to walk again, this time with greater strides. Sometime later, he turned to look back but she was gone, disappeared into the heavy mists.

3

Wills lay flat on his stomach, his chin resting on his folded forearms as he watched the ship in the distance. He had ventured as close as he dared go without detection, and for quite some time he'd lain almost perfectly still as he observed the activity. Though the sun was high, it did little to warm him; the chilled winds penetrated his thin clothing to rake against his bare skin, but he barely noticed it. He was focused on the ship itself in an attempt to memorize every aspect of it, as well as the wagons and soldiers who had been working for hours to unload its cargo.

The ship was huge, an ocean-faring ship for sure, he thought. It had three masts and while moored, the sails had been taken down and tied around them. It must be a sight to see when the sails were unfurled, and he hoped they would do it soon so he could witness it.

The English flag flew lofty and proud in the high winds. It was the first time he had seen the Union Jack, as King James had only ordered its design and use two years before; it was to be used for maritime, which in his mind further confirmed the ship was an oceangoing vessel. The flag designers had taken the previous English flag of red and white known as Saint George's Cross and superimposed it on the Scottish flag of blue and white, known as Saint Andrew's Cross or the Saltire. Since the blue cross was diagonal and the red cross upright, the result was rather striking.

The ship's deck was brimming with activity as the sailors brought up cargo from the hold. English soldiers had arrived on shore with a number of wagons and as quickly as the boxes were taken off the ship, they were packed on the wagons. Several had already left for the north; he supposed the supplies were intended for the Highlands and the English soldiers serving there.

Occasionally, he heard shouts and instructions. Gaelic was his first language and English his second, but since the latter was only spoken in the presence of the English, he had scant opportunity to use it. Now he strained to hear the words, interpreting them in his head as a bit of a game he played with himself.

The uppermost section of the hull contained a row of openings and if the light hit just right, he could barely make out the outline of the cannons. A warship then, he thought with awe; a warship delivering supplies to the English soldiers. The thrill of it made the thrashing he would receive well worthwhile.

He was so intent on studying the vessel that he did not hear the man approach from behind until he demanded in a loud voice, "And what have we here?"

Startled, he spun around.

"What is your name, boy?"

"William," he answered. "William Neely, sir."

"You speak English." It was more of a statement than a question, but he appeared surprised that Wills had understood him.

"Aye, sir."

"Are you a Highlander?"

"No, sir."

"Where is your home?"

"Wigtownshire, sir."

The man's eyes narrowed. He was short and stocky, his face grizzled and worn. "You are far from home."

"Aye, sir."

"Why are you spying on us?" He nodded toward the ship and the soldiers.

"I—I wasn't spying, sir." His mind raced. A spy could be quartered, his head impaled as a warning to others.

"Who sent you?"

"No one, sir. I came on my own. I-I saw the ship and I wondered if it was true, if you had been to lands away from Scotland."

The man leaned on the stock of a harkbus, his feet spread apart. He appeared to be weighing Wills' responses.

"I have heard tell of Ireland," Wills continued, his enthusiasm causing his words to spill more quickly "They say there are trees everywhere, that it is very green. They say it is beautiful."

A slight smile played across his lips. "What they say is true."

"And do you sail there? On that ship?"

"We do."

Wills pulled himself into a seated position and squinted up at the man. "I heard tell that a ship like that found a new world across the ocean. Is it true?"

"Ah, that would be the Godspeed. No, this ship is quite a bit smaller, I'm afraid. This one is about a hundred paces."

"A hundred paces." Wills whispered the words as if they were magical. "And the Godspeed?"

"About a hundred and fifty paces, more or less."

"A hundred and fifty paces. I have never seen a ship that large."

"Nor are you likely to," he chuckled, "unless you happen to be in London or a similar port." He held out his hand. "Stand up, lad."

Wills took his hand. His palm was rough as leather, the fingers stubby, as the man pulled him to his feet with ease. "Will you tell me about the things you have seen?" he asked.

At that, the man smiled. It was a small smile, to be sure, his lips kept tight, but Wills felt a little more certain that he would not be dragged in and quartered as a spy. For the better part of the afternoon, until the sun was beginning to dip on the far western horizon, he asked the man every question he had pondered on the long, still nights when his brothers and sisters were sleeping. He learned his name was Archibald MacGruder but he was called Archie and he, too, was from the Scottish Lowlands, albeit further northeast than Wigtownshire. They moved easily between Gaelic and English, Wills picking up new words as they talked and forming pictures in his mind that seemed so fantastic they bordered on otherworldly.

Archie had not seen the New World but he had met another who had, and he relayed information about the Godspeed's journey across the ocean, how it had taken the better part of five months, and what they had found there in a place they named Jamestown in honor of King James. Wills drilled him on lands closer to Scotland, lands he knew he would never see himself. He was astonished to learn that if the Irish Sea was calm, which it rarely was, the western coast of Ireland was only a half day away, slightly less than the time it had taken him to walk to where he stood now.

At last, the man motioned toward the ship. "We sail tonight," he said. "And I must bid you farewell."

"Aye." Wills eyed the distant horizon. The sun had not yet set but its rays had become a muted yellow, their surroundings appearing as if a blanket was being laid upon it. "And I must return home."

Archie offered his hand and shook Wills' hand with a hearty chuckle. "I hope to see you again someday, boy."

"Aye, that would be exciting. You can tell me then where else you have gone, of the things you have seen."

"That I will."

With that, he began a long stride back to the ship. Wills watched for a moment and then turned away from the vessel. He hadn't slept in more than a day and a half. The excitement of all that he had learned and seen was enough to keep the tiredness at bay for now, but it would be a long and tiring—and hungry—trek home.

He had only walked a few paces, however, before he was stopped in his tracks. "Balloch." The name was uttered in both surprise and apprehension.

Balloch did not reply but stared into Wills' face with steely gray eyes. He was a good ten years' older than Wills and a head taller. His shoulders were broad, his arms muscular. It was said his family were Gallowglass; they had mixed with the Highlanders and they in turn, with the Norsemen, resulting in men that were much larger and more formidable than the English and those that lived along the English border, like the Neelys. Though there was always a chill in the Scottish air, his arms were bare and he seemed not to notice the cold. A movement caused Wills' eyes to wander down his torso, noting the man's muscular bare legs—and the sword he held in one hand.

Wills pulled his eyes away and searched the ground around them; there were no others with Balloch, which could be his saving grace. A small flock of sheep were grazing in the pasture where the others had been taken in the darkness of night; and now that the sun was close to setting, those that had stolen the Neely sheep before they had taken them back were likely to mount a group to retake them yet again—and most likely, led by Balloch.

He pulled his sword from its sheath at the very moment that Balloch swept into the en garde. Steel met steel with a clang that reverberated over the open air. The power with which Balloch attacked was fueled by both his physical strength and a vicious brutality for which his entire clan was known. Too late, Wills realized the foolishness of returning alone to the very spot where they had seized back their herd.

The thought was fleeting as the swords drew apart for the briefest of moments before the larger man lunged. Wills was shorter, much thinner and more agile and he leapt backward in a quick retreat. The point of the man's sword came so close to his chest that he could feel the air rippling off it. Quickly, before Balloch could recover, he advanced, swinging his blade to catch the man's flesh along the side of his torso.

Balloch's thunderous grunt was a sign that the injury had done nothing more than enrage him and he lunged again. Again, Wills jumped back in retreat, wielding his sword instinctively to catch and stop the man from advancing further. They stood so close to one another, he could see the perspiration along Balloch's brow and knew he could see his own in return, could smell the sweat that now ran down his back.

There would be no retreat, no opportunity to run. It was stand and fight. The end might be inevitable but he would go down swinging.

Their swords clashed again and again, the reverberation causing the bones and muscles in Wills' arm to quiver. He felt every blade of grass, every pebble and stone, as his feet shifted and danced. He was forced backward across the rough terrain with each strike but again and again he deflected the blow, bobbing inward to graze Balloch's torso twice more.

They were both panting now, the strain bubbling on Balloch's lips as he forced the man to chase his more lithesome form in a broad circle. Back and forth they went, advancing, retreating, lunging, grappling, the tiredness wearing on his body. He saw the larger man's movements as if time had slowed; knew his intent before the sword was barely raised, twisted his body to make himself a leaner target. And as Balloch's motion became more sluggish with his own exhaustion, he was able to dart into the openings he left until the man's shirt was crisscrossed with rips, the blood turning the material red.

And as the swords met once more, Wills was forced to grab onto his with both hands. He knew it was the wrong thing to do, knew it as he was moving into the position; it exposed his torso, making him a broader target. But Balloch's arms were longer and stronger and he could no longer battle him as an equal. The steel advanced along the blade until the points kissed and air was met.

With a bellow that came from deep within, he lunged under Balloch's still outstretched arm. The larger man jerked backward and to the side in an instinctual retreat. The blade found its mark not in his chest but in his side. Wills could feel it moving through the soft tissue and hard muscle as if the blade was merely an extension of his own hand, until it had advanced inside Balloch almost to the cross-guard.

The larger man's sword shook above him and Wills withdrew his own sword quickly, catching the others' steel before he could recover. The sword was knocked from Balloch's hand and as it sailed through the air in a plummet to the ground, he anticipated his opponent's hands reaching out to grasp the sword grip before it was too late.

Instead, Balloch's knees buckled under him and he crumpled to the ground in front of him, both hands reaching to stem the tide of red blood that spurted from his side.

But before he could recover, Wills' sword was snatched from him. As he whirled around, he found himself surrounded by six English soldiers.

4

His feet barely touched the gangplank as he was hauled aboard the ship. None of the men had spoken since they had apprehended him and given his weakened state and their number, he thought it futile to resist. Two had grasped him, one on either arm, half-carrying and half-marching him to the vessel. He had no idea where his sword was nor how it had been wrenched from him but as he came aboard and saw the scores of men gathering around them, he knew it no longer mattered. His fate was no longer his to decide.

He had seen the captain watching from the quarterdeck as they approached and now Wills was shoved to a spot just below where the captain stood. He was of medium build, his shoulders appearing more substantial due to the epaulettes and cut of his uniform. His hair was such a pale blond that it verged on white, but the bit of side whiskers he sported were deep auburn, as were his brows. His face was angular, his large irises causing his eyes to appear prominent against his pale skin. He stood with his feet planted apart, both

hands resting upon the banister of the quarterdeck as
he peered down at him. Archie stood slightly behind
him.

"Do you know who I am, boy?" the captain called
out.

A hush swept through the men. Wills was reluctant
to pull his eyes away from the captain's face, so he
sensed more than saw the semi-circle that had formed
around him. The two men that had dragged him from
the meadow onto the ship had relinquished their hold
upon him and had stepped back, blending with the
crowd behind him.

"Aye, sir," Wills said. His voice carried, his timbre
deep and sure, concealing both his apprehension and
his fatigue. "You are William Stewart of Wigtownshire."

In an instant, Wills saw the man's history flash
through his mind; William Stewart was the brother of
Alexander, the Earl of Galloway who had been
designated as the 1st Lord Garlies only the year before.
Said to be distant relatives of King James himself, the
family was one of Scottish noblemen and great wealth.
Wills had seen Stewart on occasion in Wigtownshire,
though he was so far beneath his standing that he had
never come close enough to speak with him and if he
had, he didn't know what he might have said to such a
man. Unlike some of the other noblemen that treated
the average Scot as subservient, he was rumored to be
a man of compassion as well as ambition.

"And you are William Neely, I am told." Wills noted
that though they both spoke Gaelic as their native
tongue, he spoke in precise English to him.

Wills glanced at Archie, who nodded his head slightly
as though encouraging him to respond. "Aye, sir."

"Your father is a good man."

He was surprised at the mention of his father and
for a fleeting moment, he envisioned him leaving their

humble home each morning for important work with the Laird, though he never spoke of what precisely he did for him.

"What do you think your father would do if he knew of your antics here?" Captain Stewart was saying.

Wills swallowed. "He would thrash me for being here and commend me for winning."

Laughter rippled through the crowd and he thought he saw the slightest smile tug at the corner of the captain's mouth before he once again assumed a stern countenance.

"And why were you fighting?"

Wills looked beyond the ship to the meadow some distance away. Balloch was seated on the ground with two men kneeling on either side of him. A large black bag was opened beside one man that was busily wrapping Balloch's naked torso with a wide cloth. At least he was not dead, Wills thought. Killing a man under any circumstance could warrant hanging or worse.

"He stole sheep under the care of my father," Wills said. "And we stole them back early this morn."

Again, laughter rose behind him but as the captain raised one hand in silence, it quickly died away.

"And where are the sheep now?"

"Wigtownshire, sir."

"Am I to believe you walked here from Wigtownshire, stole back your sheep, herded them all the way back and then returned?"

"Aye, sir. It's the truth."

"How long did that take you?"

"We left from Wigtownshire at sunset, sir. Almost precisely this time yesterday."

Captain Stewart seemed to accept his responses but Wills couldn't be certain; while his brow did not furrow and he did not frown, his expression remained immobile and therefore unreadable. Wills' right arm was throbbing now with the efforts of the sword fight but he dared not rub the offending member. Instead, he held his chin just a little higher as he squared his shoulders.

"And these sheep, they belonged to the laird?"

"Aye, sir. The Laird of Broughton, sir."

"And I assume the Laird will confirm this?"

"Aye, sir," he answered quickly. "The Neelys are not sheep thieves, sir."

To this, Captain Stewart chuckled softly. "No. They are not." He looked down upon Wills for a long moment. "Where did you learn to fight like that?"

Wills stole another glance at Balloch, who remained seated on the ground. "I did not have a choice, respectfully, sir. He attacked me."

"That is not what I asked you. I asked where you learned to fight."

"My father taught me. And I spar on occasion with my brothers—in jest, that is."

He studied him for a long moment. Wills fought the urge to rub his right arm. Despite his efforts to appear unscathed, it was pounding now and felt as if it weighed three times its normal weight. His shoulders were aching as well, and the exhaustion was almost enough to send him to his knees.

"Why did you return here after bringing the sheep home? Did you forget something?"

"No, sir. I came to see the ship, sir."

Captain Stewart half-turned toward Archie, who smiled slightly. His movement was almost undetectable and a second later, he turned back to Wills. "So I hear."

They stood for another extended moment; the captain standing now with both hands held behind his back as if he was something to be studied, and Wills acutely aware of the threadbare clothes he wore. Self-consciously, he realized his clothing was splattered with blood but thankfully, none of his own; it was truly a miracle, he thought with a sudden sense of pride, that he had not even been nicked.

"I am in need of men like you," the captain said at last. Before Wills could respond, he continued, "We set sail tonight for Ireland. I need men good with a sword, men who will swear allegiance to King James and who are willing to fight—and die, if need be—in the King's service."

After a moment of silence, Wills realized he was awaiting a reply. His mind clouded with confusion. Was he offering him a position?

"I say, William Neely of Wigtownshire," Captain Stewart said with a barely concealed smile, "Are you willing to join the ranks of King James' men and set sail with us to Ireland?"

His mouth was as dry as a bone. He no longer felt the pain of his arm or of his shoulder, but it was as if his entire body had gone completely numb. He felt the men's presence around him acutely; the solid wood deck beneath his feet, the gentle sway as the water lapped against the ship, and the sunset just beginning to form on the distant horizon. Over there, beyond the Irish Sea, was Ireland, the land that looked like emeralds itself; a wilderness, so they said where trees grew in great groves, where fruit could be picked off the trees, where a man could make his mark upon the world.

But it also harbored a people not unlike the Scottish Highlanders; smaller, perhaps, even gnome like, or so he'd heard, but fierce fighters, bloodthirsty and as mystical as the Celtic oracles.

"Aye, sir," Wills said. His voice rang out clear and strong. "I will fight for King James, wherever you may take me."

5

If Wills thought that sleep and nourishment would be afforded him in short order, he was sadly mistaken. After swearing the Oath of Allegiance to King James VI of Scotland, who also now bore the title King James I of England, he was handed back his sword and put to work. All the cargo that had been removed through the day had left the deck in a state of dust and grime, and he was handed a mop and a bucket and ordered to clean the decks until they shone. Women's work, he thought as he set about the task, and he was much above it, as he had just proven with his victory over Balloch, but what was he to do now? His life was not his own, if it ever had been, and the sideways glances of the other men told him that he would be watched and closely.

While the aroma of hot food over open flames teased his stomach and tickled his nostrils, he was kept toiling. The arm that had been under so much strain as he held his ground against Balloch was now constantly moving back and forth in a mind-numbing exercise from one end of the ship to the other. To be sure, there were others given the same task and every now and again, he peered upward from his work to find them hard at work just as he was, but they never came close enough to one another to speak.

When the laughter and talk of the older hands reached his ears and he realized all but three, himself included, were eating their fill of fresh-cooked mutton, he thought certainly he was close to collapse. Yet he toiled on, never complaining, never inquiring when he was to eat. Life in Scotland was tough and often cruel. In the protracted winter months when food became scarce and clothing was pitifully inadequate, he learned that complaints were not only unproductive but could often result in getting his ears boxed and even less food, if that was humanly possible.

So he set his mind on the wood beneath his feet, clearing the grime until it came as close to shining as he imagined it could be.

He was dumping yet another pail of murky water over the side of the ship when footsteps approaching him from behind caused him to turn. It was Archie, and he was bearing a plate of food.

"Take your fill, boy," Archie said as he shoved the plate into his hands.

Wills did not need to be invited twice. He dug into the food with the passion of a man that had not eaten in a day and a half; indeed with the punishment his body had taken it felt more to him like an entire week without both food and sleep. It was, indeed, mutton; not much of the meat but much of the taste as it floated in a thin gravy with strange white lumps.

Archie chuckled. "One would think you had never seen a potato before."

Wills stopped chewing and pushed the white member around inside his mouth. "That is a potato?"

"It is."

"Potatoes are the devil's poison. Nightshade, is it not?"

"Spoken like a true Scot. Calvinist, I wager?"

Wills hesitated. Religion was never to be spoken about; not without a sword in the hand and a fight at the ready. And yet, with one statement he had given away his faith.

"It is alright, boy. I have known plenty. And you are right to remain silent." He picked up a white chunk from Wills' plate and held it up for both to examine. "You will find the land in Ireland is tough to farm, same as it is in the Scottish Highlands. But these vegetables grow, and they grow well. The Catholics are forced to plant them but they hedge their bets and sprinkle holy water on them as they go in the ground, and for that they declare they have been rid of the devil and are safe to eat."

"So, is this—?"

"It will not kill you, and it will not cause your soul to turn evil, if that is what you are asking. Not," he added, "if you eat it like this. But beware of eating the raw potato, most especially the eyes; for they are related to belladonna and can indeed poison a man. You will find many a Celt who will put the potato to use in their witchcraft and black magic."

Wills ate more of the fat-laden mutton. "You have known these Celts?"

"Their evil ways are against King James' law and they are dealt with harshly. If they are not performing a pagan ritual, they claim to be Catholic. And you are neither, I presume."

"Begging your pardon, sir," Wills said slowly, picking his words. "I have no quarrel with the Catholic people. I am not Catholic myself," he hastened to add, "because I do not believe in blindly following another man's faith.

I believe instead that all men should be allowed to worship their God in whatever way brings them peace— as long as their peace does not cost me mine."

A slow smile crossed Archie's face. "Well said, my boy. Your diplomacy will serve you in good form." He motioned toward one of the other young men that had been swabbing the deck. "We set sail in about an hour. Michel will show you what to do. Once we are underway, you can go below. Someone will show you where you are to sleep. We arrive along the coast of Ireland by daybreak."

✦══✦

Just as Archie predicted, they first spotted the coast of Ireland just as the sun was breaking over the horizon. Wills had spent most of the night sleeping on deck; he had been shown to a hammock below after they set sail, but he didn't last there for long. There were more men than he could count in the dim quarters, their hammocks spread between cargo and raspy snores rising like wild boars grunting in unison, but it wasn't sharing the space that so disturbed him. He was well accustomed to the lack of privacy; the one-room home he shared with his parents, brothers and sisters served multiple purposes. At night, they all bedded down on heather spread upon the dirt floor, alternately foot to head so they could fit more comfortably. Still, they had been lucky ones. Considered "kindly tenants", their home had been leased to them for generations, ensuring his brothers would have a home and he as well, had he not been conscripted; whereas most of the tenants were moved by the laird every three to five years. Those lesser homes were often erected within two days' time. His home most likely had been as well when it was originally built, but over the years they had shored it up quite nicely so only the toughest winds could threaten to topple a wall.

No; it wasn't the lack of privacy but the swaying that quickly had him above deck once more. As they moved further from shore, the currents intensified until their ferocity pummeled the ship relentlessly. While others snored around him, he made his way quickly up the ladder to the deck, where he promptly lost his dinner over the side of the ship. Long after his stomach was emptied, he alternated between dry heaving and curling up behind a massive coil of rope to keep the vicious winds at bay.

It was there that Fergus MacPherson had found him. The same age as Wills, he was a slight man with a round face and he walked with a bit of a limp. In the darkness of night, his tussled hair appeared brown but as the sun rose, he realized it was actually dark red.

"Aye, and I did the same on my first night at sea," Fergus had stated as he came to stand beside Wills. "You will get your sea legs soon enough, you will, so when you're riding a wench it will feel as though you've set sail and you're cresting a wave."

The moon was high and perhaps the witching hour was upon them when Wills noticed that the vessel had stopped moving. In his moments of inattention, the ship had laid anchor, leaving her to toss and drift.

"Why have we stopped?"

"Ah," Fergus said, leaning against the rail to peer back toward Scotland, though it could no longer be seen in the darkness. "The Highlanders are known to wander down in the darkness of night and attack the ships. No doubt they know we were there; they always do. It's safer for us to anchor at sea than spend the night ashore."

"I suppose sailors aren't fighters."

Fergus scoffed. "None of us are sailors. Oh, and I suppose maybe a few. No; we've been conscripted, same as you. Perhaps a hundred, more or less."

"You have all been enlisted to fight for the Crown?"

"If need be. Though," he hastened to add, "I would prefer to raise sheep. It has been my family's vocation for many a year and I am the best man at shearing, if I do say so myself."

"So you raise sheep as well?"

"Half the men here do. The other half are likely farmers."

All through the night there was movement onboard; under Fergus' tutelage, Wills learned that while at sea half the hands worked during the day and the other half at night. Sometime during the night, the anchor was raised and the ship was underway once more without much more than a few scanty hours at rest. A boy that appeared to be perhaps all of fourteen—if that— was stationed high above in what Fergus called a crow's nest, and it was this boy that raised the call that he had seen land ahead just as dawn was breaking.

Wills stood shivering at the ship's rail as they skirted a peninsula and he caught his first glimpse of the mystical land of Ireland he had heard so much about. At the northwestern tip were several large stones with one much larger, flatter stone laid across them.

"That would be the Islandmagee," Fergus said, eager to share his knowledge.

"And the stones?"

"Ah, that would be the Druid's Altar, it is," he said in a hushed tone. "It has been there for thousands of years. It is said the island is filled with magic, and you would not care to be there overnight, for the spirits of the ancient druids still roam."

"Will we be setting anchor there, then?"

"Oh, no. There is nothing there but the tenants."

As the ship navigated parallel with the shoreline, Wills could barely pick out a stone cottage in the thick morning mist. He was fascinated by it; unlike the Scottish homes that were comprised of very few stones and mostly mud and brambles, this one was like a miniature version of a laird's home. It was stone from ground to thatched roof and had bushes surrounding it. Bushes! As the mists shifted, he stared unblinking at the strange sight, afraid to close his eyes even for a moment lest he miss something important.

"Mac Eoin Bisset's home," Fergus said reverently.

"And who might he be?"

"It is said his family was from Scotland, though they have lived in Ireland for some four hundred years, possibly more. They have become more Irish than the Irish, it is said."

It was true, all the things he had heard about Ireland. Though the initial impression was an island of rock, he could now see that the majority of the isle—or at least as far as the eye could see—was of rolling green pastures and groves of trees. Not one tree, mind you, but many—too many to count.

"You see those rocks around the perimeter?" Fergus said, pointing.

"Aye, I do."

"It is said they are filled with caves, and pirates have concealed their bounty in them. Some have lain hidden for centuries."

"Have you explored them?"

"Oh, no. We have ne'er once set anchor there. We will sail northward to Larne, where we will likely unload cargo from Yorkshire."

Orders from the captain on the bridge and relayed by Archie to the crew interrupted their conversation and they were soon put back to work. Wills found himself running across the ship performing a myriad of errands, from ensuring the men from below were rising and taking their stations to carrying food to the officers. All the while he tried to keep one eye on the shoreline. He didn't remember a time when he had been so excited. The island rose like an emerald out of the mist—or what he supposed an emerald might look like, since he had never seen one. He wished that Beth could see it. Wigtownshire now felt squalid; bereft of trees and bushes, it was more a hodgepodge of mud and heather. It was nothing like the beauty of this land.

But isn't that why men leave? He thought. For a man that is content with his lot, one with standing in the community and a future laid out before him is rarely the man that leaves for the unknown. But take a man with poor prospects of employment, one with a doubtful future, and he has but two choices. He can remain where he is for the simple reason that he has always been there, and take what Life may send him; or he take his destiny into his own hands and set sail for the unknown in search of new opportunities and a brighter future.

They came upon Larne in short order, the sun having barely begun to clear the mists when they turned inward toward the land. He was surprised when, on one of his errands, he looked behind them to find another land in the distance, and he was further surprised when one of the crew informed him that it was Scotland. The ship slowed, the sails adjusted, as they pulled toward the mouth of Loch Ollarbha.

There, a grand castle came into view. He could barely contain himself as he tried to find Fergus in the midst of his errands. When they finally came together, their conversation was sporadic as activity on board increased.

"It is Olderfleet Castle," Fergus said, clearly excited to be sharing this information. "It is said this was once the site of Vikings, who called it Ulfrecksfiord."

"Did they build the castle, then?"

"No. The Bisset clan built it."

"The same Bisset clan as from the island?"

"One and the same."

"They must be quite a powerful clan."

Fergus shrugged. "I suppose they are indeed."

"So you have been here before," Wills prodded.

"Twice I traveled as far as Derry. But this will be the first time we will move further westward to a place that Captain Stewart has been given by King James himself. He was tasked with finding a hundred men, Captain Stewart was, to help lay claim and protect it from the hands of the Irish clans."

"So that is why he needed a good swordsman," Wills murmured. Visions of fighting gnome-like creatures began to fill his head. His dreams were short-lived, however, because they were barely moored when all hands were put to work removing certain cargo from below deck. Wills would have much preferred to walk the shore and explore the grounds, but their stop there was to be a temporary one.

As they navigated away from shore once more, Wills found Fergus winding rope. "Why are we not staying?" he asked. "Is this not Ireland?"

"Aye, it is," Fergus said. "Lend me a hand here, that's right... This is but the eastern tip of Eire. We will sail farther north and then inland to the place called Derry."

"Derry." He spoke the word in a hushed tone, committing it to memory.

"Aye. It is an old village, founded by a saint, or so it is said, and the monastery still sits, a great stone fortress." Despite the cold, Fergus mopped his brow of perspiration. "King James has shown a special interest in it, he has, and he has placed Sir George Paulet of Hampshire there as Governor not more than a year or so ago. Wicked man, he is, and I've yet to find one that cares for him."

Wills repeated the name in his mind. "So will we be staying at Derry?"

"I do not know for how long. We may remain there for a time, or we may move farther west immediately. Captain Stewart will let us know, don't you be worrying about that now."

Archie began barking more orders and Wills found himself running errands yet again, all the while committing to memory the site of Islandmagee, the port at Larne and most of all, of their destination: Derry, under the command of the King's Governor, Sir George Paulet.

6

Derry, as it turned out, was an attempt to Anglicize the original Irish Gaelic name of Daire, so named for its thick groves of oak trees. As they sailed past Culmore Fort into the River Foyle, six of those giant oaks had men swinging by their necks, a small group of women and children gathered around their feet.

"Whatever might they have done?" Wills mused.

Fergus shrugged and glanced away but not before a veil of sadness had crept over his face. "The hangings have stepped up since Paulet became Governor," he said. "Even minor infractions warrant the noose, and it's the noose the Irish dread the most. There is something about a man hanging that goes against their faith..."

There were more men as they approached Derry, some of whom appeared to have remained in place so long that the birds had picked their heads raw while the wolves had torn at their feet and legs. Derry itself sat along the northern edge of Ireland on the west bank of the River Foyle, which in turn led to the North Atlantic and some of the busiest shipping lanes of the day.

For five hundred years, the village had basked in its wild remoteness; while the rest of Europe had been engulfed in the Dark Ages, it had remained the peaceful and picturesque site of a monastery. Saint Colmcille himself had begun it in 521. The son of an Irish princess from Leinster and a father whose family had captured Saint Patrick and brought him to Ireland as a slave, Colmcille was said to have bridged two worlds. He was a member of the O'Neill Clan, one of the largest and most powerful clans in all of Ireland, and also a devout man of God and follower of the Catholic faith yet he somehow managed to achieve respect and reverence by both the Celts and the Gaels as well.

The land had been given to him, and although the O'Neill Clan held vast territory east of Derry, the monastery was situated on the west bank at the junction of the O'Donnell and O'Doherty domains. It was, perhaps, a gift from the O'Donnells to maintain peace between the two clans, which was often a tenuous peace at best, more often than not giving way to treachery and war.

No longer a monastery, Sir Henry Docwra had set out to change its history and was now considered the founder of the spirited village that had sprung up in its place since the English had begun her colonization of Ireland. From all accounts, after a dubious beginning, Docwra had fallen in love with the country and had striven to make Derry the jewel of the island; a lively port village and bustling trading post, it was a routine stop for journeys heading further west.

As they navigated further inland, Wills was surprised to find on the eastern shore vast acres of land sporting no grass and only charred trunks of trees with no branches and no foliage.

"Ah," Fergus said, noting his bewilderment, "O'Neill and O'Cahan lands were burned quite heavily during the Nine Years War. It was said once Lord Arthur Chichester and Sir George Paulet assumed their positions in Ireland, they instituted a scorched earth policy, burning everything down to the soil so the people would no longer have the will to fight."

"How do you know so much?"

"Curiosity. Same as you. For a man that is not curious about the world in which he lives is one that lives in isolation, even when surrounded by others."

As Wills watched stick-thin people observing them warily from the shore, he said, "Those people—they look like they have not eaten in quite some time."

"I understand a good many of them have starved, they have."

"Are they Irish?"

"Indeed."

"And is that a Christian thing to do, I wonder, allow them to starve?"

Fergus chuckled wryly. "It appears it's an English thing to do. Ah. And we're about to make port."

As they entered the port at Derry, he noticed that although the terrain was blighted on the eastern side, on the opposite shore was the most beautiful green meadow and forest he could ever have imagined. "And what of that?" he asked.

"That land there?" Fergus answered. "That would be Cahir O'Doherty's land, the Inishowen Peninsula."

"Who is he?"

"A Gaelic Irish Lord—a king is what his people call him."

"And his land was spared?"

"Give me a hand with the anchor," he said. "You can gawk all you want when the work is done."

The port was a hotbed of activity and ordered chaos. No sooner had they laid anchor than crates were coming up from the hold. They formed a human chain as they passed the cargo from man to man. Wills found himself quite by chance at the head of the line, where he accepted a heavy wood crate, placed it in a somewhat neat pile and had barely turned around before another was being handed to him. All around him were English soldiers and sailors as well as fishermen and merchants plying their trades. There was a distinct aroma to the place, a fresh scent of sea and salty air, of fresh flowers and pungent waste; an odd mixture of too many bodies in a small area while just beyond lay a great expanse of wilderness.

Wills caught a glimpse of rolling hills in the distance dotted with more sheep than he had ever seen in one place. He wanted to pause and stare at the oddity but the crates kept coming and it was all he could manage to keep up with them.

"Captain Stewart's ship?" The voice was formal; the speech filled with an unusual affectation.

Wills glanced up at a soldier whose shoulders were squared, his chin tilted upward so he appeared to be looking down his nose at him. "Aye. It is."

The man looked as though he had just experienced something that was quite unpleasant. "Then you will receive this cargo for him."

He added another crate to the growing pile and stepped out of the line. Fergus came up behind him, taking his place as Wills accepted a piece of paper pushed under his nose. "And what is this?" he asked as he began to read.

"Bill of Lading." The soldier motioned for men behind him to begin stacking crates on the opposite side from those being unloaded. "Simply put your 'x' there."

"I won't be signing anything I have not yet read," Wills stated. The man made an impatient puffing sound but he ignored him as he read through the half-page document. The contents were listed, along with a statement that they had received prior approval. He signed his name in full at the bottom and handed the paper back to the soldier.

"This note is for the Captain himself," the man said, "to be delivered personally." He held out a folded document sealed in wax and bearing the insignia GP.

"Aye. I'll take it to him myself."

With an exasperated huff, the soldier shoved the document into Wills' hand and strode away. Wills stood there for a moment, perplexed at the man's behavior.

"You're a Scot," Fergus offered. "Beneath his station."

Wills shook his head. "I will be back directly, after I take this—"

"—to the captain. Aye, I heard."

Wills glanced upward to find Captain Stewart watching him curiously. Stepping out briskly, he made his way along the line of men, past the cargo hold to the steps leading to the bridge. The captain beckoned for him to join him.

"For you, sir," Wills said as he offered him the document.

He took the document from him and began to peel back the wax seal. "Why did you look at the Bill of Lading and not simply sign your 'x'?"

Surprised, he answered, "I did not wish to obligate you, sir, should money be required to pay for the cargo. Once I saw that it had previously been approved by you, I knew it was safe to sign my name."

"So you can read?" The slightest furrow appeared on his brow. His question was simple and yet filled with incredulity.

"Of course, sir." As he spoke the words, he realized his own voice had assumed the same tone.

"Can you write as well?"

"Aye, sir. I can indeed; in two languages, Gaelic and English."

Captain Stewart leaned back on his heels. "William Neely, you are filled with surprises, aren't you now?" Not knowing what to say, he simply waited to be dismissed. He understood the inference; Scotland, like England herself, was very much a class system. A man was born into his destiny; it was based entirely on what his father was and who his father was before him. Nobility followed one path; lairds, another. Common folk had their own lives mapped out and the Neely family had been one of farmers for as many generations as they had walked the earth, or so he had been told. Farmers had little need to read and write and yet, for whatever reason, he had an innate curiosity about nearly everything. It had been that trait that had led him on a path from a young age to learn the alphabet, arithmetic and once, he had even found a dog-eared, worn book. Oh, and it was a prized possession, to be sure, and read numerous times before it served another purpose in the dead of winter when there was nothing left with which to keep the fire pit going. He still thought of that book and the pitifully short time it had kept them warm, far more briefly than the words contained within had warmed his heart and his thoughts.

The captain was talking and he jerked himself back to the moment. "I am in need of an aide that can read and write," he was saying. Having read the brief note, he was refolding it. "Archie, good man, show young William here a better suit of clothing. We have a meeting in Derry and my aide must look the part."

Wills had not noticed Archie standing on the bridge behind the captain but as their eyes met, he realized that the older man had been observing the exchange. He winked at him before motioning for him to follow him to the quartermaster.

Lord Arthur Chichester of Dublin Castle, Lord
Deputy of all of Ireland, was a man of privilege. Wills
had heard of nobility throughout his life but it had
always been from a distance, rumors and innuendo
passed along so many times that stories from London
or Edinburgh were likely to contain as much fiction as
fact. As he stood now in the home of Sir George Paulet,
Governor of Derry, he felt completely out of his element
as he tried not to stare at the bizarre clothing and opulent
room.

He was content with his position behind Captain
Stewart; as an aide, he would not, he presumed, be
asked his opinion or be invited to sit. This provided an
opportunity to commit everything he could to memory;
for certainly someday he would return to Wigtownshire
and he should be prepared to tell of this day in great
detail and flourish.

Chichester was semi-reposed in a chair like none
other Wills had ever seen; the tufted back was taller
than the man, the arms ornately carved. He was,
perhaps, around 45 years of age; his hair was dark and
long but thinning, the hairline receded. His face was
very narrow, made to appear even more so with a short,
well-groomed beard that accentuated the heart shape
and pointed chin. His eyes were dark, his brows arched,
as he looked from Stewart to Paulet and back again.
His eyes had not once landed on Wills but flitted through
him as if he was completely invisible.

He wore layers of clothing and a neck collar unlike
anything Wills had ever seen before, reminding him of

the banty rooster that awakened his family every morning just as dawn was beginning to break. He was hard pressed to determine what possible usefulness such a collar could provide and he found himself stifling a laugh as he envisioned the man beginning to crow for certainly he seemed as full of himself as that old banty rooster always was.

He shifted his attention to Sir George Paulet in an attempt to remain solemn. Paulet appeared to be older, perhaps by as much as ten years, though it might have been his shiny, nearly bald head that made him appear thus. He was a tiny thing and had he been Irish, Wills would have confirmed their purported gnome-like appearance was fact not fiction. He and Chichester were in a spirited disagreement regarding the man named O'Doherty.

"There is nothing to be gained by insulting Cahir O'Doherty," Chichester was saying impatiently, as if he had stated the same many times before.

"He is naught but a minor leader of natives—closer in intelligence to monkeys than to men," Paulet answered with equal impatience. He brushed at his clothing as if clearing specks of dirt. His snub nose was wrinkled in disdain, appearing more like a monkey than the people he described. "It serves no purpose to pretend he is anything more."

"There are more than a few grumblings, as you will soon hear, Captain Stewart." Chichester turned his attention to the captain. "Eire is a wilderness filled with savages—"

Paulet interrupted. "They know nothing of civilized society," he said in disgust. "They wander like vagabonds and they are so filled with superstition that nearly everything they do must be blessed by their 'priest' beforehand."

"Yet," Chichester continued, "they have elected their own 'lords' so they call them, men they are all no doubt related to as there is much inbreeding, and Cahir O'Doherty is considered by fellow Irishmen to be the Lord of Inishowen. Had it not been for England's involvement here, I daresay he would be called the King of Inishowen. And might I remind you—" his voice rose as Paulet attempted to interject once more "—he is known as the Queen's O'Doherty, because he did, in fact, fight on behalf of Queen Elizabeth during Tyrone's Rebellion, which was a bloody nine years' war, I must say. And when O'Doherty fights, his men fight with him." He turned back to Paulet. "You would do best to keep the man on our side."

"Appease him, you mean."

"Exactly."

"I sit here on this squalid land," Paulet said, waving his hand toward the window, "when just beyond is the most beautiful of all of Ireland. Tell me why I cannot simply annex his lands and call them my own."

"You know perfectly well why you cannot," Chichester answered. "The Queen—and more recently King James—reaffirmed that he was to keep possession of that land in payment for his services—and his men's, I might add—during the war. It has, after all, been in his family for more than a thousand years."

"What does he want from us?" Captain Stewart asked.

Chichester waved his hand dismissively. "Not from us, but from King James. He applied for a position with the Prince of Wales, which, in the prince's great wisdom, he will no doubt decline. So he remains here in Ireland, a thorn in our sides to be sure, but one with which we must walk a thin line: give him enough with the right hand while we taketh away with the left."

A slender young woman quietly entered the room, balancing an enormous tray. She was stunningly beautiful, Wills thought. She was perhaps all of five foot two with dark auburn hair and voluminous green eyes. Wills made a move to assist her but Paulet held up his hand. "That is beneath you," he said, his eyes flicking over him for the first time. "Let the wench do it."

Wills reluctantly resumed his place behind Stewart as the men continued to talk, feeling uneasy as she laboriously eased the tray onto the table. She glanced at Wills briefly, her eyes and her smile conveying her gratitude for the gesture he had been unable to complete. Then with shaking hands, she set the tea cups in front of the men.

Paulet held his palm out as he raised his chin, his jaw tightening.

Deftly, she removed his cup from the table and placed it in his palm. She then hurried back to the tray to retrieve the pot, returned to his side and began to fill it with trembling fingers.

"—would be better off without the lot of them at all," Paulet was saying. As he spoke, his hand moved as if he intended to gesture with it. The servant exclaimed at the same time as the hot water spilt onto his hand and forearm and with a shout, he bolted up from his chair and tossed the bit of water already in his cup into her face. "How dare you?" he shouted before flinging the cup against the far wall. As it crashed, he slapped her full across the face; as petite as she was, he was nearly her height.

Wills instinctively stepped forward but he felt Stewart's hand firm on his forearm, holding him back. It was all he could do not to break free of the captain's hand and help her anyway as thoughts of his mother and Beth raced through his mind. Women were the fairer sex, were they not, and meant to be treated kindly?

"Pardon me, Lord Chichester," the captain interrupted. "I am rather perplexed as to the relationship of this man O'Doherty to my ambitions."

"I will show you," Paulet answered grudgingly. As the woman wiped the water from a face now inflamed with the heat of it, he spat, "Clean that mess up. I shall deal with you later." He then took long strides to a bookcase in the corner of the room, where he extracted a roll of parchment. He motioned toward a table in the far corner.

Wills waited for the captain to join Paulet and Chichester and then stood behind them, an arm's length from the captain in the event he was needed. Out of the corner of his eye, he watched as the woman picked up the fragments of the cup from where it had been tossed, set out a fresh cup and fill them. When she left the room, she was biting back tears. He wondered if she was Irish, for certainly Paulet treated her with complete disdain but on the other hand, she was beautiful and not the half-human creature he had been told the Irish were. With a heavier heart, he maneuvered himself so he could view the scroll as it was unfurled and the corners weighted down with bric-a-brac.

"This is Inishowen. It contains two hundred thousand acres—more or less." Paulet pointed to a peninsula that jutted off the northwest corner of Ireland. "As you can see, it borders the village of Derry. Moreover, the land granted to you is in Donegal, here." He pointed to the other side of the peninsula. "When you set sail for Donegal, you must navigate around O'Doherty's territory—or what he perceives is his territory. And on the other side of the lough is MacSweeney and then O'Donnell lands."

"We are most definitely in the process of colonizing it," Chichester added hastily. "But you see here, when you reach the most northerly point of the island, your ship will be in the Atlantic Ocean and the waters there are deadly, the coast rugged. Inistrahull Island was once connected to the peninsula, so you'll want to remain well outside them both, for the land juts up under a ship and can easily capsize it."

"I see." Captain Stewart rubbed his chin.

"But there is more," Paulet said. "When you reach the northernmost point, you must turn southward so your ship will be navigating the Lough Swilly here, between Dunaff Head to the east and Fanad Head to the west."

"Ah. That is the lough that divides the MacSweeneys and the O'Donnells from the O'Dohertys?" Stewart asked.

"One and the same. And when the lough divides and you see an island in your path—that would be Inch Island—you will turn to the west and enter Drongawn Lough. It is here—" he drew a circle with his hand on the western shore "—that you and your men will colonize."

"So what you are telling me is this 'lord' of the Irish people, Cahir O'Doherty, will have in his charge the land between myself and my men and the village of Derry."

"Precisely."

"And this land here—which is most obviously a shorter journey overland from Derry to my property— is not the more feasible way of navigation?"

Paulet chuckled dryly. "Most definitely, you will not want to travel overland, Captain. It is wild and untamed; and the Irish are as undomesticated as the wolves, of which there are plenty of both though we tried our best to burn them out as well. You are far more likely to have your throats slit in your sleep should you venture overland. Besides, you will have need of your ship to navigate around the island."

"I see." Stewart stood for a long moment, thoughtfully rubbing his chin. Then he motioned for Wills. "Mister Neely, can you repeat this drawing?"

"Aye, sir."

Paulet signaled for one of his servants. "Fetch the man some parchment and ink."

As Wills settled in to draw the map, the others retreated to the sitting area once more. Their words ranged from boisterous disagreement to pleasant laughter, but he no longer heard their conversation. He was busy recreating the peninsula, shaped rather like a man's fist, bordered by Lough Foyle on the east, which led to Derry, Lough Swilly and Drongawn to the west— and MacSweeney and O'Donnell territory. Captain Stewart's land grant would be in the westernmost part of Ireland. His eyes scanned quickly to the east, where he spotted Wigtownshire on the Scottish coast. He would be a long way from home. For a fleeting moment, he pictured Beth on their final walk together and wondered whether his father and brothers had searched for him when he had not returned. They certainly would learn that he had been placed into King James' service, for word had a way of traveling through Scotland as if every dale and glen had eyes and ears and a mouth for retelling.

Once the map had been drawn, he drew a light circle around the area designated as Captain Stewart's land. He assumed the captain would be given a more precise set of boundaries but from what he gleaned from the gentlemen's discussion, the location could be problematic. It rested along the shore near a basin, which meant the only way in or out by water was northward right past three chieftains' tribal land—and the overland route would be no better.

His mind was still with the young servant girl as he walked with Archie and Stewart toward the ship, and he was only now beginning to appreciate how small a village Derry really was. The majority of inhabitants appeared to be soldiers and whether they were stationed there or simply passing through was impossible to tell. Most of the homes were small and built of wood, though a few—such as Paulet's home—had been built of stone and were quite ostentatious. There were two buildings that appeared to be dormitories for the single soldiers, one in the Upper Fort, as it was called, and one in the Lower Fort.

They rounded a corner and he nearly bumped into a man with a bulbous nose; despite Wills' apologies the man rushed off in a near panic as though he had been the one at fault.

"That is odd," Wills said to Stewart before realizing that the captain had stopped in his tracks. Following his line of sight, he realized there was a small crowd gathered around a square and in the center of that square was a scaffold from which a young woman hung. Her head was bent at an unnatural angle indicating that she had died from a broken neck. Her long blond hair had been twisting in the wind so that it was wrapped around her face like so many layers of a spider's web. Her simple gown drooped from her body and had either been made for a much larger woman or she had lost so much weight that it no longer fit her. Sickened, his first impulse was to immediately cut her down and cover her body, but standing there a moment longer, he grew even more repulsed at what he observed.

Two young children cried as they clutched at her ankles and calves and perhaps it was their constant pulling that had caused her clothing to slip down from her shoulders, exposing part of her breasts. Both were repeating, "Máthair! Máthair!"

Incensed, Wills spoke to the closest man. "What is the meaning of this outrage?"

The man's eyes widened and for a moment, he thought he had not understood his words so Wills repeated his question in Gaelic. He glanced around as if wishing to flee but apparently seeing no escape, he answered in Irish Gaelic, "She stole a piece of bread to feed her children."

Stunned, Wills could only stare at the man. Something flitted across his eyes—perhaps a sense that Wills was as saddened and sickened as he—and he shrugged his shoulders and shook his head.

"Cannot someone cut her down?"

"Oh, no, no," the man answered. "You see that man over there, near the corner? That would be Sheriff Hamilton. Should anyone move to cut her down, they would hang beside her, they would."

"But—but the children? Surely, he could show some decency!"

"He acts on the orders of Governor Paulet." Suddenly his eyes grew wider. "But I have said too much." With that, he rushed from the square.

Wills turned to Stewart, who was obviously as appalled as he. "Sir—"

"I understand how you feel, lad. But this is Paulet's village and we cannot interfere."

"But surely someone can do something for those children—"

"Come." He placed his hand on Wills' shoulder, almost leading him away from the square.

Though he tried to erase the image from his mind, he found that he could not, and somehow he knew those two tiny children would remain in his memory forever. They could not have been more than two or three years of age, he thought, and certainly a mother stealing a morsel so her children could live was worth something? Surely, Paulet and his man Hamilton could have found some decency in their hearts?

He began to look at each face that passed by and slowly he began to realize that not one of the men or women appeared as they had been described in Scotland. On the contrary, they were of the same height and build—though many very noticeably thinner—as the English and Scots. The only way, in fact, that he could tell the difference was in their expressions. The foreigners walked as if they owned the world and their eyes carried insolence in them. The Irish, in contrast, looked at the ground. Their faces were crestfallen, their eyes—if one glanced his way—were the eyes of one who had suffered and suffered badly.

What have I gotten myself into here? He wondered as they approached the ship. It became a constant refrain even after they set sail once more.

7

The skies were an arctic blue and the winds crisp as they navigated past the Isle of Doagh on the northwestern edge of the Inishowen Peninsula. The rocks jutted out of the ocean depths, black and craggy, forbidding any vessel from coming too close to O'Doherty shores. Some sported strange shapes; Galician Art, he was told, swirling motifs and concentric circles some three thousand years old, an era that gripped his imagination, taking him back in time to the Early Bronze Age and Late Neolithic period, an epoch when perhaps another type of people roamed those shores and traversed these waters. He wondered what the art meant, for surely it must mean something; certainly the intricate patterns that could only be seen from the sea were intended as a message for mariners. But what if, he thought, what if these patterns were all over the island? What if some ancient culture had left these symbols not at random but as an archaic alphabet of some sort?

A formidable stone structure came into view as they circumnavigated the Isle, a structure that could only be Carrickabraghy Castle, one of many castles owned by Cahir O'Doherty, the young lord of the O'Doherty Clan. It was easily the largest structure he had ever seen. He counted seven towers that soared high above the rock, though he was certain it had more. Upon its labyrinth of parapets Wills could clearly view soldiers stationed, watching their approach with growing interest. A flurry of activity bespoke of their distrust of strangers, as if they anticipated an imminent attack from the sea; but as the captain instructed the crew to continue about their business, those men along the parapet and at the base of the castle seemed to reluctantly return to theirs.

Children playing on the castle grounds were not so eager to turn their backs but watched the ship as though it was an oddity from the heavens, and indeed they might have very well looked as though they were from another universe with their English ship and strange flag. Women walking with baskets on their hips also stopped to observe their passing and though Wills tried to focus on his tasks, he found himself wanting to stare back, to study them even as they studied him.

Paulet had called them monkeys and he was hard-pressed to understand why he had made the comparison. They were not gnome-like creatures, as tales had been told in Scotland by men who had presumably been in positions to know better; they did not appear to be shorter or slimmer than those on board the ship but appeared much like the Scottish Lowlanders and English—and aye, for sure, some were large enough to be Highlanders, they were. The women, even from the distance of the sea, were something to behold with their long, dark hair that caught on the breezes; slender yet shapely, they begged a closer look. From the comments of some of the crew, they, too, felt the attraction; perhaps, Wills thought, it was the same pull the Vikings had felt so many centuries ago, the same allure that caused them not to pillage and leave as they had so many other places, but choose to remain on this Emerald Isle among the Irish people. As he spotted several with red hair, he recalled the adage *Red on the head where the Vikings tread*, a reference more aptly used with the Highlanders that had intermarried with the Norsemen.

The call came out from the bridge to turn the ship southward, and they found themselves slowing as they left the ocean and navigated into the Lough Swilly. He looked to the sea to observe the dolphins that had frolicked in advance of the ship for more than an hour, the gentle swell caused by the slow-moving vessel creating currents the mammals used for the pure pleasure. They disappeared, diving deep, before leaping clear out of the water's depths, whistling and clicking as though they were laughing with joy. Now they jumped in well-coordinated acrobatic teams as if to say good-bye.

The shorelines on both sides of the Lough Swilly were filled with more seabirds and geese than Wills had ever seen in one place and perhaps because of the racket a ship full of men could make, a skein broke loose from the treetops, creating undulating patterns in the skies overhead. It was a glorious day to be sure; one that Wills had no doubt would remain in his memory forever. Ah, but there were many memories this day, weren't there? Some beautiful, some not, and all held power over him.

He took the stairs at the captain's order and stood just behind him alongside an Irishman they picked up in Derry by the name of Tomas Gallagher. It had been yet another surprise at the appearance of an Irishman, for the man looked unexpectedly like himself; and again, as he looked at the man, he recalled all the talk in Scotland where he had imagined Irish men to be half his height, bent and rather gnome-like. Instead, Tomas was taller by an inch, perhaps two; with his sharp blue eyes under black lashes and raven hair, he set a striking pose. His shoulders were squared and his chest and arms well-muscled as they strained against the confines of his shirt. He moved back and forth between Gaelic and English so many times in the same breath that Wills had to focus on his every word, which was never difficult to do considering their topics of discussion. Wills' curiosity was insatiable and Tomas seemed perfectly willing to attempt to satisfy it. What's more was Fergus and Tomas seemed to go back a bit and greeted one another like old friends.

As they moved farther south, the trees appeared to come alive. It was otherworldly, Wills thought, because in one moment, ten men stood within the shadows of the forest and in the next instance, they were gone. It occurred again and again until he wondered aloud whether his eyes were playing tricks on him.

"Oh, no," Tomas responded, laughing. "That would be more of the Clan O'Doherty. They are only watching us and what we're about. I have spotted perhaps fifty thus far in addition to the men at the castle."

"Fifty." Wills strained to see them. "Are we on their land?"

"Depends on who you would be asking." He pointed to the land on the opposite shore. "Now that land there was O'Donnell land. For centuries, this lough went back and forth between the two."

"*Was* the O'Donnell land?"

"Aye, until the Flight of the Earls." At Wills' puzzled expression, he added, "You are not familiar with that, then?" He leaned against the bridge railing. "Ah, but there are some very powerful families in Eire, including the O'Donnells. Hugh O'Donnell was the King of Tyrconnell and once owned all that you see on the western side—though he granted some lands to the Gallowglass MacSweeneys. Sometimes, he was even considered the overlord of the O'Doherty's though there would be some that would dispute the inference, they would."

"A king, you say?"

"Aye, and with as much power as your King James but admittedly with much smaller land holdings. His son Hugh Roe O'Donnell ruled until 1602, when Rory O'Donnell succeeded him. That one pledged his allegiance to King James in London and was designated as the Earl of Tyrconnell. Well, wouldn't you know it now but that The O'Donnell's enemies here in Eire as well as noblemen in England protested greatly at this appointment, and stories abounded of a plot against the Crown, though none, the O'Donnell's claimed, existed.

"And then on a stormy night when the skies were black as pitch and it's said the banshee were heard up and down the coasts of Eire, The O'Donnell got word that he was to be arrested and tried for treason and imprisoned in the Tower of London. So he gathered up his friend and ally, Hugh O'Neill, the Earl of Tyrone, whose land holdings were just as great if not greater, and ninety or so of their family members and closest allies and fled the country, he did."

An island rose before them upon which rested a stone structure. "When did this occur?" Wills asked as he searched the narrow windows for movement. "The Flight of the Earls?"

"Less than one year ago. Aye. That would be Inch Island you'd be looking at and that would be another of Cahir O'Doherty's castles there…"

"He has more than one?"

Tomas chuckled. "Aye, I believe he has eight but my count might be off... So anyway, The O'Donnell and The O'Neill fled to mainland Europe, along with a third — The Maguire. It has been rumored — but on good authority, mind you — they are raising an army with the help of the Spaniards."

"Raising an army to do what?" Wills asked.

"Why, to reclaim their lands, of course."

"These lands?" he prodded, jabbing his thumb toward the western shore.

"Aye. These lands."

"The very lands we are going to now?"

"Aye. Those very lands."

He fell silent for a moment, his mind in turmoil. Oh, he didn't mind a scrap or two and he would never run from a skirmish but if he had his druthers about it, he had just as soon know who he is to be fighting and why. "So you say they were to be arrested and tried for treason," he mulled. "And who might be the accuser?"

"Ah, the new Lord Deputy of Ireland, Sir Arthur Chichester himself, and of course, wouldn't you know it, everything Chichester says is embellished quite lavishly by George Paulet, God help his wicked soul." He crossed himself.

"Is that so?"

Tomas cocked his head. With a glance toward Captain Stewart, he lowered his voice as if he was sharing confidential information for only Wills' ears to hear. "It is said that Chichester not only wanted their lands for Plantations — the very reason you are here today — but also to diminish the Irish lords' authority among their own people. He most especially had it in for The O'Neill. And these are proud folk, don't you know. They submit to no man. So it's said that Chichester threatened them with treason if they did not submit, something to do with gunpowder found — never proved, mind you, that the Earls were behind it."

As they drew closer to Inch Island, he spotted a small ship at anchor along its shores. Several men were standing just beyond the ship and appeared to be in a heated argument. Fergus joined them at the rail to watch.

"Oh," Tomas said, shaking his head, "I cannot believe they are doing it again."

"Doing what again?"

"George Paulet has been eying Cahir O'Doherty's land and castles since the day he arrived in Eire."

"The Bible says do not covet your neighbor's property," Fergus said.

"I think that's 'do not covet your neighbor's wife'," Wills said.

"Property. Wife. Not any difference, 'ey?"

"Oh," Wills answered, "my mother would love to educate you on that, she would. And you'd know the truth of it by the time she was finished."

"In any event," Tomas continued, "Paulet sent a group of men to Inch Island and finding the castle was vacated—as it often is, if The O'Doherty is at another— they made themselves at home. Settled right in, they did. And when Cahir O'Doherty returned to find them there, sleeping in his bed and partaking of all that was his—well, let's just say it was not a pleasant sight."

"What happened?"

The shouting grew louder as the ship began to pass and then the group grew silent as they all observed Stewart's passing.

"Once The O'Doherty had thrown them off his land, he went straightaway to Derry and it's said the shouting match was heard throughout the whole village. But Paulet would hear none of it. He seems to think anything owned by an Irishman is his for the taking."

"How did he escape punishment?" Wills asked. "Even if it is his lands, I've seen for myself that Paulet is not an honorable man."

"Cahir O'Doherty is a protected man," Tomas answered. "He is known as The Queen's O'Doherty, and though she has passed and King James reigns, the designation shields him still."

"So you say Paulet did not back down?"

"He did not. And the next we knew, The O'Doherty had taken a ship all the way to England and traveled overland to London. And there in King James' court, he argued his case."

"And what became of it?" Fergus asked.

"He returned to Derry with parchment in hand under the King's own seal. The Inishowen Peninsula— including Inch Island—is Cahir O'Doherty's and his alone."

They had passed Inch Island and the shouting had begun again. "So what is that all about?" Wills asked.

"It appears some of Paulet's men do not agree with King James' order."

"That's not for them to pick and choose, is it now?"

Tomas chuckled. "I would say The O'Doherty feels the same as you."

The shouts had grown distant by the time the order was called to bring the ship to land, abruptly ending their conversation and leaving Tomas' last words hanging in Wills' imagination like so many apparitions intent on resurrecting themselves.

"Retrieve the surveyor," Captain Stewart directed Wills as he ordered the gangplank lowered.

"Aye, sir." He hurried down the steps to the few cabins to find Mister Parsons imbibing with zeal and accompanied him back to the bridge. Once the gangplank was in place, the captain, the surveyor and Wills disembarked. They strolled for a few minutes as if simply taking in the fresh air while Archie's voice boomed behind them, issuing orders to the crew in securing the ship and lowering the sails. Wills had to admit that the walk on solid ground was much needed and deeply appreciated, and he marveled that he had left Scotland swabbing the deck only to find himself one of two men strolling about with the captain himself. He had yet to find his sea legs, though thankfully the roiling of the ship had not churned his stomach since that first night.

Then abruptly Captain Stewart stopped in his tracks, almost causing the surveyor to run headlong over him. "Mister Parsons," he said, "as you know, I have been granted one thousand acres from that shoreline." He pointed toward the ship before turning around. "And fifteen hundred acres in the area of Boilage and Banagh, which should be just to our southwest, if my calculations are correct. There is a further matter of land in Aughentaine in the former Earl of Tyrone's holdings, I believe, southeast of Derry."

"Aye, sir." Mister Parsons shifted the large ledger he carried in his arms. "I have it all mapped out, sir."

"At the break of day, you are to take a group of men and physically survey it. I wish to know what inhabitants are here and what business they are engaged in, as well as the topography."

"Aye, sir. Of course, sir."

"Young William, you are to report to Archie with the task of securing our most able men to accompany Mister Parsons. They are to go armed and ready for whatever awaits them."

"Aye, sir."

"And absolutely no spirits are to accompany them. Is that understood, Mister Parsons?"

The surveyor appeared aghast but quickly composed himself. "Of course, sir. Of course."

"Archie is to direct the rest of the men to keep their watch this night. At first light, we shall meet on board to direct their activities. We shall remain here indefinitely."

"Aye, sir." Wills stole a look back at the ship, where Archie was still issuing orders from the bridge. Indefinitely sounded like a very long time; a very long time indeed.

In the 5th century, some one thousand years prior to the Stewart ship landing on these shores, Saint Patrick struck the shield of Prince Conall Gulban with his crosier, forming the sign of the cross just prior to baptizing him. He bestowed a blessing upon him as well; that if he followed that cross, he would always remain victorious in battle. A Constantine shield bearing Saint Patrick's outstretched hand holding the cross became the O'Donnell coat of arms and the clan was to indeed rise to tremendous power. It was Conall Gulban that was the ancestor of Rory O'Donnell, whose father had been the High King of Tyrconnell and who himself had been given the title of Earl of Tyrconnell by none other than King James I; the very same Rory O'Donnell that had escaped Ireland in the Flight of the Earls and was now, at this very moment, gathering a Spanish force to lead back to Ireland and reclaim the lands from the English—lands his family had ruled for more than one thousand years.

And now as Wills stood before the coat of arms of The O'Donnell, he felt a shiver shooting up his spine.

"Drafty in this place, isn't it now?" Captain Stewart remarked.

"Aye," Wills answered. "I will find more timber for the fire."

"You needn't go far," Stewart chuckled. "I have ne'er seen so many trees in all my life."

As Wills made his way through the Great Hall of the O'Donnell Castle, one of seven castles once owned by the clan, he couldn't help but feel as if he was a usurper there. It had been vacant when the surveyor located it, which had not been difficult because all paths appeared to lead to it, and Stewart immediately proclaimed that he would live in it until the fort, which was under construction nearby, was complete. Truth be told, Wills would have preferred to have remained with his newfound friends—Fergus and Tomas—but the captain understandably wanted him near at hand, for an aide couldn't be much of an aide if he was off gallivanting about the countryside, now could he? Archie also moved into the castle and the three men found themselves in a vast labyrinth of ancient stone whose ceilings felt enormously high, the stairwells unending, the hallways filled with shadows and the nights filled with the ghosts of all that once walked here.

To be sure, a nobleman from England would have found it primitive, the roughhewn stone too simple and crude, the utilitarian style of squares and turrets too meek and unsophisticated. But to a lad from Scotland that had known nothing more than a one-room house easily compromised by strong winds it was beyond anything he might have imagined.

According to Tomas, once it was quite apparent that The O'Donnell had fled the country with The O'Neill and Maguire, the castle was ransacked by the remnants of the O'Donnell clan—and no doubt, their enemies as well. Depending upon the storyteller, the valuables were hidden for safekeeping or had found their way to a hovel where a coat of arms now hung above an earthen fire pit or an ornate chalice now graced a crude block table.

The people who were left were surprisingly friendly, though Tomas warned not to take their smiles too literally. They lived in tiny enclaves of huts comprised sometimes of limestone, sometimes of wood and sometimes they seemed mostly of mud. It had been Captain Stewart's first order to gather as many as could be found so that he might speak to them as their newly appointed lord. Now as Wills moved from the Great Hall into the sunshine, his eyes fell upon the open area in which Stewart had stood atop a stump to address them. The stump was still there, now surrounded by men busy with efforts to establish a colony.

Stewart had proclaimed the lands granted to him to be a Plantation. He had spoken to them in Scottish Gaelic, which was more or less understood by the Irish — at least a good sight better than English — and he had encouraged them to remain on the property if they did so in peace. There would be changes, however; in lieu of the mishmash of scattered enclaves, there would be more orderly villages erected in the style of the English and connected by proper roads.

Wills gathered an armload of kindling from a pile set near the open square. The sunshine felt good on his head and shoulders and for a moment he hesitated, reluctant to return to the frigid rooms of the castle where the stone seemed to absorb the chill and spit it back out when one least expected.

Around him was a flurry of activity. The next order of business was to erect a fort not far from the castle, along with a series of homes for the men. It was rather curious, Wills thought; he had pictured a soldier's life as one of sleeping beneath the trees and always on the move; but Stewart wanted permanent homes to repay the men for their loyalty to himself and to The Crown. What loyalty he referred to, he was sure he didn't know, as he had not fought a battle yet and of those that had, they spoke as if it had been years ago during something called the Nine Years War, an ingeniously imaginative name if he ever heard one.

They had set about erecting a place they would call Fort Stewart, surrounded just outside the walls by these permanent structures. They were quite solid, Wills thought with amazement; unlike the homes most Scottish working class erected within a day or two, these were built with precision. Limestone was easily found, enough for entire villages, also helping to clear the land for farming, which would begin in the spring—which appeared to be weeks away at most. Trees, as Stewart had pointed out, were also so thick that at times a man had to use an axe with which to clear the way. A team was now busily felling them in a broadening circle around the site of the fort, stripping them of branches which would become fuel for fires and preparing the trunks for use in construction.

"Need some help there?"

The voice brought Wills back into the present moment and he turned to see Fergus and Tomas approaching him.

"Aye," he answered. "It is good to see the likes of you two vagabonds again."

Tomas gathered an armload and started toward the castle. "You are living the life of a king now, 'eh?"

Wills chuckled. "It is not what I might have expected of a king's life, for sure."

Fergus also gathered an armload. "The ship's cook has gathered some women for use in laundering and cooking," he said with a wide smile and a quick wink.

"Irish women?" Wills immediately stood a couple of inches straighter.

"What else might there be in this wilderness?" He leaned in closer and whispered, "I do not know how long I can be trusted around them, and no doubt a hundred men feel the same."

Tomas chuckled. "You'll find them loving and faithful, for sure, but don't you dare go crossing them.

An Irish woman can fell a man faster than a sword with just the ire off her tongue."

The three crossed an expanse of green before pausing at the door to the castle. Tomas glanced behind them and then stopped cold, his face turning ashen.

"What is it?" Wills asked, looking behind them.

The crowd of men working on construction had parted, allowing a group of strangers on horseback to approach the castle. One man rode ahead of the others, as if they remained a decent pace behind out of respect for their leader. He was larger than they and sat proud and tall upon a gray stallion; as he drew near, Wills noted his firm, squared jaw, ample mustache and thick auburn brows from which unwavering eyes peered out at him. They were eyes that had seen much, he thought; they drooped at the outer corners over high cheekbones, as though they had seen much sadness but they were also eyes of resolve and conviction. His dark auburn hair was long and straight, reaching past his shoulders, and was parted in the middle and swept back from his face. He appeared, Wills thought, much like the Scottish Highlanders.

Stewart's men were gathering behind the small group as they all converged in front of the castle.

"It's Niall Garbh O'Donnell himself," Tomas said under his breath.

"He'll require a larger army than that," Wills answered.

"Oh, don't be getting cocky with yourself now; he's not here to fight," Tomas whispered hoarsely. "Had that been the case, we'd be picking up the dead before we knew he was here."

Niall Garbh stopped his horse a few paces from them. Without a word, he dismounted. His shoulders were broad, made even broader still by a fur that rippled with the wind. Approaching them, he stated in perfect

English, "I am here to speak with Captain Stewart. My name is Niall Garbh O'Donnell."

"Aye," Wills said, made suddenly self-conscious by his armload of kindle. "Won't you come with me, please?"

As Niall Garbh followed him into the castle, Wills was conscious of more footsteps behind them. Glancing over his shoulder, he noticed The O'Donnell's men had followed them inside, and at his first opportunity, he allowed the kindle to slide out of his hands and onto the stone floor. His sword was across his back, as it always was, and he noted with satisfaction that Tomas and Fergus had taken up positions behind the men and were already flexing their fingers in the event of an assault. Behind them were the faces of the others, some of whom had climbed the step to the door and were awaiting Wills' instruction.

"Captain Stewart," he called out. "Niall Garbh O'Donnell is here to see you, sir."

The captain strode across the Great Hall. He was lithe and graceful though he cut a much smaller figure than the imposing O'Donnell.

"Won't you come in," he said, grasping both The O'Donnell's hands in his. "I am Captain William Stewart."

Niall Garbh nodded silently. His eyes moved slowly from the captain's face to the Great Hall, where he seemed to be performing a mental inventory of all he saw. It had to be difficult, Wills thought, for a man to lose his home to an invading force, most especially one that had sheltered his ancestors as well as himself.

"Wills, some ale please for The O'Donnell and his men."

"Aye, sir." As Wills busied himself preparing the ale, he motioned for Fergus to stoke the fire. Women's chores yet again, but this time he was glad for it as it afforded him the opportunity to remain close and observant.

There were only five men with Niall Garbh, too few to mount an insurrection and upon examination of the strangers' expressions, he supposed it wasn't likely they had arrived like a Trojan horse without the horse to commence a surprise attack. One looked like a younger version of Niall Garbh himself; he had the same shade of auburn hair and the same high cheekbones and squared jaw, though he was a slighter man perhaps close to Will's age.

As he placed several tankards upon a long wood table, the young man was introduced as The O'Donnell's son, Neachtain.

Captain Stewart invited the men to sit. He seemed unsurprised by their appearance and quite at ease. Archie had been summoned and now that he had joined them, he was eying their visitors as he sat beside the captain, displaying all the suspicion in his dark eyes that Stewart did not.

"Take some men," Wills whispered to Fergus, "and search the area. There may be more hiding just beyond our sights."

"Aye," he said simply as he made his way to the door. As the crowd outside parted to allow him exit, Wills noted several men began following Fergus.

He turned to Tomas. "Find some of those Irish lasses you've been chattering about. We need meat for our visitors."

A short while later the Irish servants had covered the table in fowl that had been cooking for the night's supper. Ale was flowing and there was a steady stream of warm bread loaves. He noted the women kept alert eyes on The O'Donnell and his men, but they averted their gaze each time one of the visitors looked them in the face as if perhaps they were considered traitorous for serving the foreigners, even if they were not the exact lot that had driven them from the family castle. He took up a position just behind the captain; his feet spread wide, his sword ever present. Fergus had ordered several men inside the Great Hall; they fanned out in a loose semi-circle behind the Irishmen like silent sentinels.

"I have heard much about you," Captain Stewart was saying.

"Then you are aware," Niall Garbh answered, "that while my cousin, Red Hugh O'Donnell, was fighting the English in the Nine Years' War, I sided with the English."

"I am aware of that," the captain said, taking a bite of bread and washing it down with ale. "I have heard about your display of humanity to the English at Derry." He turned slightly as if speaking to Archie. "Sir Henry Docwra, the previous Governor of Derry, found himself and his small band of men completely surrounded by Irish clans bent on his destruction. Niall Garbh O'Donnell provided valuable information—along with Sir Cahir O'Doherty—against The O'Neill and his cousin, Red Hugh. It enabled us to land an English contingent by sea as well as direct men marching from Dublin, ultimately guaranteeing English victory at Derry."

Niall Garbh lifted his tankard in a brief tribute to the captain's knowledge.

"I know also," Stewart continued, "that upon the signing of the Treaty of Mellifont, you were offered the Lordship of Tyrconnell by Charles Blount, 8th Baron Mountjoy."

"The predecessor of Lord Arthur Chichester," Niall Garbh added.

"But you were not satisfied with that. You also wanted to be declared Lord of Inishowen, supplanting The O'Doherty though he helped us, too."

"The spoils of war," Niall Garbh answered smoothly. "Is that not the way of the English, as well as the Irish? Or the Scottish, I should say, *Captain* Stewart?"

"It is. And it is not for me to second-guess Lord Mountjoy. You have, perhaps, petitioned Lord Chichester?"

Wills felt his body grow tense with their talk. It was a dance; one partner stepped forward, the other back, only for the process to be reversed and repeated.

"Your Lord Chichester has quite the reputation with the Irish peoples."

"You are referring to his scorched earth policy, I am sure," the captain replied. "I did not agree with his tactics."

"I believe his words were that swords would not do as much harm as famine, something to that effect."

"As I said, I did not agree with that."

"Yet you are here, on O'Donnell lands."

Captain Stewart leaned back. "That I am."

Their eyes locked, each with a steely conviction. The air grew tense and then Niall Garbh laughed. "I did not come here to claim my lands," he said, glancing over his shoulder at the captain's men. "As you know, King James has also granted lands to me."

"I am aware, yes."

"I came only to see the great Captain Stewart for myself."

The air lightened with Niall Garbh's laughter but Wills remained vigilant. It was a forced gaiety; as he studied each man in the Great Hall, he had no doubt that every last one of them — Irish, Scottish and Englishman alike — knew of the charade. He quietly made his way toward the door, where he peered outside to the courtyard and beyond. The crowd had thinned no doubt due to the men Fergus had taken with him to search the area. Those that remained were back at work erecting another section of a stone structure. The air was still—too still, he thought. This turn of events did not bode well with him. It did not bode well at all.

8

Wills, Tomas and four other men waited at the stables beyond the castle; their horses at the ready. They had converged when it was apparent that The O'Donnell and his men did not intend to remain overnight and now they waited as the Irishmen bade their farewells to Captain Stewart. Wills watched from the corner of the building until they had begun their journey back from whence they had come, noting they paused for a long moment to witness the construction underway for Fort Stewart. Once they reached the tree line, he motioned for the others. It was time.

Mounting his horse, a fine specimen of Irish equine, he led the men along the path The O'Donnell had just taken. The Irishmen traveled southward along the shoreline of Drongawn Lough while Wills and his men hung back a fair distance and kept to the shadows of the trees. He noted that Niall Garbh rode tall and proud; he and his men did not look behind them or seem to survey their surroundings but traveled as though the land still belonged to the O'Donnell clan and there was nothing to fear.

They eventually reached the lower basin. Wills signaled for the others to stop and observe; rather than continue due south, they turned eastward, disappearing into a copse whose path was obscured from where they sat. They quickly lost sight of them and after a brief moment in which he was certain the Irishmen could not turn their heads and notice their followers, he spurred his horse onward.

The skies were roiling with gray clouds and a fine mist began to fall. Nighttime would soon be upon them and Wills found himself anxious to discover Niall Garbh's destination before the sun had set. They entered the forest along the same path the Irishmen had taken minutes before; a path set obliquely so it could be seen from one direction and only then when in close proximity. The branches hung low here, often crossing the path to join with a tree on the other side like two arms outstretched in an embrace, compelling him to lean forward to avoid injury to his neck and head. The thick foliage blocked the sun, throwing the riders into lengthy black shadows.

He tried to peer up ahead, tried to discern any movement of flora that would expose the Irishmen's position but once a horse passed through, the branches appeared to shift immediately back into place like veils falling, creating a cocoon around each rider. A glance behind him easily led to the false conclusion that he was completely alone, though he knew the others followed him in single file.

As the branches caused him to lean ever lower, he studied the ground beneath the horse's hooves. The undergrowth was thick, the path the horse followed so narrow and winding that had he not seen the men enter it with his own eyes, he might have been convinced it was not a path at all. Yet as he peered to his left and to his right, he knew there were no openings in which they might have turned.

Eventually and abruptly, the forest parted and he found himself in a small clearing. As the others converged behind him, they quickly filled the tiny area. Thinking the path would logically continue on a straight path, he made for the opposite side, only to find brambles so thick it was impossible to penetrate them. They all fanned out as much as possible in the small space, searching for the continuation of the path but they found none. Much to Wills' dismay, even the path they had traveled to reach this point was now completely obscured.

He looked heavenward for signs of the sun pointing westward but the trees reached into the skies, blocking his view. They were the tallest trees he had ever witnessed by far, he marveled, and wondered at their possible age. The trunks were so broad that three men joining hands might not be able to encircle each one, and their branches, like those along the path, appeared to reach for one another like prison bars coming together.

"You, there," Wills said, motioning for one of his men, "climb that tree and get our bearings."

"Sir." The young man slipped off his horse, selected a tree and was preparing to climb when The O'Donnell appeared before them.

It happened so quickly that Wills blinked, believing his eyes were playing tricks on him. But there in front of him, standing with his feet set apart and his hands on his hips, was The O'Donnell himself. The foliage had not moved and did not move now; one moment the space was empty and the next, he simply appeared like a phantom out of thin air.

He heard a gasp behind him and the scuffling of horses' hooves, and as he took in the clearing, he noted his men had surrounded them. They did not have swords drawn though they were but a hand's length away, but they stood like their leader with feet spread, hands on their hips and slightly bemused expressions.

"You might have inquired where I was going," Niall Garbh said.

Wills did not respond. There were an equal number of men on each side, something he had planned in advance of their departure, but he was dumbfounded as to how they could have dismounted and surrounded them. There were no signs at all of their horses, and no indication how they could have appeared through the brambles.

"Had I wished to attack," Niall Garbh continued, "I would not have approached with a small contingent but with an army."

"We are not here to harm the Irish people," Wills said. "We plan to improve their lot. You will find Captain Stewart to be a man of honor, honest and fair."

He thought he perceived the slightest upturn of Niall Garbh's lips, but he could not be certain in the lengthy shadows. A sudden noise erupted overhead and instinctively, he looked upward to find a flock of startled black birds taking flight from the treetops, their numbers so large that they blocked any remaining light. After only a second, he returned his gaze to the ground, only to find Niall Garbh O'Donnell was gone.

Backing up his horse, he looked to his men who were also searching for signs of the others. They had all, in the space of a second's time, simply disappeared.

⊬⇒⇐⊬

They were utterly lost.

Wills tamped down his impatience for the umpteenth time. Never in all his life had he been lost.

He knew the signs of moss and sun and knew instinctively that he needed to travel west until arriving at Drongawn Lough and then northward to return to Fort Stewart and the castle, and yet he and his men were hopelessly turned around.

They had not encountered another clearing, nor were there any signs of The O'Donnell and his men. He tried not to imagine that they were just beyond the next set of trees, snickering at the foreigners' stupidity, and yet the feeling persisted until it became absolutely maddening. What they thought were trails seemed to lead nowhere but had simply served to guide them in serpentine patterns that had them traveling in circles, their progress impeded at every turn.

The sun had long ago set and with its absence, whatever warmth had been left in the forest seemed to have been inhaled by an invisible force that left the branches swirling over their heads as though coming alive. They ushered in frigid winds that raked their skin, causing even the most stalwart among them to shiver. Even the horses sensed the disturbance, their snorts growing panicked in the thick forest.

Just as he was considering stopping the men where they were to wait for the moon's rising, he caught a whiff of wood smoke. Turning to Tomas, he knew he sensed it as well; they turned their faces upward as if they could determine from which direction it came. As they circled in place, he spotted the faintest red and orange and signaled his men to follow it.

After a few minutes, they found themselves in the same clearing in which they had encountered Niall Garbh O'Donnell and his men. Wills swore under his breath, a sentiment that was echoed in the voices of his men. They had traveled for hours, seeming to cover miles of landscape only to find themselves back where they had begun.

But this time, a small wood fire was cackling in the center of it.

"We stop here," Wills directed. "We'll wait for the moon to rise and lend us light."

A low chortling sounded from the edge of the trees and he reached instinctively for his sword. "Who goes there?"

As he peered into the tree line where the voice had seemingly originated, the answer came from behind.

"It is I who should inquire who you might be."

Startled, he turned around to find a man only slightly older than himself standing beside the fire. He was without doubt the tallest man Wills had ever encountered; perhaps towering six and a half feet tall. He was made even taller still by an unusual metal hat from which a single elaborate feather emerged. He had a long, oval face almost completely obscured by a neat Ducktail-styled beard and a mustache in the English style. His hair was long, combed straight back from the temples and was quite possibly red though Wills could not be certain in the dancing light cast by the fire. He wore breeches and boots, a shirt that reached to his knees and a cape with heavy brocade. He noted he wore a belt fashioned around his shirt from which several knives hung in their sheaths.

"I am William Neely, aide to Captain William Stewart, cousin to King James I. And who might you be, sir?"

"I am Sir Cahir O'Doherty, ruler of the Inishowen Peninsula and a friend to The Crown."

"No," Wills said before he could catch himself. "You are only slightly older than I. It is not possible."

At that, the forest erupted in a wave of quiet laughter.

"Twenty-three," Cahir said. "I joined the English army at the age of fifteen and received a knighthood at that age as well, for bravery and services performed during Tyrone's Rebellion. You are on Clan land, sir. May I inquire as to your intentions?"

Wills swallowed. They were clearly surrounded; he could hear the laughter continuing but could not see any man—nor had they seen signs of any as they had wandered for hours. "Begging your pardon," he said. "I did not intend to encroach. I am reluctant to admit—though I must—that I am lost. I must return to Captain Stewart, who is—"

"—living in O'Donnell Castle," Cahir finished. He cocked his head. "It is but a short piece." He nodded toward one corner of the circle.

Wills looked in the direction he indicated. He could have sworn he had been that way already and had naught to show for his efforts except a silly look on his face. "Might I—?"

"Indeed you might," Cahir responded as if reading his mind. "My man Phelim will guide you as far as Drongawn Lough. From the shoreline, I take it that you can find your way home?"

"I can indeed. And I thank you for your generosity."

"Not at all. As my land borders yours, it is my desire to have friendly relations with Captain Stewart and his clan."

"Please," Wills said, "visit us. We welcome you and your men."

Cahir nodded.

The brush parted and an older man that appeared similar enough to Cahir to be his father rode into the clearing on a blue-black horse. Like Cahir, he was tall in stature with broad shoulders; his beard was much longer, nearly raking his chest and his mustache jutted out past his cheeks. His hair was lighter, perhaps a light auburn. But the shape of the face, the eyes and the expression were almost identical. "At your service," he said simply before turning the horse in the opposite direction. Wills motioned for the others to follow. When he turned to thank Cahir O'Doherty once more, he was gone.

9

The morning sun's rays crept through the open doors of the Great Hall in a wide swath, illuminating the dust and grime that was impossible to keep out. It crawled upward along the expansive wood table until it fell like a giant claw across the map of Eire.

"I'm glad you agree, Captain," Wills said. "Now, according to this map, the O'Doherty lands are surrounded by water except for here, along their southern border. Our lands are located within the old O'Donnell territory, so there is only this area here—" he drew a line with his finger across the region where the O'Doherty peninsula of Inishowen joined the mainland "—which will need to be surveyed."

A shadow crossed the table and Wills glanced up to see Tomas and Fergus joining them at the table. He looked at the other men—Captain Stewart, Archie and the surveyor, Mister Parsons—briefly before returning his attention to the map. "I suggest that a contingent be sent to Cahir O'Doherty to convince him it is in his best interests to assist us in determining the clan boundaries. Once that has been achieved, we should clear the land to that point. The forests are too thick and lend themselves too easily to enemy attack."

"We can begin clearing immediately," Captain Stewart said thoughtfully. "This land is uncontested so we will begin around the castle and fort and move outward in a circumference until the forests have been cut back. This will immediately provide us safety, as no man will be able to approach without detection."

The others around the table offered their agreement.

"By the time we reach the southwestern edge, here along the Drongawn Lough, The O'Doherty's men will have assisted us in determining the boundaries. We can then—if he is willing—cut back the forest at that juncture."

"I wish to lead the contingent," Wills offered.

Captain Stewart looked up, surprised.

Before he could question his intent, Wills continued, "He might have killed us. We were completely surrounded, and yet he and his people are able to move freely through the forest without detection. It is—and I do not say this out of superstition, mind you—but it is as if they are mythical creatures who are able to appear and disappear at will. I have never encountered such. And yet," he continued, "he did us no harm, even providing us with an escort—a man by the name of Phelim MacDavitt, who saw us safely within sight of the castle."

Stewart nodded. "Archie, do you have any objections?"

"I do not. In fact, I believe young Wills will represent us well."

"Fine. Then take Mister Parsons, Fergus, Tomas, and three or four others with you. But this time, you are not to travel overland."

"My thoughts precisely," Wills said with relief.

"If I may, Captain." Tomas inched closer to the table. "The O'Doherty clan owns many castles, but it is generally accepted that Cahir prefers that of Carrickabraghy Castle. It is located here, on the Isle of Doagh; the castle the ship passed on our journey here."

"On that island?" Captain Stewart said, leaning in to peer more closely at the position on the map where Tomas pointed. "I recall the structure; quite impressive. It seems to be an odd place for the head of the clan to choose, being somewhat removed from the rest of his holdings."

"Not truly an island," Tomas offered. "It was at one time, thousands of years ago, but with the receding of the ocean, there is land between the isle and the Inishowen Peninsula—though it cannot be walked except at low tide. We passed by the castle closer to high tide as we turned southward into the Lough Swilly."

"Ah," Wills said. "Then if we might use the ship, Captain, we can simply sail north from Drongawn Lough into the Lough Swilly and then moor here, along the Inishowen Peninsula's northwestern edge."

"I must warn you," Tomas interjected, "the same craggy rock that connects the Isle with the mainland is one that can easily batter a ship and split her in two. The castle was only built some eight years ago as a defense against the English; they keep the bulk of their livestock on the Isle because it is precisely so inaccessible."

"Then what do you suggest?" Captain Stewart asked.

"Moor here, at the entrance to the Lough Swilly. There is a beach there; we can walk along the shoreline. The first low is shortly after midnight; the second, shortly after noon. We will be watched, regardless of the day or night. Best we take as few men as possible so they do not believe it is an invasion."

"You raise a good point, Tomas."

"You see," Tomas continued, "An invasion did occur there just one year after the castle was built on the old friary site. It was a clan matter, to be sure; when Cahir's father died, Cahir was only fourteen years of age and two factions of the clan fought over who should become the clan's leader. They attacked along the sand plain here, at Pollan, not far at all from the castle… Cahir's forces were victorious, of course, and Sir Henry Docwra—Sir George Paulet's predecessor—proclaimed the boy the Lord of Inishowen."

Wills looked up as Tomas finished speaking. "I agree with mooring here," he said. "It is but a short sail and if I take not more than six men total, I will leave one man with the ship. The others will accompany me to Carrickabraghy Castle."

"And if Cahir is not there?" Captain Stewart prompted.

"Then we will make our case to the man he left in charge, and urge that he visit us here at the O'Donnell's castle to make plans for the survey. I believe, sir, it is important that he understand why we are clearing the land and that we do not knowingly encroach on his."

"I agree. Then gather your men and arrange to set out to meet the afternoon's low tides."

+≡≡+

The skies were a vivid blue along the horizon with the fluffiest of canopies so close it seemed as if the men could reach out and touch the clouds. Wills noted they were white, without the slightest appearance of gray or black, which boded well for their return journey. However, he had learned the Irish weather was like a woman's mood, changing in a mere heartbeat, and he would feel the better for it once he had successfully met with The O'Doherty and was safely on his return trip.

The ocean to the west of the Lough Swilly was black and churning and as they prepared to turn inward to moor along the Inishowen Peninsula coastline, the waters a short distance away parted as a killer whale broke the surface. The orca was so massive that as its body cleared the water, the resulting swell sent the ship teetering to one side as though it was only a tiny vessel and not one that had carried a hundred men westward. It was magnificent, Wills thought, as all eyes turned to watch it. The sun caught its body, causing its black back to sparkle with a brilliance the likes of which he had never seen before. It was massive; easily the length of their ship, well over twenty foot. It expelled the contents of the blowhole with such force that the vapor sprayed at least fifteen feet into the air before it completely left the surface. For one amazing second, he could see the entire whale with its white belly, a patch of white under its chin, and another smaller patch near its eye.

Then it was gone, diving deep before they could catch their breaths.

"I would wager he was six tons," Fergus said in awe.

"We'd best pull to shore as far as possible," Wills said, "or we may return only to find the ship has been blown to sea." He turned back to gauge the distance to shore when another sight caused him to suck in his breath. "Lads, we have company."

The shore was filled with men. They stood a few paces from the tree line and nearly shoulder to shoulder. Each stood with the same stance, their feet spread wide, one hand on a shield and the other holding a weapon.

"Take the helm," he directed Fergus.

He made his way down the steps to the deck and toward the bow. "I am here to see Cahir O'Doherty," he called out loudly to be heard above the swells as they prepared to moor. "The Lord of Inishowen," he added.

"Good move," Tomas whispered hoarsely. "It shows respect for their leader, calling him by title and all."

"Ah," Wills said as an older man broke away from the line. He walked briskly and was followed a few paces behind by two others. "Phelim MacDavitt."

The older man waited until the ship was within a fair distance of the shore and with a simple nod of his head, a half dozen of his men moved forward to help secure the vessel. Wills turned toward Tomas. "Make certain he sees every man; he no doubt will be counting." With that, he made his way to the captain's cabin to gather the surveyor's papers.

⊹⫸⫷⊹

Carrickabraghy Castle was set close to the coastline atop formidable cliffs and roughhewn rocks that would make an attack from sea nearly impossible. It was even more imposing now that he stood before it than it had been from sea, consisting as it did of an elaborate rectangular stone structure with a tower at the end closest to the sea and perhaps seven towers in all. As Wills approached with an O'Doherty escort far outnumbering his tiny band, he noted soldiers atop the parapets watching them approach just as they had when their party had sailed past on their initial approach to Stewart's land. The beachline was brief at best before giving way to some of the most rugged landscape Wills had encountered; it was wild and hilly, the dips and growths having no rhyme or reason to them but seemed rather like God's giant hand had gathered all manner of pebble and brush and simply scattered it onto the earth. Where each fell began outcrops of rock that sometimes was smooth as a woman's leg while at other times rough as a man's stubble and in between climbed all manner of wild underbrush and foliage. It was most definitely some of the most inhospitable terrain he had ever witnessed.

Once they gained entrance to the keep, they found themselves in a large courtyard surrounded by activity. Sheep, horses and a few cattle grazed alongside chickens pecking at the ground. An old woman sat at a spinning wheel erected just outside the door of a smaller structure and others tended to a boar on a spit over an open flame. The women, in particular, peered at them out of the corner of their eyes with poorly concealed curiosity.

In one corner, a variety of crops were growing and in another, the sounds of a blacksmith forging filled the air. They were led past soldiers practicing their sword-fighting skills, an activity Wills would have enjoyed observing, had they been present under different circumstances. He was still a bit unnerved by the Irishmen's habit of simply appearing in numbers as if out of thin air as they approached a set of open doors.

Cahir O'Doherty himself met them at the threshold, welcoming them inside the Great Hall as if they had been long-time allies. In short order, ale, boar and venison were set upon the table by two serving wenches, one with blue-black hair and the other with wavy red. Both were careful to focus on their tasks but when Wills felt eyes upon him and looked to his left, he caught the wide green eyes of the redhead studying him. She quickly cast her eyes downward, only to shift upwards again.

"You remind me," Cahir was saying, "of another man that was here representing the Crown. Do you know Henry Docwra, by chance?"

"Unfortunately, I never met the man, though I have begun to hear quite a bit about his time here," Wills answered, taking a deep swig of ale.

"A pity. I suppose he must have returned to England shortly before you arrived... He understood Ireland; understood the Irish peoples."

"Please enlighten me."

"You are Scottish, are you not?"

"Aye, I am."

"On your island, you have the Highlands, the Lowlands, England, Wales... Ireland, though a smaller island, has been divided into hundreds of 'countries' for many a century. We stay within our boundaries—more or less—establishing alliances with some neighbors and clashing with others. Each 'country' elects their own leader, sometimes peacefully, sometimes not. The differences," he continued, leaning forward, "are that our countries are called clans and our leaders, chieftains or lords. But it does not make us inferior simply because we do not use the identical verbiage of the English."

"I do not believe I have ever heard it explained in those terms."

"Henry Docwra understood this. Oh, he had a rough time of it when he first came to Eire and set his encampment at Derry, for sure. But later, he took the time and he made the effort to learn where each of our boundaries exists in Ulster, if not the whole of Eire. He forged relationships with some chieftains, warred with others, much as we have been doing for centuries."

"And, if I may ask, how do you view the English and the Plantations?"

Cahir shrugged. "They are but another set of chieftains to me—most likely, to all the Irish. Henry knew this, understood it and respected it."

"But Henry has been replaced by Sir George Paulet."

He growled. "Paulet is a weasel and a bastard."

"I beg your pardon?"

"He respects no man. And particularly in disrespecting a man who has won the gratitude of the Queen, he has demonstrated that he does not respect The Crown as well."

"You are referring to having been knighted by Queen Elizabeth?"

"I am. Do you know how old I was when I traveled to London to receive knighthood? Fifteen. During the Nine Years War, I was a valuable ally to the English. I fought against other chieftains—Irish chieftains, many more powerful than I—on behalf of the Queen, and now I have pledged allegiance to the King."

"How did you find London?" Wills asked, hoping to steer the subject to more pleasurable conversation before the deadly combination of rhetoric and ale ignited into unchecked anger.

"Terribly dreary." He tore off a hunk of venison. "Very dirty place, London. I have been to Paris, to Valladolid and Madrid. Those are beautiful places. Opulent. Even decadent." He chuckled. "It is interesting; the French and the Spaniards look at England with disdain, believing their country to be backwards and coarse. The English, in turn, look at the Scottish as if they are boorish. And both look at Ireland, believing it to be beneath them all. Every man must have someone else to look down upon, it seems."

"You sound much like my sister Beth," Wills said thoughtfully, emptying his mug.

"Ah, then no doubt I would enjoy conversing with her."

The serving wench immediately stepped forward to refill his mug before making her way around the table, topping off the others' tankards. "I prefer to judge each man individually," Wills said, "not by the God he chooses to worship, the language he speaks or the customs he practices."

"Ah, but you are a rare one," Cahir said. "But because you have an open mind, because you are curious about the Irish and you do not seem to be here purely for the sport of eradicating Eire's native peoples, you will go far."

"Tell me," Wills said, choosing his words carefully, "you have only just met me. How do you know of my curiosity or my intentions?"

He shrugged. "The trees have eyes and the winds have ears, William Neely of Wigtownshire. You would serve yourself well to remember that."

"Tell me, sir, how did your peninsula get its name?"

"Inishowen?" He leaned back. "You have heard of Niall of Nine Hostages?"

"I am afraid I have not."

"He was once a High King in Ireland more than a thousand years ago. He had several sons, one of whom was named Eoghain. He gave him this peninsula and called it Inis Eoghain—the island of Eoghain—and it was since anglicized to Inishowen."

"Ah. I had an inkling there was a story there."

"You will find a story associated with everything and everyone in Eire." He raised his tankard in a brief salute. "And I am a descendant of Eoghain so you see, this land has remained in my family for more than a thousand years."

"I see," Wills responded, raising his tankard in turn. "That brings me to the purpose of my visit."

"Ah."

"I have with me here a set of surveys that illustrate Captain William Stewart's landholdings." He motioned for the roll of parchment and waited until Mister Parsons had spread the uppermost map upon the table. "We do not wish to encroach upon your land and my apologies again for crossing into your territory—and my gratefulness again for the escort home." He met Phelim's eyes, nodding briefly. "It is our desire to clear our land of the forested area and I am here to ask for your assistance in determining the precise border between our lands."

Cahir's eyes narrowed. "Clear the land."

"Aye." Wills looked from one man to the other.

"Eire has already been sacked and burned," Cahir said. "When Paulet and Chichester replaced the Earl of Essex and Henry Docwra, they began systematically burning our forests and our homes, killing livestock and wild animals alike, starving us until they hoped we had no fighting spirit left."

"That is not our purpose in clearing the land. You see, Lord O'Doherty, wool is demanded in England. It is a ready market. We intend to raise sheep by the hundreds if not thousands and transport the wool to English markets. If we can clear much of the forest, we can provide suitable meadows for our sheep. And," he added, "it might be something for you to consider as well."

"Farmers of sheep." He looked amused. "When you clear the forest, there is nothing to hold the soil."

"Ah," Tomas said, "but there is. The English have a system which we will be pleased to show you."

A long moment of silence ensued. Then Cahir thumped his fist good-naturedly on the table. "But of course we will assist in identifying our borders. And if you choose to clear your own land of the forest, it will be only you that wallows in mud and muck. And without the trees on O'Donnell land, it provides a lengthier sight with which we can spot you before you reach O'Doherty ground."

Before Wills could respond, he thumped the table again. "More ale!" he called. "Let us celebrate."

10

Wills was beginning to doubt the wisdom of his suggestion regarding the clearing of forest land. With the tables turned, he realized too late that what Cahir had detected in his shrewdness was indeed true: the O'Doherty clan could remain in the shadows and shelters of their trees and easily watch the activities of Captain Stewart and his men as well as the former tenants of The O'Donnell on vacant land.

There was also the matter of physically clearing the land, which served to be more problematic and time-consuming that it appeared when first advocated.

As Captain Stewart had ordered, they began in two circles; one around the castle and the other around what was becoming known as Fort Stewart. The ground was uneven, filled with rocks and limestone, often backbreaking work. It took weeks to reach the area of the border, at which point they sent word to The O'Doherty. He appeared personally alongside Phelim, who was looking and acting more like a father or older brother to them all, the different last name notwithstanding. They seemed to have brought with them every clansfolk; women and children watched from the safety of O'Doherty soil as if it was the most amusing spectacle they had ever witnessed.

Some of the O'Doherty men even joined in to clear O'Donnell property from the line they drew, eager to push back the forest from another clan's land. They were so enthusiastic about it that Wills made a mental note to investigate the history between the O'Donnell and O'Doherty properties. He couldn't seem to get it out of his head that the Irish expected Rory O'Donnell to reclaim his estate at some point in the not-too-distant future with the support of a Spanish army and when they did, the O'Doherty's would certainly have the advantage.

That advantage, Wills thought as he helped to heave another tree over, extended over Captain Stewart as well. But the captain had been adamant, even calling together the hundred or so men that had accompanied him to Eire to lay out a plan.

England was indeed clamoring for wool; they could not seem to get enough of it. Wills learned that it was not only his sword fighting prowess that had attracted the captain's attention but also his background in herding and his willingness—obligation, more like it—to go after the sheep stolen by neighbors.

Each man would be rewarded for his efforts with a home and a tract of land. The homes would be erected in rows so each had a stoop and a small back courtyard; the close proximity to one another would provide safety. The land would be divided vertically just as it was in Scotland's Lowlands: each man would receive land at the top of the hill as well as the bottom so it was divided into strips. Therefore, no man would receive the plumper grass at the top while another would obtain marshland at the bottom.

Captain Stewart announced he also planned to rotate the land during the initial years. A man would remain in his home indefinitely—unlike Scotland lairds that had a tendency to move most tenants every three to five years—but the land upon which the sheep would graze would be rotated every three years so in the event that one man did have a more desirable lot, he would not retain control of it in perpetuity.

Further, each man would keep a share of the income provided by the shearing of the sheep with the remainder, albeit the much larger portion, going to Captain Stewart. They would work together as a community to shear the sheep and they would also be expected to farm some crops in which all would share.

It seemed like a perfectly reasonable plan, honest and well thought out, and the type of plan that a Scot such as Captain Stewart would have envisioned, having witnessed both the advantages and trials of the system used in Scotland.

Moreover, Wills was beginning to learn just how backward some of the Scottish techniques or lack thereof—truly were. In Scotland, marshy land was marshy land. It was God's will and nobody questioned it or sought to improve it. But now he was learning through the English settlers a method of drainage. It was ingenious, he thought when he first witnessed the trenches that syphoned the water into Drongawn Lough, and it was near impossible to resist traveling all the way back to Wigtownshire for the pure pleasure of educating his father and neighbors on this sensible strategy. Unable to do that, he placated himself by watching the water being whisked off the land during the heaviest rainstorms, satisfaction rising in his chest with each drop that spilled into the lough.

11

Derry was a hotbed of activity. More English soldiers had arrived, necessitating more pubs and more permanent living quarters. In one corner of the village, women gingerly raised their skirts to their ankles to dodge the worst of the muddy paths as church bells chimed while on the other side, drunkenness, petty brawls and brash music were a constant threat to Sheriff Hamilton's order. Accents of women and men alike revealed their origins from the precise diction of the English to the earthier tones of the Scottish and the melodic charm of the Irish.

Wills had spent the morning running errands for Captain Stewart; now that sufficient land had been cleared, he was arranging the import of sheep from other regions of the island. Derry would, along with Donegal, become the destination for the wool and already a burgeoning industry had begun to spring up. Potash pits were smoking between the forest and the village, tended by scores who would turn the lanolin from the sheep's wool into soap while others were spinning, carding and felting wool that would eventually find its way to Scotland and England and points further east for use in clothing and bedding. There was talk of a tiny settlement closer to the eastern shore—a place called Belfast that the Irish claimed giants once inhabited—but it was not much more than talk. Plans to develop industry around the wool trade there had fallen short after Sir Thomas Smith had been granted the land once it was seized from The O'Neill after the Flight of the Earls, but Smith had never ventured to Eire to take proper custody of it.

Captain Stewart returned to the ship they had anchored in the harbor and had graciously given Wills a rare afternoon's leave. He had hastily tracked down Fergus and Tomas, joining them for a much-anticipated meal in a loud and chaotic pub. It was a sharp contrast to the quietude of Fort Stewart, other men and building sounds notwithstanding. The ale was cool and slid down his throat easily, helping to warm his belly along with a bowl of fat-laden stew and hot baked bread.

A raucous laughter sounded behind him and he leaned back in his chair to observe a group of soldiers sharing bawdy jokes. The room was a sea of men; the handful of tables were full and those unfortunate enough not to have a seat had chosen to improvise with plates of food in their hands while they stood. Several tankards of ale had been unceremoniously pushed onto their table by those whose hands were full with the task of eating and it was not uncommon for one slightly inebriated or simply clumsy to bump into the tables, threatening to send its contents flying.

The occasional serving wench wound her way through the crowd, ignoring the slaps on the derriere at times and at other, retorting with feminine threats that only made the men bolder.

As Wills studied the crowd, his eyes fell on a distant table set in the far corner and against the wall where two men seemingly oblivious of the pandemonium played a game of chess. One man was unfamiliar to him; he was a tall fellow with tawny hair held in a tail at the nape of his neck. The other was Sir George Paulet.

While Tomas and Fergus swapped stories and laughter, Wills quietly observed the two men. There was something off-putting about Paulet that he couldn't quite put his finger on. His skin was rather pasty and his eyes darted about under heavy dark brows as if he were suspicious of all those around him. His mouth was small for his face and he held his lips in an odd shape, something between a permanent smirk and a scowl. His right hand was poised above the chessboard, revealing an outsized ring and lace cuffs, his little finger unnaturally posed. He had an air, Wills decided, of affectation.

A soldier moved from the bar toward the front of the pub and Paulet leaned closer to the wall as though he was concerned the man would brush against his clothing. As the soldier wandered past, Wills caught sight of another figure: Cahir O'Doherty was standing only a few feet away from Paulet, leaning against the bar with a mug in his hand, watching the chess game with Phelim.

His own ale gone and the serving wench now nowhere to be seen, Wills stood. "Another, anyone?" he asked his tablemates.

"Aye, aye!" Tomas answered.

"One for me as well," Fergus said.

Wills maneuvered through the throng of pressed bodies until he had reached the bar and was only a few feet from Paulet and O'Doherty. He raised his mug in greeting to the latter.

"Ah, William Neely!" Cahir said, raising his mug in return. "And your land is cleared now, is it?"

"We have started, aye. We will begin raising sheep soon and preparing to plant."

"Excellent." His eyes grew dark as he watched Paulet, who had finally made his chess move. Setting his empty mug on the bar, he stepped to Paulet's table. "Pardon the interruption, Governor, but we have a matter to discuss."

"Off with you," he responded, waving his hand in dismissal. "Can't you see I am a very busy man?"

"So I hear. Each time I have visited your office, I am told you are too busy to speak with me."

"Has it ever occurred to you that I do not wish to speak to you?" Paulet said haughtily.

"I can assure you, sir, the feeling is mutual. However, there is the matter of Inch Island. King James was quite explicit in that the island belongs to me."

"King James was quite explicit that I am the Governor."

"The Governor of Derry; not the Governor of Inch Island."

"You have no need for Inch Island and I do."

Wills noticed the men around the table had become quiet as Paulet's voice had risen. All eyes were now turning to the two men.

"Whether I have need for it is of no concern of yours," Cahir was saying. His face was reddening and it was apparent that he was trying to keep his temper under control. "The facts are that I own Inch Island and I have expressly forbidden your men to make use of it without requesting and obtaining my permission."

With that, Paulet leaped from his chair, nearly toppling his ale. He barely reached to Cahir O'Doherty's muscled chest but as Wills watched, both his feet left the ground as he leapt forward and slapped O'Doherty hard on the cheek.

The pub grew completely silent and for a moment, Cahir stood perfectly still as if he was stunned. Then his face began to redden with a mixture of anger and humiliation.

Paulet's face was also deep crimson as he seethed in anger. "How dare you!" he spat. "I need never ask permission of an animal such as yourself."

Cahir made no move to remove the spittle from his clothing but he merely glowered at the man in silence. It would obviously be a grossly uneven match as Cahir could most likely lift the smaller man and toss him like a child, but Wills noticed that no one stepped forward as if to assist the governor.

Phelim tapped the younger man on the shoulder and whispered hoarsely, "Let us take our leave."

"Yes," Paulet said, his voice rising. "This establishment is not for Irish monkeys. It is only for those who serve the King—the only King." He attempted to lift the mug from the table but toppled it instead. "Here! Here! To King James!" he shouted as though he was raising his mug high.

Cahir's hands balled into fists. "What did you call me, sir?" he asked. His voice was steady but menacing.

Paulet slapped him a second time across the face, this time so hard that spittle escaped from O'Doherty's mouth. "An Irish monkey," he repeated menacingly. "Or does your infantile brain not know what a monkey is, perhaps?"

Cahir made a move for the sword he carried across his back, but Phelim held him steady. "Not here," he said, the pressure on Cahir's shoulder visibly increasing. "Pick your place and time."

After an awkward moment, Cahir glanced meaningfully at the chess board and said, "You have allowed yourself to become flanked." With that, he reluctantly shifted his eyes away from Paulet and slowly continued toward the door. When Wills turned back to the bar, he found three mugs waiting and Fergus had joined his side.

"I'll just be taking these two," Fergus said, his large hands grasping two mugs.

As Paulet returned to his chair, he shouted, "Serving wench! Where is that disgusting bint? Bring me another ale. Someone has absconded with mine!"

Wills made a move to pick up the fallen mug but Fergus moved into his line of vision. "Don't," he said. "Stay out of it."

"I am afraid," Paulet's chess partner stated, moving his bishop to capture Paulet's king, "that the ruffian was quite correct. I flanked you, dear George, and now your king is finished. Checkmate."

Wills left the necessary coins at the bar and grabbed his ale. As he passed by Paulet once more, he could hear the man cursing. Making his way back to his table, he spotted a man rising from another table that had been nearly concealed by the throngs of standing soldiers. He strode purposefully after Cahir and Phelim, his eyes not wavering from the men's backs as they opened the door and stepped into the sunlight. It was Niall Garbh O'Donnell.

He set his tankard on the table as Fergus was settling back in beside Tomas. "I will be only a moment." Before either could respond, he was passing through the crowd to the door.

The sunlight hit him full in the face, a sudden departure from the smoky atmosphere of the pub. He stepped into a path littered with horses, carriages and pedestrians moving, it seemed, in all directions at once. Peering around the crowd, his eyes came to rest on Niall Garbh's dark brown overcoat just as the man turned onto a side street from the main road. He kept his eyes on the corner as he followed Niall Garbh's path but as he moved onto the side street, The O'Donnell was nowhere to be seen. He was just about to return to the pub when he spotted him rounding yet another corner.

By the time Wills had reached the next intersection, he heard voices coming from the other side of the building and he stepped back, moving into an alcove.

"How dare him!" Cahir was saying. "Have I not proven my loyalty to both Queen Elizabeth and King James? How dare him speak as if I—and the Irish—are subhuman!"

"There is a time and a place," Phelim answered, "and it is not in a pub when we are outnumbered by English soldiers."

"I would rather suffer death," Cahir responded heatedly, "than be met with such insult and dealt such dishonor. A slap! One slaps a child, not a man of my distinction—and not once but twice, as if I was nothing more than a schoolboy!"

"Phelim is right," Niall Garbh's voice rose above Cahir's. "Bide your time. The opportunity will present itself and we will crush him."

"The man does not represent King James," Phelim added. "He represents only himself; he is loyal to no other."

"Then allow me to take him out."

Both men objected in unison.

"Perhaps we can petition the king for the return of Henry Docwra," Phelim suggested.

"Ah," Niall Garbh said, "but you know why he is gone and why this tyrant has taken his place. The king thought Docwra was too lenient because he sought our cooperation instead of our rage."

"But I have been a loyal subject," Cahir argued, "even turning against my own flesh and blood to align myself with the English. I fought and killed many an Irishman and had it not been for my efforts, the English might not have won the Nine Years War at all."

"And don't I know," Niall Garbh said. His voice sounded menacing. "My own clan has lost the bulk of their lands to an English settler on account of your actions."

"Now, now," Phelim said, his voice conciliatory. "Let us put the past behind us and decide how we can unite to ease the yoke of English oppression."

The voices lowered and though Wills strained to hear more, he concluded that they were moving further down the street and out of earshot. He took a deep breath and exhaled slowly as he considered their words. Then remembering that Fergus and Tomas awaited him at the pub, he stepped out of the alcove briskly, promptly colliding with a pedestrian making her way in the opposite direction.

She was petite, a full head shorter than Wills so that when he rammed headlong into her, his chin grazed the top of her head. The aroma of rose hips wafted upward and for the briefest moment, he found himself staring down at her golden hair. It was pulled straight back, the long tresses gathered into a braid along which ran a slender crimson ribbon.

He stepped back. "My deepest apologies. Are you quite alright?"

She gazed up at him with voluminous green eyes. Her face was heart-shaped, her cheekbones high and her chin elfin. A long, slender neck led to a v-shaped bodice that revealed more of her bosom than a man had the right to see, and yet Wills could not tear his eyes away from her.

As she opened her mouth to reply, a gentleman moved through the crowd toward them, swiftly taking her by the elbow. He appeared to be at least twenty years older than she and had graying hair. Wills bowed his head slightly and murmured, "Sir."

The man did not respond but continued walking. As the beautiful young woman was whisked along, she peered over her shoulder at Wills. Her lips curled upward in a shy smile and then she was turning away from him again. He found himself watching her until the crowds obstructed his view and even then he tried valiantly to find her again, to watch the gentle sway of her crimson skirts and the way the sunlight played across her hair.

He was still standing there when Fergus slapped him on the back, jolting him back to the present. "So you are forgetting your friends, are you now?"

Wills shook his head. "I just overheard a conversation between The O'Donnell and The O'Doherty."

Tomas sidled alongside them. "Oh, the two of them have quite the history, they do."

"Oh?"

"Aye, indeed. A sorted one. The O'Donnells were a powerful clan and though the O'Dohertys had their own and their land was almost cut off from the others due to its location on the peninsula, you know, the O'Donnells were considered their overlord prior to the English invasion."

"What exactly is an overlord?" Wills asked.

"Let's just say a level above. Every now and again the O'Donnells pressed the O'Dohertys into paying them tenancy."

"But how could they do that?"

"Size, pure and simple. The O'Dohertys did not have the numbers to fight them. Anyway, after the English invaded, Cahir sided with the English even as Rory O'Donnell fought against them. Cahir alleged that Henry Docwra had promised if he helped the English win the Nine Years War, he would give him the O'Donnell land in payment."

"The O'Donnell land? The land Captain Stewart has been granted?"

"Aye," Tomas said, laughing. "Ironic, isn't it now?"

"But—"

"Well, obviously, Cahir did help the English and even received knighthood from none other than Queen Elizabeth herself but the lands were given back to the O'Donnells after the war."

"Why?"

Tomas shrugged. "Rory O'Donnell agreed to submit to King James and in the Treaty of Mellifont he was given back the clan's land."

"Then how did Stewart get it?"

"The Flight of the Earls, plain and simple. Even after the Treaty, the English were convinced that Rory—along with Hugh O'Neill and The Maguire—were continuing to plot against the Crown. Rumor had it they were to be arrested, which is why they fled. And once they deserted the island, their lands were declared available for the Plantations."

"And that's when Captain Stewart was awarded his property on former O'Donnell land."

"Ah, you're not just a pretty face are you now?" Tomas laughed, jabbing him in the shoulder.

"Come on," Fergus said, "I've someplace to go. We are wasting precious time on our rare journey to civilization." He urged them toward the outskirts of the small village while they continued to talk.

"Derry? So you'd be calling Derry civilization?"

"It's a damn sight closer to it than Fort Stewart, I can tell you that."

"So what's the story of Niall Garbh O'Donnell?" Wills asked, turning the attention back to the previous subject.

"Oh, he's a duplicitous one, he is," Tomas answered. "You never can be quite sure if he is on the side of the English or the side of the Irish and truth be told, he is on the side of Niall Garbh O'Donnell and that's that. He attempted to betray Rory and seize the chieftain role for himself and it took King James to sort it. He gave

Niall Garbh a land grant bordering on your own but gave Rory a Lordship, which did not set well with Niall Garbh at all."

"And what's the story between Niall Garbh and Cahir?"

Tomas shrugged again. "It depends on the day and the hour. They have fought against one another and beside one another and it is anyone's guess where he will be next."

"Ah, here we are." Fergus stopped and puffed out his chest.

"Where are we?" Wills asked, perplexed.

Fergus pointed at a wood structure at the end of the street. "Best brothel in all of Derry."

Wills laughed. "Then enjoy yourself, lad. I've work yet to do."

"No, Wills. You don't get to Derry all that often now. A man has needs and it isn't healthy to pass up the chance."

Wills waved his hand as he started back up the street. "See you this evening," he called over his shoulder. As he walked out of sight, he might have considered turning around and going back had it not been for that gorgeous waif he had just encountered. He could still smell the perfume in her hair. No doubt about it, he had to find her again.

12

Ireland was beginning to feel like home. As Wills made his way from the far fields to Fort Stewart, he was amazed at the transformation that had taken place. With extensive deforestation had come the unveiling of a new landscape; both were beautiful in their way but now he could look out over the hills and valleys to forty shades of green under a constantly shifting sky.

Oh, the women had helped, to be sure. As if a bulletin had been erected at Dublin Castle, they came in wagonloads—primarily English but many a Scot as well. They were not looked upon with favor by the Irish lasses and a few catfights had ensued before the captain had put a stop to the nonsense. There were more than enough men to go 'round and more than one dance and celebration had transpired to prove it, in which many a lad paired up with a female. It was survival, was it not? Wills pondered. A man has needs, as Fergus had so brashly proclaimed, and they went beyond his bed. He had clothes to darn and a belly to fill and now, thanks to Stewart's vision, a home to clean and tend to.

But though he danced more than one night away and saw his image catch the fancy of many a lass, none had struck his heart and imagination like the dainty fairy in crimson skirts.

He sighed. He'd spent the morning in weapons training, like he and all the other men had done for weeks now, though it was difficult to justify it in his own mind sometimes, as peaceful as things had remained. Still, the use of the harkbus was being drilled into each of them along with more sword practice. He had never fired a weapon before but now each morning after herding the sheep to the field, he was required to shoot time and again at designated targets and by God, he was damn good at it, he was. Oh and for sure the targets were mostly trees that stood perfectly still and waited for the volley but he would do himself a disservice if he did not recognize his growing proficiency.

After the target training came the formation training, which just served to prove that men could turn killing into a highly regimented art form. They were each assigned a number that was his to keep, a number that determined which of three lines he would always serve in, and where within that line he would be positioned. The lines were formed one behind the other with the first—which he served in—at the front. Their weapons would be fired in unison upon command and then they would drop to their knees and reload while the second row directly on their heels would fire before dropping to reload as well. The third row would fire but had no need to kneel during reload. Then it would begin all over again with the first row, second and third. Ingenious, he thought. It kept up a constant volley but with no enemy in sight, he wondered at the import placed upon it.

Tyrone's Rebellion, or The Nine Years War as some called it, had been over for six years now and though wounds were fresh in some men's minds, it seemed as distant as his own buried past. Oh, sure there were grumblings but for the most part the Irish had grown accustomed to William Stewart's lordship. The settlers, as the English and Scottish were called, had brought with them curious forms of drainage and dividing up each man's plot but they had been beneficial and even he could see the foundations laid for greater progress ahead.

Why, even a glance at the hillside in the distance spoke of the advances they were making. Once forested, it had been stripped of its trees, roots and underbrush and for a while had appeared like a big brown breast rising above the valleys below. But they had erected intricate natural fences along the vertical incline, dividing it from top to bottom into a dozen plots. He paused in his walk to watch the men at work there now, tilling the soil with cows made thin from the winter and preparing the soil for planting. Under all those trees and amid all those rocks was rather decent soil, certainly far better than the Scottish Lowlands.

Most of the crops would be potatoes, as England had an increasing demand for them which made a ready market. There were so many things one could do with a potato. They could be boiled and eaten or boiled and mashed or boiled and mashed and used in bread. They could be set among the embers, providing a smoky flavor or used in stews with thick meat drippings. And with England's love of them, the future looked bright indeed. There would be enough left over for the tenant farmer and his family, and enough land set aside on each plot for other vegetables such as turnips, carrots or beans.

He smiled as he looked at the fencing along the slopes. It was hardly visible from this distance but perhaps in a year or two or certainly within ten, it would be substantial as it was a living, breathing fence. He remembered when two of the men had brought some branches into camp one eve, showing the variegated leaves to one and all. They called it Griselinia, and by taking sticks from the fallen trees, putting them in the ground every few inches and the Griselinia plantings in between, it formed a miniature hedge that one day would grow into a taller, fuller one that might even be sufficient to keep sheep and cattle corralled.

The thought of livestock caused him to turn away from the hill and peer into the valleys below, where other men were tending to sheep. Each man was questioned as to his preferences, with some choosing to grow plants while others chose to herd sheep or cattle. He had selected sheep. He knew their habits and how to provide the care they needed; he had shorn too many a sheep to count in Scotland and had helped to birth many a wee lamb. England's desire for wool had created another ready-made market and his heart felt light and his mind at peace as he envisioned the years ahead.

He worked long days, to be sure, but it seemed to agree with him as he'd put on the weight of a man and he could see it in others' eyes that he could no longer be considered a lad at'al. Up before dawn, he and other shepherds moved the herd from pens near the fort into the open valleys. They each had their plots and his, like the others, ranged from fertile grass to rocky climbs to mud and muck that required constant tending to drain. Why, they even had dogs! He shook his head at the thought of it. Dogs had almost become extinct in the Lowlands of Scotland; life had grown too difficult and food too scarce.

But here the dogs were a necessity. They tended to the herds during the day while the men played at warfare in the unlikely event of another Irish uprising, and they protected the livestock from wolves and foxes, which were plentiful. In the late evenings when the sheep were safely corralled next to the fort once more, bellies were full and men retreated to the tiny homes they had built themselves, often accompanied by a willing lass, he enjoyed a solitary walk under the moonlight when the air was alive with the sounds of wolves howling. Occasionally, he saw them—large, furry gray creatures with eyes that could glow in the dark. They were often drawn to the bleating of the sheep, necessitating both dogs and men standing guard during the darkest hours.

His work as an aide to Captain Stewart was erratic at best; he and Archie tended to matters for the most part, but occasionally he was brought in to ride to Derry with a message—horseback having been made possible once the lands had been cleared. There still existed some forest at the bottom of the Inishowen Peninsula on O'Doherty lands but he knew now how to navigate them and the clan accepted that he was only passing through and meant no harm to them and theirs.

He spotted two horses moving across the distant fields and he watched them now with growing curiosity. They did not divert around the plots—which even a blind man could see were carefully laid out—but rode straight through them, scattering the sheep and riling the dogs. Watching their route, he realized they were heading straight for Fort Stewart.

He took the shortcut to the fort, no longer seeing the farming or the livestock, stepping around the chickens in the yard by instinct, as he made his way to the large stone house where William Stewart now lived. The O'Donnell castle was vacant for the most part, save for the occasional wanderer that drifted into its empty rooms. The best of the furnishings had been moved to Fort Stewart which was deemed more defensible as it was closer to the water and outside the deepest forests that had not yet been cleared.

Wills had barely announced the presence of visitors than they were appearing at their doorstep.

"Ah!" one man said as he dismounted, "and what a beautiful ride it was through Eire today!" He took a moment to remove one glove before offering his hand to Captain Stewart. "Christopher Saint Lawrence, 10th Baron Howth," he said. "We met while in London a few years ago."

"Yes," Captain Stewart replied. "I recall our meeting. It occurred sometime after the Nine Years War. You have been abroad, I hear?"

"For some time, yes. In the Spanish Netherlands. I have only just returned to Eire this past month."

"Come, come," Stewart said, beckoning him inside. "You must be hungry and thirsty."

"No woman to greet us?" Howth murmured as he followed Archie and Captain Stewart inside the house. "Quite unusual."

The captain's response was lost on Wills, who was already busy with arrangements for their unexpected visitors. Truth be told, the captain had set his eye on a lass by the name of Francis Newcomen. Born in Dublin, she was the daughter of English aristocrats and she had not traveled by wagon with the other women out for their future but with her parents to welcome Captain Stewart to Eire. Unfortunately perhaps for the both of them, she was compelled to return to Dublin with her father but there was many a night in which the captain wrote long letters with a satisfied smile on his lips which left no doubt as to its contents or its intended recipient.

The gentleman that had accompanied Howth was his personal manservant, Richard Scott, and as the man followed his master into the house Wills quickly delegated the care and feeding of their horses. Then he made his way to the rear, where he found two Irish ladies that tended to the captain's food and housekeeping, instructing them to prepare a meal for their guests along with ale to be served immediately. Brushing the grime off his clothing from the day's activities, he discreetly moved into the doorway of the dining hall. Captain Stewart signaled him and Wills made his way into the room where he stood a few paces from the captain in the event his services would be required.

Four men sat at the table: Howth, Richard, Stewart and Archie.

"You must tell the story of your capture, Baron," Stewart was saying. "Archie here would enjoy hearing the tale."

Howth was clearly pleased with the request. As he settled into his chair, he asked Archie, "Have you ever heard of Grace O'Malley? Perhaps you would know her better by her other name, Granuaile, the Pirate Queen."

"I have heard tales of her," Archie said. "Please. I am intrigued."

"I should begin at the beginning. I spent much of my childhood at Howth Castle, which has been in our family for more than four hundred years. I was but a child of eight when one eve I was playing on our property, which was, by necessity, surrounded by a rather tall and imposing wall. This rather eccentric and forceful middle-aged woman appeared at the gate demanding to be allowed inside."

One of the Irish servants appeared with a large tray and he paused as he watched her place a mug of ale in front of each man. "Thank you, my dear," he said as he accepted his mug. "She rather looked a bit like you," he continued, his eyes wandering down the length of the woman's hair. "Her hair was jet black, just like yours, and her eyes were black as well. Very striking, as her skin was the color of alabaster. Well, the servant at the gate told her the gate was locked, as my parents and grandparents were at dinner. I, having been fed by my caregiver some time earlier, was the only one about."

He took a long swig of ale. "Well, the next thing I knew, she had enticed me to climb the wall to speak with her, and I, being the curious sort I am, particularly when it comes to the ladies, could not resist. She was bewitching to me, even at that tender age. Before I quite knew what was about, she was claiming me as her hostage!"

A glance at Richard told Wills that the story had been told many times before but Archie and Stewart and even the Irish servant, Aoife, were mesmerized.

"Why, what on earth did you do?" Archie prompted.

"Well, there was naught I could do. She spirited me away, all the way to Galway, I might add, incensed at the discourtesy she had been shown. It took weeks for my parents to get me back, and she only released me after they had issued a formal apology and vowed to keep their gates open in the future. After that, they always set an extra plate at the table just in the event she was to show up again!"

"You must have been frightened silly," Aoife breathed.

"Oh, not at all. For all her reputation as the Pirate Queen, she was quite proper. Why, to this day I have not encountered anyone with as much property as she had amassed. More than a thousand head of cattle—"

"A thousand!" Archie shook his head.

"Her castle was absolutely stunning; spectacular views of the ocean. Her ships were constantly coming and going—"

"Her ships?"

"Oh, yes. And did I mention there were a number of castles owned by the O'Malleys? They all faced the ocean, as I recall. They had an extensive trading business and they also taxed fishermen wishing to use their coastline. And they paid the tax, too, because it was the best fishing for days around, it was. She was pure nobility... Do you know how she came to be known as Granuaile?"

"I do not," Archie said, clearly enjoying Howth's tale.

Howth waved a finger toward Aoife, who stood in the doorway with a jug of ale as if she was captivated. "You know, m'lady, Granuaile is Gaelic for bald. Well, so the tale goes, when Grace O'Malley was but a young thing she asked her father if she could accompany him on one of his expeditions. He declined and rightly so, as she had such long and flowing black hair, he claimed it would be an impediment on a ship. So what did she do? She chopped it off herself, aye, with her own hands she did! Chopped it right down to the scalp. It is said he had no further recourse but to take her with him."

The others laughed and a short silence ensued. Then Archie asked, "Whatever became of her?"

"Oh, she was a colorful figure, indeed she was. Wealthy beyond description. Married several times and she purportedly had a string of lovers as well. Quite insatiable, I understand. And quite the fighter as well. She could lead men into battle like no man I had ever seen before or since... What became of her, you say? She passed not five years ago. Despite all the battles she led and the Irish insurgencies she supported, she died, it is said, of old age. She must have been about 73 years of age..."

Another servant appeared in the doorway and the two women set out plates of venison and rabbit, along with several loaves of bread.

"And what do we owe the pleasure of your company?" Captain Stewart asked as they ate.

"Well, as I said, I have only recently returned to Eire and I am about, determining who my friends are..." At that, the table became silent and remained so for the duration of supper.

+≈≈+

It was early the next morning before Howth and his manservant prepared to leave Fort Stewart. Wills was returning from driving his sheep out to pasture, yearning for a hearty breakfast and a warm mug of tea when he encountered them mounting their horses.

"Now remember, Captain," Howth was saying, "what I have told you about Phelim MacDavitt. There might have been peace these last five years, but I tell you on good authority he is hatching a plot against the king. He is a dangerous man and should be arrested immediately should you encounter him."

"Aye," Captain Stewart nodded. "We shall indeed remain at the ready."

They bade farewell and as Wills stood beside the captain watching them ride off, he said, "Would you like for me to do anything for you, sir? Perhaps regarding Phelim MacDavitt?"

"I am not certain what Baron Howth told me is accurate," he said thoughtfully. "The man has a penchant for exaggeration. What has been your assessment of MacDavitt?"

"He and the O'Doherty clan have been very cooperative. You recall their assistance in clearing our land... I have not once felt threatened by them. Yet, when we were last in Derry, I did overhear a rather curious conversation."

After Wills had relayed the event to the captain, he was silent for a moment and appeared deep in thought. Then, "Send word to The O'Doherty that I would like to have a word with him, at his convenience either here or there. Perhaps we can put this matter to rest and promptly."

13

When Cahir O'Doherty responded, it was under the giant oak tree a few paces from Captain Stewart's home. He arrived with Phelim and a small band of men, jovially bantering with the English and Scottish settlers as he made his way to the captain, who had set a small desk and chair under the tree and was busily tending to his books in the fresh open spring air.

After warm greetings, Stewart caught Wills' eye. With no more than a slight nod, Wills understood his task. He excused himself on the pretext of acquiring food and drink for the group and quickly located Tomas and Fergus.

"We must separate Phelim from Cahir so the captain can speak with The O'Doherty alone," Wills said. "Find an excuse."

"Aye," Fergus said as they returned with Wills to the large oak tree. "It is just a shame that the brothels are not at Fort Stewart, 'ey?"

The opportunity presented itself only a few minutes later. Satisfied with ale and food eaten on the ground in the massive shade of the oak, Phelim turned the conversation to the sheep they had passed on their way to Fort Stewart.

"What has happened to their wool?" he inquired. "They seem to be all colors of the rainbow."

Tomas chuckled. "Aye, and I thought the same when the English first taught us. The lambs are being born, you know, and it is important for us to keep the lambkin with the mother. You know the lanolin that is pulled from the wool during processing?"

"Aye, aye; it is used in soap."

"Well, it turns out it is used for much more. We can take the lanolin and mix it with dye from wild berries or the tannin from bark. We apply the mixture to both the mother and lambkin so we know they are to be kept together. We make one color for each shepherd and change the pattern of the mark for each couple."

"And it does not wash off with the first rain?"

"No, not at all," Fergus added. "It adheres to the wool and lasts through sun and rain."

"No."

"Aye; would you like for us to show you?"

As Fergus, Tomas and Phelim rose, Cahir set his mug down as if to join them but the captain leaned over and whispered something only he could hear. As they set off toward the cauldrons filled with the lanolin and dye, Wills encouraged the other men in their group to join them, leaving only the captain, Cahir and himself under the oak.

"You wished to speak with me?" Cahir asked once they were out of earshot.

"Aye," Captain Stewart said. "I have been informed that Phelim MacDavitt is plotting against King James."

Wills kept his eyes on Cahir, watching his expression and mannerisms for anything that would, perhaps, reveal dishonesty or an attempt to conceal information. The man's eyes grew wide as he shook his head.

"That is not possible," he said. "He does not act without the consent of the clan and treachery is not something we have discussed."

Stewart was silent for a moment as he kept his eyes locked on Cahir's. "He is not dissatisfied with the settlers here?" he asked.

Cahir tore his eyes away and stared thoughtfully at the ground beneath him for a moment. Then he said, "Is this situation perfect? Of course it is not. Are we completely satisfied—Phelim, my clan, even me? Certainly not. But the truth of it is that for too many centuries to count, Irish lands have changed ownership countless times. A drought or a flood could bring about the demise of many a king. Border disputes could push one clan further in any direction while driving another back. We have fought the Spanish Armada while other Irish clans have embraced them. The O'Dohertys— myself included—fought on the side of Queen Elizabeth and again under King James—killing our fellow Irishmen. We were promised many things in return, some of which we received and much more that we have not. But I can assure you that we are not plotting insurrection."

Fast-moving clouds parted, allowing the sun to find its way through the branches of the oak. They fell on Cahir's eyes with precision, revealing an expression of incredulousness.

"And Phelim feels the same as you?" Captain Stewart pressed.

"He does," he answered without hesitation.

"And he does not bear ill will against any settler?"

Cahir chuckled. "Ah, now I did not say that. You cannot brush all Englishmen with the same stroke. Some—such as Docwra—were as good as their word. They respected us just as we respected them. Others, I am afraid, are not as reputable."

"Governor Paulet of Derry," Wills interjected.

His expression grew irritated. "Is that where this rumor originated? Paulet is accusing Phelim of treason?"

"No," Wills said. "This did not come from Paulet."

"Well," he said, his annoyance at the man's name only slightly receding, "now that you have mentioned the man, I—and my clansmen—find him to be arrogant, disrespectful and filled with hatred for all things Irish. It begs me to ask why he remains here when he hates Ireland and the Irish people so?" Without waiting for a reply, he added, "But that is between Paulet and my clan. Not between The Crown—King James—or the rest of the English settlers or Scottish settlers such as yourselves."

"Then why are we hearing these rumors?" Captain Stewart asked.

"I do not know." Cahir looked down once more. When his eyes returned to look first at Wills and then at the captain, they were moist. "Tell me, what is it that I must do to prove myself and my loyalties? During Tyrone's Rebellion, I was known as the Queen's O'Doherty. I fought for nine years against other Irishmen. I have been knighted. I am married to an Englishwoman of nobility. Yet due to accusations from both Paulet and Chichester, Viceroy of Ireland— accusations that cannot be proven because they are utterly false—I have been forbidden to leave Ireland so I cannot even plead my innocence at King James' court. Instead, I must live with this cloud of suspicion over my head." He extended both his hands, palms up. "Tell me, Captain Stewart, what is it that I must do to prove my clan's loyalty once and for all?"

Stewart did not answer immediately. As the silence fell among the three men, Wills could hear the others laughing and chatting in the distance, unaware of the serious accusations against one of their own.

"If the accusations persist against Phelim MacDavitt," Stewart said, his voice calm and measured, "then I must urge you to turn him over to the proper authorities—"

"And who might they be? Paulet or Chichester? The same men who have accused me, fined me and yet have never provided any evidence against me?"

"No," Stewart answered. "A third party. Perhaps authorities at Donegal. I will plead your case—provided you can guarantee me that there is not a one amongst you plotting against the Crown. I will take it to King James himself. By turning him in, you can set events in motion to clear his name and yours."

Cahir nodded but did not seem convinced. The voices grew louder, Phelim's laughter rising above the rest. As the other men joined them once more, he wiped at the edge of his eye. Then he slapped his thighs and rose to his feet. "Thank you for your hospitality, Captain Stewart," he said. "I am afraid we must now take our leave as we wish to return to Carrickabraghy Castle before nightfall."

Wills met Fergus' gaze. Fergus cocked his head and parted his lips slightly, the unanswered question paused. Wills managed a faint, almost indiscernible nod.

The small group comprised of Wills, Tomas, Fergus and Captain Stewart accompanied the O'Doherty band to the outer edges of the fort. "We will be visiting Donegal tomorrow," Captain Stewart said. "I have not ventured there yet and I understand there is much to see. I hope to learn of ways in which we can transport our potatoes and wool to England; I understand there are a number of cargo ships there, and frankly, I wish to avoid Derry for obvious reasons."

"Aye," Cahir said. "I understand and you will find Donegal to be much more hospitable."

"Perhaps we will see you there," Phelim added.

"Oh?" Captain Stewart said, surprised.

"Aye. You have inspired us, you have," Phelim continued. "We plan to clear Canmoyre Woods. It is a wilderness, to be sure, harboring fox that prey on our chickens. Our blacksmiths are skilled but we have heard tell that in Donegal we will find the newest, sharpest axes and we will certainly need them to clear such wilds."

"Axes, you say." Stewart's eyes narrowed.

"Would you like some assistance?" Wills ventured. "In clearing Canmoyre Woods, that is?"

Phelim clasped his hands. "Oh, no. But we thank you just the same."

The sun was beginning to dip on the far horizon as they said their final goodbyes. Watching their backs until they were out of sight, Wills couldn't shake the feeling that Canmoyre Woods held a more sinister role. As he turned back to look at Captain Stewart, he saw his own doubts mirrored in his. A frown had turned his mouth downward and had furrowed his brow, but before Wills could request additional orders, he turned his back and strode silently toward his home.

He watched him for a brief moment before realizing that the setting sun also meant it was time for the sheep to be driven back to the fort and corralled before nightfall. Tomas and Fergus were already halfway across the meadow when Wills caught up with them but their banter fell on deaf ears.

14

Henry Hart had an impossibly high forehead, his hair having receded to somewhere back of his head. His eyes were sharp and studious under thin and straight brows and as if to compensate for the lack of hair on his pate, he sported a full red beard and a neatly trimmed mustache. He was not an imposing figure but around him swirled an air of nobility, of privilege and of wealth. Like Stewart, he had risen to the rank of Captain and had fought in the Nine Years' War. He was now the Commander of Culmore Fort north of Derry at the mouth of the River Foyle and so it caught Stewart by surprise to find him nursing a mug in a smoky pub in Donegal. Friendly and obviously pleased to see his old friend, he insisted that the captain along with Archie and Wills join him for a late lunch.

Donegal Town was situated on Donegal Bay at the mouth of the River Eske. It had been the seat of power for Tyrconnell until the Flight of the Earls in 1607, and now a large portion had been granted to Captain Basil Brooke, an Englishman tasked with developing a

Plantation similar to Fort Stewart. It reminded Wills of the foothills of Scotland where one could gaze upon the Highlands because in the distance the rugged Croaghgorms rose, their hue an odd shade of blue that led to their name. The English simply referred to them as the Blue Stacks and it was said it was always better to go around them than through them. The Irish, Wills was learning, could be a superstitious lot and their tales of the Croaghgorms were no different; they were filled with faeries and gremlins and the ghosts of all those that had perished there in centuries past.

The town of Donegal was as bustling as Derry, if not more so, and it had a more peaceful atmosphere without Paulet and Hamilton. There were none hanging and the Irish here worked alongside the settlers with a seemingly greater degree of mutual cooperation.

In the town center was Donegal Castle, once the stronghold of The O'Donnell and now in the hands of Captain Brooke. On the southern shores of the Eske another imposing stone structure stood that served as a Franciscan Abbey, and it was said that many records from across Europe had made their way there throughout a thousand years of dark European history. Books and records had been burned throughout Europe as part of a wave against intellectualism, which was considered to be an enemy of the Catholic Church's ideology. Had it not been for the scores of men who transported them to western Ireland at great risk and to the friars that hid them for centuries, much of Europe's history might have been lost.

The records were purported to be there still, painstakingly copied page by page by Franciscan monks, and Wills wanted nothing more than to visit those great stone halls and see the records for himself. Alas, he thought with a great inward sigh, the chances of that were slim to none as Captain Stewart had kept him at his side throughout the entire day.

A meal of chicken and potatoes was just arriving when Cahir walked in alone. Henry immediately rose, as did Stewart and Wills, and much to Wills' surprise he patted Cahir on the back and insisted that he join them.

"I have known this lad since he was—what—all of fifteen?" Henry said. "There was many an occasion when we fought side by side." He tore off a piece of bread and pointed it at them briefly. "If ever you wanted someone you could trust, it would be Cahir O'Doherty here."

"I can say the same for you as well," Cahir said. "It has been my pleasure to serve with you."

"So tell me," Wills said, nudging Cahir, "how did the two of you meet?"

"Ah," Henry began before Cahir could reply, "I remember it like it was yesterday. Here comes this lad across the field with his clan behind him, a flag bearer holding high the British flag. I couldn't believe my eyes. Nor my ears when I heard he was their leader."

"I remember that day as well," Cahir said, chewing a hunk of chicken thoughtfully. "There was many a man that did not trust me or my clan, but you did. You allowed me to prove our loyalty on the field that day— and many days and years afterward."

"And how is Mary?"

"Ah, Mary." Cahir's expression turned tender. "She is well indeed."

Turning to Stewart, Henry said, "Cahir's wife, Mary Preston, is the daughter of Viscount Gormanston and I must say, one of the most beautiful women I have ever laid eyes upon. Have you met her?"

"I'm afraid I have not." Stewart glanced at Wills.

"Nor I," Wills added. "She was not at Carrickabraghy Castle when I was there." As he spoke, he raised one brow to Cahir.

"You are quite right," Cahir responded. "She had traveled to Dublin to visit friends. She was quite disappointed that she had missed you."

"And what brings you to Donegal?" Henry asked. "A bit far afield, are you now? And completely alone?"

"Oh, not alone for long, I'm afraid; just a brief respite. I came with a few others. We have need of a few tools and Fynbar Campbell's reputation has made it all the way to Inishowen."

"Ah, Fynbar. Yes. He is a good man. He forges a fine sword; I own several of them myself. What need have you of swords these days?"

"Not swords but axes."

"Not planning to crack a few skulls open, are you?" Henry chuckled as he said it but his eyes became veiled.

"Ha! Cracking a few tree trunks is more like it."

"I hadn't realized that you traveled without Phelim," Captain Stewart interjected. "You two always seem to be together."

"That is because Phelim is Cahir's foster father, isn't he now?" Henry said.

Cahir nodded and reached for another slice of chicken.

"Is that so?" Stewart asked.

"The MacDavitts and the O'Dohertys go back a long, long way," Cahir said. He met Stewart's eyes. "We have married into one another's families for generations. He was one of my father's finest friends and when my da passed, he supported my claim as lord over the O'Doherty clan."

"I have heard tell you are blood relatives as well as he becoming your foster father," Henry added.

"Blood relatives many times over no doubt," Cahir said with a laugh.

Wills was silent as he observed the men. So that was why Phelim looked like an older version of Cahir, he thought. He had noticed it the very first time he had spotted them together in the clearing. That seemed so long ago now; much of that forest had since been cleared, affording them a view that reached almost to Derry.

"You know, I lived for a time in one of O'Doherty's castles," Henry said.

"Oh?" Stewart said with surprise.

"Aye, Burt Castle. Did you know it belongs to the O'Dohertys?" Without waiting for an answer, he continued, "It was also known as O'Doherty's Castle but by God, they have so many of them it was difficult to tell which one we were speaking about so we've come to call it Burt's Castle. You know where it is, William, near Culmore Fort."

"Ah, yes." Stewart peered at Cahir curiously. "I had not realized that also belonged to the O'Doherty's."

"It does indeed," Cahir said. "And when I leave here tomorrow, I shall be returning there."

"Is Phelim there now?" Stewart asked.

"He is here in Donegal but will return to Burt Castle with me."

"I shall be returning to that area tomorrow as well," Henry said. "I am needed at Culmore Fort. I command the garrison there, or did you know that already, William?"

"I heard something of the sort," the captain said, mopping the chicken juices with a slab of bread. "I was surprised not to have run into you at Derry on one of my many trips there."

"That is because, I'm afraid, I steer clear of Derry — Paulet, you know. It is simply not the place to be these days, and I find myself on a variety of trips elsewhere."

"Trips here to Donegal?"

"Mostly to Dublin."

"Dublin?"

"Aye. Chichester sends for me on a regular basis."

"Say," Stewart said, his eyes moving pointedly from Henry to Cahir. "You have Chichester's ear, do you not?"

"As much as anybody—or as little as anybody."

"Cahir?" Stewart leaned forward in his chair.

The O'Doherty did not appear to have noticed the conversation and spent another minute chewing a bite of potato before he answered. "I believe, dear Henry, the captain wishes for me to discuss a matter of grave importance with you."

"Oh?" Henry wiped his mouth with a piece of cloth and laid it on the table. He leaned back with his mug of ale.

"It appears there is a rumor that Phelim is plotting against the Crown."

"Phelim?" Henry chuckled. With the others continuing to look at him with all seriousness, he grew somber. "Is he?"

"No. Absolutely not. I would bet my life upon it," Cahir said.

"Well, then. There surely is nothing to be concerned about, 'ey?"

"I'm afraid there could be," Captain Stewart said. He relayed the conversation with Baron Howth to him.

"Howth!" Henry said in dismissal when he had finished. "The man can exaggerate anything. He is the wrong sex, if you ask me. God should have placed him in petticoats; he is such a perpetual gossip."

"Still," Stewart pressed, "I have advised Cahir that if the rumors persist, he should turn over Phelim to someone he trusts and request that the man's name be cleared."

"It is that serious?" Henry asked.

Cahir shrugged his shoulders.

"Cahir, dear boy," Henry said, leaning forward once more, "should it reach that point, you can count on me to vouch for you both. I doubt that anything will come of it, but should you choose to turn him in, I will be at Culmore Fort the day after tomorrow. I will personally escort him to Dublin and plead on his behalf—provided you give me your word that neither of you nor your clans are planning any insurrection against King James."

"You have my word on it," Cahir said without hesitation. "You have known me all this time, Henry, and you know that had it not been for me, Docwra and his men most certainly would have perished at Derry."

"That is true. You turned against The O'Neill and Hugh O'Donnell to rescue him."

"And you know that ever since, I have been true to the Crown—first to Queen Elizabeth and now to King James."

"Aye. You have indeed."

"Then surely you would know there is no reason at'all for me to turn against the English now."

The two men's eyes met across the table. "I believe you," Henry said. "I have trusted you with my life, and I trust your words now."

After a moment, Cahir cleared his throat. "I must, I am afraid, take my leave. Phelim and the others will be waiting for me. No doubt they have selected their tools by now."

As he stood, the others stood as well, shaking his hand in turn.

"Please be my guest at dinner," Henry said, holding onto his hand just a moment longer. "Frances has been asking after you and Lady O'Doherty; you know how she enjoys both your company. Besides, she complains that she does not have another Englishwoman with whom to chat, and she adores Mary so."

"I would like that," Cahir said. "I will be but a stone's throw from you when I return to Burt's Castle. And Mary would enjoy seeing your lovely wife again."

"Good. Then she will send you a proper invitation."

They watched him depart and then settled back at the table. "Now, where were we?" Henry asked.

Wills called for another round of mugs. As he leaned back, absentmindedly patting his full belly, their conversation seemed as though it was a thousand miles away. His mind was following Cahir through Donegal and he found himself wondering why the axes the O'Doherty blacksmiths forged were not sufficient enough to fell a few trees.

15

ergus slapped Wills on the back. "Can you imagine?" he asked. "Can you even imagine? We came here with nothing and this time next year we shall have more money than we can stuff in our pockets, for sure."

"That would be nice, 'ey?" Wills said. "Who knew the price of wool would be so high?"

Fergus puffed out his chest. "In one year's time, I shall have enough of a standing to attract a lady to be my wife."

"Getting a bit carried away with yourself, don't you think now?"

"Ah, you just wait and see."

"And have you someone in mind?"

"Not as of yet. But I shall meet one that catches my eye and me hers. And then I shall set about making as many little Ferguses as a man has a right to."

The stables were at the edge of Donegal and while they waited for Captain Stewart and Archie to join them, they led them into the roadway where Tomas joined them. It had been a productive journey. They had learned that most of the wool used in England had customarily come from Spain, as even the Scottish Lowlands could not supply enough to keep the English satisfied. With England and Spain constantly at odds and more likely to be at war than not, the arrangement had become problematic and was a major reason King James had initiated the Plantation colonization of Ireland. It seemed that even with England and Wales turning to sheep herding, their appetite for both mutton and wool was insatiable.

"And don't forget the potatoes," Tomas added. "I have planted my lot and I am anticipating quite a good crop. And what a blessing it is to have the English ready for them just as quickly as I can plump them up and get them out of the ground."

"Aye," Wills agreed. "Who would have thought a member of a poisonous family could become such a staple, 'eh?"

"Between raising sheep and raising potatoes, this will become the richest country in all of Europe!" Fergus proclaimed.

"Oh, it is a bright future I see, for sure," Tomas agreed.

"It is, indeed," Wills added. He adjusted the blanket on his horse's back. A bright color caught his eye and he peered past his horse's muzzle to a sapphire gown. A young woman was exiting a mercantile across the way, her skirts swaying as she dodged the worst of the mud. His breath was caught in his throat. He would know that sway anywhere.

"Are you listening to us?" Fergus said, stepping in front of Wills.

"I'll be thanking you to move your big mug," Wills said, trying to peer around him.

He looked over his shoulder. Laughing, he stepped to the side. "It appears that one of the female persuasion has caught his eye," he said to Tomas.

"Who is that woman?" Wills whispered hoarsely.

The older gentleman he had seen with her in Derry followed her out of the shop, pausing to close the door behind him.

"That would be Rhiannon Ó Dálaigh," Tomas said reverently.

"And the man with her? That old man is her husband?" Wills asked painfully, watching him grasp her elbow and lead her down the road.

Tomas laughed. "Are you daft? That is not her husband; it is her father, Varney Ó Dálaigh hisself."

"Her father," Wills breathed.

"Oh, now don't you be getting any wild ideas," Fergus said. "She would not be interested in the likes of you; she is quite obviously of a higher society."

"We'll see about that." He barely registered that he had handed off his horse's reins to Fergus as he crossed the street and followed, brushing imaginary dust and grime from his clothing. He had not a clue what he would say or do when he neared them, but it appeared the fates were with him because the man hesitated outside a shop, said something to his daughter and then stepped inside, leaving her alone.

She stood with her back to the shop's door, gently swaying back and forth as if she was unable to stand perfectly still. She held a diminutive parasol that matched her sapphire gown so that it dangled against her lower body; it seemed impossible that something so small could possibly shield her from the sun's rays. As he neared, his eyes raked over her blond hair; it was pulled away from her face into a bun at the back, leaving only a few wisps of rebellious curls framing her ivory face. At least he thought it was a bun, but it was hard to tell as it appeared as much hair was determined to escape it along her nape than remain in it. He had a sudden urge to pull her to him and thread his hands through those silk tresses. His face grew hot and he almost turned around and headed back to his friends when she suddenly looked directly at him.

"It's you," she said. Her voice was soft and melodious as only the Irish accent can be. It took his breath away.

"I wanted to properly introduce myself to you," he managed to say, "and to make certain that I did not harm you when in my clumsiness, I ran into you at Derry." His words sounded rushed and he wished he could take them back and prepare a proper statement.

"And you are—?" she prodded.

"William Neely," he said, bowing slightly.

"William Neely," she repeated. He loved the way his name sounded on her tongue; his cheeks grew hot despite the chill in the spring air.

"My name is Rhiannon. Rhiannon Ó Dálaigh." Her eyes darted toward the shop her father had entered. "You must travel quite a bit, William Neely."

"I suppose I do. And the same could be said of you?"

She laughed. It was a soft laugh, one that sounded like it could float away on the lightest of breezes. "I'm afraid not. I live here in Donegal."

"But Derry—"

"We have family in Derry; my father's sister. She is all alone, and I remain with her sometimes as a companion."

The door opened behind her. Mister Ó Dálaigh looked from his daughter to Wills, his face darkening. Clearly, he was not amused by the younger man's attentions.

"Sir," Wills said, bowing slightly, "my name is William Neely. I am an aide to Captain William Stewart."

"William Stewart," Mister Ó Dálaigh said as he stepped onto the road and closed the door behind him. "A great war hero."

"Aye, sir. He is, sir."

"Are you Scottish?"

"Why, I am."

"I thought I detected the accent."

"You are not Scottish—?"

"No, but I have traveled quite a bit in the Scotland Lowlands. You are from—?"

"Wigtownshire, sir."

"I see. Same region as Captain Stewart."

"That is correct. He—requested that I accompany him to Ireland."

"He did, did he?" His eyes narrowed just a bit, enough for Wills to feel as though he was being sized up. "Well, your—friend—seems to be heading in this direction."

Wills glanced behind him to find Captain Stewart and Archie walking at a brisk pace toward the horses.

"Aye, sir. I am afraid I must go. I just—before I left—"

"Sir?"

"I—I would like to—perhaps—see your daughter—with a proper escort, of course."

Mister Ó Dálaigh did not respond. His face was expressionless and Wills found his eyes wandering back to Rhiannon. She was blushing and when their eyes met, she nodded her head and smiled.

"Next time you are in Donegal," he was saying, "send word. Perhaps you and Captain Stewart could join us for supper."

"Aye, sir. I will indeed." He bowed once more and then bowed to Rhiannon before backing away. "Good day, miss."

He turned just as Captain Stewart was mounting his horse and was relieved that Rhiannon and her father could only see the back of his head for he knew his face must have turned forty shades of red. Fergus was still standing with his reins in his hand as he approached. With a formal, stiff bow, he handed the reins to Wills. "Sir," he said in his most proper tone.

Before he could respond, he had ducked behind the horse and was mounting his own.

"Wills, I must speak to you," Captain Stewart said, clicking his horse into an energetic walk.

As Wills pulled his horse alongside the captain's, he began a set of instructions regarding the shearing of the sheep. Tomas and Fergus fell in behind them. As they passed by Rhiannon and her father, Wills bowed his head in farewell. It might have been his imagination but he could have sworn that she was blushing more deeply. She raised one brow and smiled before her father once more took her elbow. He could feel their eyes on his back as he and the captain conversed. He had never before wished he was a war hero but now he yearned that he was something more than a tenant farmer's son from Wigtownshire.

No matter, he thought as they rode out of sight. I will win her heart and her father's respect. He knew it in the depths of his soul.

16

The chants went up as Wills and Fergus squared off, each with a woolly sheep. Then Archie raised his hand high. "On the count of three! One—two—three!"

Time stood still and time sped past and when Wills stood up and released his sheep, he was surprised to find that Fergus had barely started. "What the devil?" he said. "I thought you said you were a shearer!"

Fergus struggled to keep the lamb under control. "She keeps jerking about!" he complained.

"Let me show you," Wills said, laughing. "I have already won, anyway."

Fergus cut a mean glance at him but said, "Take her."

"Oh, dear Fergus," Wills said. "How many of you here have sheared a sheep, 'ey?"

A few raised their hands but most shook their heads.

"Well, so you're about to get a fast lesson." He kept his hand firmly entwined in the wool about the sheep's neck. As Fergus moved out of the way, Wills dropped to his knees and pulled the sheep against his chest. "First of all, treat her like a woman you want to coddle." After the laughter died down, he continued, "And just like a woman, you want to keep her off her feet." Again the crowd chortled and giggled. "If she's off her feet, she won't be running away from you."

He held the lamb against his chest, cooing to her as he worked. With all four feet off the ground, he knew the lamb would not try to get away. "First is the belly, 'eh?" He sheared off the wool as close to the skin as he could comfortably get it. Then he pulled her into a different embrace so he could reach her side. Still cooing to her as though he was merely petting her, he sheared her wool off in one large piece—one side, then the back, and then the remaining side. When he was finished, he helped her back onto her feet but instead of running, she simply stood there as though she could blend in with the crowd.

"The trick is," Wills said as they admired his quick work, "to keep the lamb from panicking. It should not be a stressful process but one they learn to tolerate—or even enjoy, if done on a warm enough day. They will be glad of the shearing over the summer. Oh, and one more thing—shear when they're dry. Wet wool will not shear, I'll tell you that."

Several men moved forward and Wills continued his instruction. "You'll get it yet," he said. And to Fergus, "Just imagine her to be the woman you'll meet when all this wool has turned to coin in your pocket."

Once the first set was done, more men moved in until they were making a decent headway on the shearing. The women in camp busied themselves with gathering up the fallen wool and carrying it to nearby mounds, one for each shepherd. Each would be weighed when they reached Donegal and the men would receive their payment, the amounts carefully recorded in ledgers that marked not only the payment for the shepherd but the larger amount for the lord.

He noticed one woman hanging back from the crowd. She wore a cape that covered her from head to toe, the hood casting her face in shadows. Though his own shirt was thin and pulled above the elbows, her clothing made it appear as though winter might still be about instead of the spring sun that did its best to warm them. She caught his curiosity, she did, and as soon as he could break away from the others, he began to move toward the opposite side.

"Mister Neely," she said in greeting when he came near.

He nodded in response. "And would I be knowing you now?"

She turned away from the others and allowed her hood to part just enough from her face for him to get a glimpse. He recognized the red hair first; it was wavy and bright and almost assuredly would have cascaded over her shoulders had she not contained it. Her eyes were voluminous and as green as the meadows.

"Aye," he answered his own question. "I remember you. You served my men and myself at Carrickabraghy Castle, did you not?"

"I did, sir."

"But I don't recall being properly introduced to you."

"Elan."

"Elan. Do you have a last name, Elan?"

Her smile held promises, he thought, though he was hard-pressed to understand what they might be. He'd had many a maiden show her intentions to him, especially after having arrived in Ireland, but there was something about her expression that was different somehow. There were dark secrets there and he had a sudden urge to leave her standing and return to his duties.

"Could you please," she said, her words coming fast as he turned away from her, "introduce me to Captain Stewart?"

A frown furrowed his brow. "Pardon me?"

"I have business to conduct—with both you and the captain. Please."

He hesitated a brief moment. "And what's this about?"

Her tongue flicked over her lips as if her mouth was dry. "I may have news of an insurrection."

"Come with me."

As he passed Archie, he whispered, "I am escorting a lady to see the captain."

Archie cut his eyes over to Elan but her hood had once again placed her face in shadows. "Aye. You'll find him in his study writing letters." As Wills turned to go, he added, "But you'd best be back soon. Those sheep won't shear themselves, you know."

+=—=+

The gray stone walls and the tall, narrow windows made the study feel cave-like, requiring candles to light the desk though the sun shone brightly just beyond those walls. Captain Stewart sat on one side of his desk, his writing papers still laid out before him. His eyes, however, moved slowly from Wills to Elan and back again.

Once inside, Elan had removed her hood so her hair tumbled across her shoulders. She kept her hands folded neatly in her lap. She had declined an offer of ale or food, though she appeared to have traveled on foot from Carrickabraghy Castle. Though Wills knew all too well how the Irish could find footpaths that seemed barely wide enough for a cat, it would still have taken many hours for her to journey the perimeter of Drongawn Lough. As she settled into her chair across from Captain Stewart, he moved to the window, his eyes searching the surrounding area for others that might have followed her.

"I came alone," she said as if reading his mind.

"Forgive me," Captain Stewart said, "Lady—"

"Just Elan," she corrected.

"Elan. Of course I am not as familiar with the terrain as you, but wouldn't it be risky for a woman such as yourself to be traveling alone?"

She smiled. "Not necessarily, Captain. It all depends on who you know."

He nodded so slightly that his movement was almost imperceptible. "And what would bring you here today?"

"I won't waste your time, Captain." As Wills seated himself across from her, she continued, "Nor yours, Mister Neely. I am sure you have heard rumors of an... insurrection."

Stewart met Wills' eyes. "Pray continue."

"I work at Carrickabraghy Castle. I serve in the Great Hall and I overhear conversations. Are you understanding me?"

Stewart stood. Rubbing his chin, he made his way around the desk. "Are you telling me that you have heard talk of a revolt at Cahir O'Doherty's castle?"

She cocked her head. "That is exactly what I am telling you, Captain."

"A revolt against The O'Doherty?"

"A revolt against King James."

Wills readjusted himself in the chair so he was nearly perched on the end of it. "Supposing you have heard as much, why would you risk coming here to Fort Stewart to inform us of such?"

"I am a loyal English subject," she said, her eyes meeting his without so much as a blink. "I have spent more than half my life surrounded by war, and these last few years of peace have convinced me that I would rather see peace come permanently to Eire even if it means we are ruled by an English monarch."

"Are you telling me that Cahir O'Doherty is plotting a war against the English—and against us Scottish settlers?" Stewart asked.

"I am afraid that is exactly what I am telling you, Captain."

"Have you heard their plans?" Wills pressed.

"I know only that The O'Doherty is raising an army."

"How is he raising it?" Stewart asked.

She tossed her hair back. "He has land holdings, Captain Stewart. They may not be as extensive as The O'Donnell's or The O'Neill's but there are hundreds of men who live under his lordship. They will fight for him. They have followed him into battle before and they will follow him again. All they need—all they have ever needed—is for him to ask for their sword in battle."

"But why?" Wills asked. His eyes sought hers, silently imploring for an answer.

She shook her head. "I do not pretend to know what emotions are felt within a man's heart. I only know the words that have left his lips."

Stewart crossed the room yet again, both hands clasped behind his back. He paused at the window, his eyes racing over the terrain just outside. After a moment, he turned back. "When?"

"I do not know."

He nodded. "Can you obtain additional information?"

"I do not know. I have told you all that I have heard."

"It isn't enough," Wills said. "Forgive me, Lady— Elan. But I believe what the captain is saying is that we need more. We must know where he plans to attack and when. We need numbers of men. And if possible, we need to know why."

"Mister Neely is correct," Stewart said, returning to her side. "And I am asking you to return to Carrickabraghy Castle, to keep your eyes and ears open and report back to me when you have more."

She stood. "I can try, Captain Stewart. I cannot make guarantees because I do not know what else will be said in my presence. But I will report back to you should I have more."

As she began to move toward the doorway, Stewart asked, "May I provide an escort for you?"

She pulled her hood over her head, quickly tucking in her red tresses. "Absolutely not, sir, though I appreciate your kind offer. But I would attract far more suspicion should I arrive back on O'Doherty lands in the presence of another than if I navigated my way alone."

Wills glanced at Stewart only momentarily before following her into the sunshine. As she murmured her farewell and strolled toward the edge of camp, he quickly found Fergus, who was covered in grease wool. "Follow her," he whispered. "I want to know who she is, what last name she carries. I want to know her role in the O'Doherty clan."

"Aye," he said.

"And you'd best be brushing off your clothes, lad, else she'll think a sheep has followed her home."

17

County Donegal was a place like no other on earth; Wills was convinced of that. Though Captain Stewart's land holdings were not far from the village of Donegal, the journey overland with a caravan of wagons loaded with grease wool was too daunting to imagine. There were no roads, only the same types of trail on which he and his men had been so hopelessly lost when following The O'Donnell. It was a land of extremes, to be sure, of pristine white beaches and formidable cliffs, of mountains made entirely of quartzite that peered down upon bogs that could sink a man's wagon and his livelihood right along with it. The lakes and the forests each held their allure and their perils and often both were intertwined with the other.

So it was that the caravan lined up at the ship and each man's wool was carefully catalogued and loaded with burlap dividing one lot from the other, and the wool would be unloaded in just the same manner, weighed and catalogued and an amount agreed upon.

Oh, for sure it might have been only a bit longer to sail around the opposite side of the island and take the wool right on into England herself, but there were advantages to selling it in Donegal. An industry far larger than Derry's had sprung up there; too many boiling cauldrons to count would separate the wool from the lanolin; soap was a burgeoning enterprise as was spinning and by the time the wool had made its way into England, it would be a mix of woven materials and spun threads ready for whatever it was the English had use for. It would take up far less space in the ship's hull once the grease wool had been properly refined and separated, making each journey count that much more.

Ah, yes, it was best to leave all of that up to those whose livelihoods had grown to depend upon it and once the grease wool was weighed and catalogued, the men with Captain Stewart would have their coin all the faster. And no doubt but that Derry would have been closer to Fort Stewart but in addition to its smaller industry, it was a different flavor altogether, wasn't it now? Derry was political as if a heavy cloud hung over it, soldiers and civilians alike reflecting the negativity, mistrust and sheer vitriol of the man at the top, Sir George Paulet. But Donegal, ah Donegal, it was everything he might have hoped for: beautiful, isolated, wild and unfettered; despite the ocean's penchant for rolling in thick mists and heavy rains, they were not the clouds of hatred but of cleansing and merely a continuation of the open seas herself.

And so it was that Wills stood at the bow as the ship sliced through the water, the mists heavy with salt fanning his face and yet he could not breathe deeply enough to inhale all that he wanted from the Atlantic Ocean. The whales were out again; enormous pods of them with so many plumes reaching into the skies from their massive blowholes that it appeared the entire horizon was filled with them. The skies were blue, the clouds fluffy and white, though it was said that all four seasons could come to Donegal in a day's time and he knew it was more likely than not that by afternoon, they would be drenched if they had not yet found shelter in which to ride out Nature's moods.

But shelter he would have and the best kind for sure, because after the work was done and most of the men would find their way to the local pubs, he would retire to the boarding house to make himself presentable and then along with Captain Stewart, they would hail a carriage that would transport them to Varney Ó Dálaigh's home. And there around a proper table and conversation, he would sit across from Rhiannon Ó Dálaigh herself.

Aye, and it was a good life.

+≍≍+

Varney Ó Dálaigh was all of 58 years old and proud of it and all that he had accomplished. Though he was not arrogant or boastful as Paulet tended to be, the conversations centered around his life's experiences to date, including a knighthood. He and Captain Stewart had a lot to discuss, for there was fame to be had in fighting for the English monarchy; there was fortune to be had in the resulting land grants and industry; and there was pleasure to be explored in the wild western edge of County Donegal. Being an Irishman, he was ready and able to answer any and all of the captain's questions, which turned out to be quite numerous.

"And would you care for more meat?" Lavena Ó Dálaigh asked, her astute blue eyes focused on Wills.

Before he could respond, an Irish servant expertly lifted the platter and carried it to his side, where he dutifully picked off one more shaved slice of venison, though he had barely touched the food already on his plate. Lavena nodded her approval from one end of the long table but her husband, who was seated at the opposite end, did not appear to have noticed the exchange as he continued his long-winded conversation with Stewart.

Two beautiful young ladies sat across the table from Wills, but he only had eyes for one. Rhiannon might have been the spitting image of her mother had their eyes been the same color. They both had soft blond hair that caught the sunshine as it found its way into the ample dining hall; both had eyes that were so large and perceptive that they almost appeared otherworldly. Both had heart-shaped faces with high cheekbones, not at all like Varney's squared jaw and narrow green eyes. But while Lavena had her hair styled in an elaborate braid, Rhiannon's was simpler, almost girl-like, as it cascaded in gentle waves over her shoulders.

Her sister Ginessa sat next to her; two years younger, she seemed more adolescent still. She was called Ginny and she was a tiny thing, if he said so himself; so slight that a brisk wind might have carried her away. She was very talkative and quite eager to share stories of her talents, which ranged from music to sewing, while Rhiannon sat quietly watching him with a small, contented smile on her lips.

"Ah, yes, I know much of both The O'Donnell and The O'Doherty," Varney was saying. "You would be best to keep your eyes and ears open, for sure. The O'Doherty is trustworthy, I'll give him that; he's earned King James' respect and the Queen's before that. But his land is his land, make no bones about it, and he'll defend it with vigor."

"That has been my assessment of the man as well," Captain Stewart said. "Then pray tell, what is the animosity between Paulet and Cahir?"

Varney waved his hand in dismissal. "I am certain with Paulet, it is nothing personal. He would hate his own mother, I am convinced of that."

"Varney, darling." Lavena raised her glass of wine to her lips but did not sip it.

"Ah, but it is God's honest truth," Varney said grudgingly.

"And Phelim MacDavitt? What do you know of him?"

"Quite a bit, I'm afraid." He leaned back and placed both hands upon his belly. "Phelim Reagh MacDavitt. He fought against the English initially; his land holdings were more threatened than Cahir's. But then one of the most powerful chieftains in Ulster—Red Hugh O'Donnell—kidnapped Cahir. And, well, that was that."

"Please," Stewart said after a moment's silence. "Do continue."

"Phelim is Cahir's godfather. It's said that he swore allegiance to Cahir when he was but a babe, pledging to protect the lad with his life. After the elder O'Doherty died, he became known as the lad's foster father and had it not been for Phelim, Cahir most certainly would not have ascended to become chieftain of his clan."

"What did he do?" Wills asked. "When Red Hugh kidnapped Cahir, that is."

"Oh, yes. Well, they changed sides. They mounted quite the impressive rescue, so I'm told, liberating Cahir from The O'Donnell's dungeons. They took him straightaway to Derry, to Sir Henry Docwra, who was Governor of Derry at the time, and Docwra declared Cahir to be the chieftain and lord of the O'Doherty clan. In return, both Cahir and Phelim fought on behalf of the English and against Red Hugh and The O'Neill and The Maguire, as well."

"So that's how he came to fight on behalf of the English," Stewart said thoughtfully. "I had wondered at the allegiance there."

"Aye, and Red Hugh, O'Neill and Maguire fled the country not one year ago."

"I have heard," Wills said, "that the three Earls are in Spain gathering a Spanish force to overthrow the English here and gain back their lands."

"Ah, it will never happen," Varney proclaimed.

"How can you be certain?" Wills pressed.

"Why, the Battle of Gibraltar changed everything. Truth be told, the Dutch had already destroyed the Spanish fleet at Gibraltar even before the three fled to the Continent, but I am certain you have noticed that word reaches these parts at a snail's pace, sometimes a full year after the event has occurred. With an uneasy peace having been declared between England and Spain and the Dutch having devastated the Spanish fleet, the Spaniards were—and still are—weary of war. It is unlikely that they will come to the Earls' aid and invade Eire."

"Unlikely," Wills repeated the word slowly. "But it is not impossible."

"No," Varney said, taking a hearty swig of wine. "Nothing is impossible on this island, I am afraid. But one must ask himself, what would be gained by their invasion? An island of rock and bog? What would be the strategic importance of that?"

"What of the wool trade and potatoes?"

"Ach, the English need those. Not the Spaniards."

"Or its proximity to England?"

"Perhaps at one time they might have considered it, but when the Spanish Armada was destroyed off the coast of Eire and the English routed the Spaniards from one end of the island to the other—well, that was that. I doubt seriously if they would attempt it again."

"Enough of this talk," Lavena interrupted. "If you men must speak of politics, surely you can retire to the drawing room and have your fill of it there. But," she added hastily, "to do so now would rob you of the most delectable part of the meal." Her eyes twinkled as she glanced at Rhiannon and Ginny. "The girls have made lingonberry pie."

"No," Wills said in awe. "Where on earth did you get the berries?"

"One of the advantages of living in an active port such as Donegal," Rhiannon beamed. "Ships from the north were unloading them just this morning."

"Macha," Lavena said, ringing a bell at her plate. When the Irish servant quickly appeared, she directed, "We shall have our pie and tea now. It is such a beautiful evening and the weather has turned warm. Shall we have it in the gardens, gentlemen?"

⊶═══⊷

The gardens were indeed beautiful. It was the beginning of April, a time when the island should only have been awakening from the winter chill, but today was an unusually warm day. As Wills wandered through a maze in the English design, behind him the cleaned plates and half-emptied cups were being gathered by two servants. Captain Stewart and Varney had returned to their talk of politics and the economy and Lavena had insisted that Rhiannon and Ginny show Wills the gardens, which he was certainly eager to do as it afforded him a bit of time away from the observant eye of Sir Ó Dálaigh, even if Ginny was to be part of the mix.

As they rounded another corner and up another incline, he found himself at the apex of a cliff overlooking the sea. Directly below the cliff face disappeared into the churning waters of the Atlantic but just a short distance away an outcropping of rocks rose like stepping stones. They were almost completely covered with seals fat with their unborn.

"The ocean must be swarming with fish, 'ey?" Wills said as the large creatures, clumsy on land, slipped into the waters with grace only to reemerge a moment later carrying thrashing fish.

"Aye, and it's what attracts the seals, you know. Da says they will give birth in another month or so. This is one of my favorite places, especially when the calves are about."

"Is it now?" He glanced around them. "Where did Ginny get off to?"

"Oh, she's moved forward through the maze." She smiled demurely yet there was the hint of something else. Ah, Wills thought. Dare he hoped that dessert in the garden and the idea to explore the maze was not so impulsive after all?

"Ginny prefers the sights and sounds of Donegal," she was saying, pointing off to their left. At an angle below them was all of Donegal Town, close enough to be seen yet far enough removed to be completely out of earshot. And if he strained his eyes, he could just make out the Stewart ship moored in the harbor.

"I agree with you more," Wills said, turning back toward the seals. "I much prefer the scenery of the ocean and the seals."

"Come," she said. "There is a bench back here where we can watch the ocean waves and smell the salt in the air." She reached for his hand as if to lead him.

At the gentle touch of her soft skin on his, he felt a warmth swell over him like a liquid bolt of lightning had suddenly struck him, causing his insides to melt inside. He glanced over his shoulder toward the house but the hedges blocked his view—and in turn, her parents' view. She tugged at him, laughing quietly, as if perplexed why he stood still. And the truth be told, he was all of a sudden concerned that if he took one step in any direction at'al, his knees would simply dissolve altogether, leaving him a pool of molten man right there in the hedges.

"Are you quite alright?" she asked, her eyes growing wide. "You're looking a bit flushed."

"Rhiannon," he breathed. His voice had grown quieter, deeper. With her hand still on his, he pulled her to him until her body was pressed against his. Not wanting to let go of her hand, afraid the moment would pass if he did, he instead wrapped his free arm around her. She tilted her face up to his. The pupils had grown large, the green of her irises reflecting the brilliance of the sun overhead so they shone as though the pupils were edged with emeralds. Her lips were full and red and as he looked down at her, she parted them slightly, the tiniest bit of a smile turning them upward.

By God, she felt good in his arms. Without even realizing it, his hand left hers to caress her long, slender neck as she watched his face. And then his hand was on her jaw and he was leaning down to meet her lips with his own. If there was a softer, fuller mouth in all of Eire, it was certainly more than a mere man could handle. At her acceptance of him, he felt as though he could lose himself in her embrace. Gone was the house, the others and all of Donegal and in its stead was only the two of them atop the cliff, high above the ocean waves as they crashed against the shore with an intensity that matched the beat of his heart.

Then her lips were opening wide and her passions met his with such abandon and desire that he forced himself to pull back before he had crossed a threshold in which he could not turn back; one that would have her flat on her back in a grassy knoll, her skirts pulled up while he made love to her under the flight of the seagulls and the ocean breeze.

He pinned her against him but as her arms encircled his neck, he wondered who was pinning who exactly, for she wanted him every bit as much as he wanted nothing more than to take her right there, right then.

"Rhiannon dear?"

At the sound of Ginny's voice, they pulled apart abruptly, both turning to look at the seals once more, their faces ablaze as Rhiannon's younger sister joined them once more. She chuckled as she entered the tiny clearing. "So very sorry to interrupt," she said in a voice that betrayed that she was anything but, "Mother and Da must be wondering where we've got off to."

⊹══⊹

They heard the voices even before they had rounded the last opening in the maze.

"So this young man William," Sir Ó Dálaigh was saying, "who is he precisely?"

"William Neely," Stewart answered. "His family is from Wigtownshire, same as mine."

"And yet I have ne'er heard of the Neely family before." His voice was tinged with doubt. "Is he a field hand?"

"No. He is not. He is my aide—"

"Before he came to work for you, I'm asking."

"His family were graziers."

"Not gentlemen planters?"

"You can do no better than Wills," Stewart said. His voice remained amicable but firm. "He is an honest man, a hard worker. He has risen fast in my employ and I've no doubt he'll rise faster still."

"Yes, but the Neelys—"

"Oh, Da," Rhiannon exclaimed as they came around the last hedge to find themselves back on the terrace, "the seals are out in abundance today. It won't be much longer before they have calves!"

As they settled back into their chairs, Lavena reached for the teapot. "Here," she said, shooting a glance at her husband, "you must have more tea." As she poured the hot liquid into Wills' cup, she nodded toward a tray that had not been there prior to their exploration of the hedge. "And do have some biscuits. It certainly won't do to have you leave hungry this evening, would it now?" As they dutifully selected a biscuit, she continued, "And did Rhiannon tell you she's to be in Derry over the summer?"

Rhiannon shot a glance at Wills. "No, I didn't have the chance."

"Derry?" Wills asked. "All summer?"

"Aye," Lavena said before Rhiannon could respond. "She's to remain as a companion to my sister-in-law there until the end of the season."

Wills took a bite of his biscuit while his mind raced. "Whatever will you do in Derry?"

"Oh, I'm sure I'll think of something," Rhiannon replied. He caught the twinkle in her eye as she tilted her tea cup. Lord help him for he could think of things for sure as well and there was something about the mischievousness in her voice that made him wonder if they didn't have the same thing in mind.

18

The sun had not yet sliced through the morning mists when they set sail for Fort Stewart, their pockets heavy with coin. Captain Stewart was in a particularly good mood, no doubt considering the expressions on the men's faces when they returned bearing news of exceptionally high prices for wool, and most especially because they were the first to have brought the spring's bounty to Donegal this year. Aye, and the English were clamoring for the stuff after a cold winter—a season still ongoing, most especially in dreary London, despite the fact that the north of Eire was already turning to spring. They were begging for meat as well and there had been a vigorous discussion at breakfast regarding hunting parties. Now was the time for sure, before the trees were full with their leaves once more and the underbrush was thick, and with the clearing of so much land the deer and the wild boar were out in the clearings appearing befuddled. Perhaps in a few more weeks they could return to Donegal with salted slabs destined for England.

"Mid to late July," Tomas was saying, "and I will be as rich as the two o' you. I am expecting quite the crop of potatoes, I am."

"Between the wool and the potatoes, we shall all be rich!" Fergus declared, slapping Wills on the back. When he didn't respond, he came to stand in front of him. "And what's it with you this morn?"

"Ah," Wills said, averting his eyes as he tightened the rope for the sails. "'Tis nothing."

"You have been unusually silent since you returned from dinner last eve," Tomas said. "Things didn't go well with the lass?"

He sighed. "They went well with her, aye. 'Tis her father I am worried about."

"What's the story there, 'ey?"

With the ropes secured and a short stretch of northward sail before them, Wills leaned against the railing and looked his friends in the eye for a moment. "I am afraid he could be looking for a nobleman for his daughter."

"Ha! And didn't we tell you?" Fergus said. "What would she want with the likes of you? More importantly, what would her da want?"

"What of your family?" Tomas pressed.

Wills shrugged. "Truth be told about it, they are tenant farmers—same as the three of us are here. Oh, and for sure, the Neely family has a decent reputation, one that has served us well. It has been a long time since our house and lands were rotated, so the house is sturdier than most and we've served the same laird for several generations now, we have."

"Ah, but there's the rub, 'ey? Sir Ó Dálaigh is looking for a nobleman for his daughter; a landowner. And a tenant farmer never owns the land himself, now does he? He tills it or he ranches it for the pleasure of the laird, and at his displeasure, he can be sent packing. 'Ey?"

He nodded and turned to face the ocean waves. The mists were heavy this morning, the skies gray like his heart at the moment. After a moment, he mused, "But Rhiannon Ó Dálaigh was born in Ireland."

"So what of that?" Tomas asked.

"What are you saying?" Fergus asked. "That he would give away his daughter because she was Irish born?"

"No. Not that at'al." He stared out at sea for a moment longer. "Varney Ó Dálaigh has lived in Donegal for two decades, at least, but I had the impression his family was not of there."

"Aye?"

"So why does a man leave all he has ever known for the wilderness of Donegal?" Without waiting for a reply, he jabbed his finger in their direction. "I'll tell you this, I will. No man leaves home if there is something there for him."

"Are you suggesting—?"

"I am suggesting that Varney Ó Dálaigh is a self-made man himself. See, here's the thing: when a man is at the top of the heap, there is no reason for him to leave that. He may own lands, a manor house or a castle, even; he might have the ear of his noblemen neighbors, a place in his community. Why would he give up all of that to travel to a place so vastly different?"

Fergus and Tomas grunted but whether they approved of his logic, Wills couldn't tell. After another moment of thought, he added, "It isn't a far stretch to leave the inhospitable soil of Wigtownshire for the rich beauty of Eire. But his family has been in Ireland for generations, apparently, and on the east side of the River Shannon. So why did he not leave for Dublin, which was far closer and far more civilized, but for the wildness of Donegal instead?" He shook his head. "No, gents, I'd be willing to bet, I would, that Varney Ó Dálaigh had nothing to keep him close to his family for a man does not leave home unless he sees a brighter future for himself and his children elsewhere. He brought his wife to Donegal as well, which means at the time he knew he would not likely be returning, and with his two daughters having been born in Donegal, I believe it's safe to say that he has determined he is better off now than he was before."

"So where does that leave you?" Tomas asked.

"Truth be told, I left Wigtownshire for the same reason, I did. Perhaps at the time, I felt I didn't have much of a choice, Captain Stewart having observed me running a man through. But, no, the feeling went deeper still. I knew I was leaving. I just didn't know when or how."

"But that doesn't answer the question, now does it?"

"Oh, I have an answer alright. I do. I came to Ireland to make something more of myself than I figured I could do where I was. And that I will do, or die trying. It's just now the timetable has sped up a bit, 'ey?"

A sudden gust of wind and a roll of the sea had them scrambling to adjust the sails so they weren't in danger. But as their conversation was replaced with orders from the bridge and vigorous activity, Wills' thoughts remained on that grassy knoll at the top of the cliff.

19

ills was in the fields tending to the sheep when he spotted the figure weaving between the trees in the distant forest. He thought initially that his eyes were playing tricks on him as the sun had been peeking through the clouds all afternoon. But as he watched the shadows, the movement appeared too deliberate and when several birds left their treetop nests to circle overhead, he made his way down the hillside and toward another copse. He did not look to the northeast in the direction of the figure but kept his head turned due east, though he cut his eyes to the side a few times. Satisfied that the individual was continuing its advancement, he waited until he, too, was in the shadows of the trees before he began making his way around the southern edge of Drongawn Lough.

Ah, but it was a woman, he thought as they drew nearer to one another. Now he could make out the outline of the cape and hood and as the figure crossed through a sliver of sunshine, he could plainly see a shock of wavy red hair tumble from underneath the hood.

Elan, and he was no closer to discovering her full identity than he had been the first time they'd met.

Their paths converged at the edge of the O'Doherty woods.

"Mister Neely," she said in greeting. "Nice of you to meet me here in the woodland."

"Were you coming to see the captain again, perhaps?"

She glanced over her shoulder. His eyes followed hers but he detected no movement other than their own.

"This is better," she said warily.

"Why is that?"

"I bring you news." She slipped her hand inside her cape and extracted a badly weathered paper that was torn at both the top and bottom as if nail rods had once been hammered into it. Wills received it from her outstretched hand and quietly unfolded it.

The top half contained an artist's rendering of Phelim MacDavitt but had it not been for the name underneath, he would not have recognized him from the picture as it bore little likeness to the man himself. The bottom half contained only seven words besides his name:

Wanted for Treason
By the King's Order

"Where did you get this?" Wills asked.

"It's one of at least four erected at each corner of O'Doherty land," Elan answered.

Instinctively, he glanced through the trees.

"You won't be finding another," she added hastily. "The O'Doherty himself ordered them removed."

"So Cahir knows about this already, does he?"

"Aye. He does."

"And where is he now?"

"Carrickabraghy Castle as I was leaving."

Wills studied the paper for a moment longer, though he needed the time more to steady his mind than to memorize its contents. They were plain enough. "So do you know if The O'Doherty intends to turn him in?"

She chuckled dryly. "Hardly. They are rounding up all the clan's men as we speak."

"What do they intend to do?"

"I would imagine they intend to attack, wouldn't you?" At his silence, she added, "They were already planning an insurrection. This proves they have been found out—at least Phelim has. They have no choice now but to follow through."

"It makes no sense."

"It makes perfect sense."

"But Cahir—he's the Queen's O'Doherty."

"*Was* the Queen's O'Doherty. And a lot has changed since her death some years past, in case you haven't noticed."

He swallowed and looked toward Fort Stewart. He could barely see the smoke rising from the fires there. Surely from where he stood, he was halfway between Carrickabraghy Castle and Captain Stewart, and time was of the essence. "Where will they attack?"

"I heard The O'Doherty mention George Paulet."

"Derry, then?"

She shrugged. "Make of it what you wish." She pulled her hood forward and tucked her hair underneath. "I must get back before I am missed."

"Is this attack imminent?"

She hesitated, peering momentarily at the paper. "Would you make it imminent, if you were Phelim?" Without waiting for a reply, she turned and a moment later, she was once again a shadowy figure, darting between the trees as she made her way back to Carrickabraghy Castle.

+⊱═⊰+

There are times in a man's life when he knows that his decision could change the course of history; oh, and sometimes it is not world history and maybe not even a country's or region's history but certainly that of himself and his closest acquaintances. Such were Wills' thoughts as he watched Elan until she was out of sight.

He stood at a triangle of sorts. He was a bit closer to Fort Stewart and the captain than he was to Culmore Fort and Henry Hart, but only a bit—an hour at most. At the pinnacle of the triangle lay Carrickabraghy Castle and Cahir O'Doherty, approximately three times the distance from Culmore Fort. It was perhaps the least desirable of the three and yet something deep inside him begged him to verify Elan's words; certainly he could not cause Stewart or Hart to rally a hundred men or more against O'Doherty without evidence, now could he?

But truth be told, he wanted to go to Carrickabraghy Castle only to see Cahir welcome him in, assure him all was well and convince him he had heard only another rumor. And yet he knew if he made the wrong decision, events could spiral out of control; at its worst, at least one man could die.

He had begun to walk back toward Fort Stewart, perhaps out of habit more than anything else despite the fact that those voices inside him grew more frantic at every step he took to further him from the O'Doherty castle. As he cleared the forest and found himself once again in the open, he paused.

In the meadow some distance away, his sheep still grazed and if he did not herd them into the safety of

Fort Stewart by nightfall, they were easy prey for the wolves that roamed here in abundance, hungry and alert.

A voice and a whistle called his attention to another spot where Fergus was driving his sheep to a grassier area on his slice of the hill with the help of a border collie. Never one that preferred walking, Fergus was mounted atop his horse. As he glanced in Wills' direction, Wills found himself waving frantically with both hands. His friend hesitated, stopped his horse to peer at him for the briefest of moments and then began a full gallop toward him.

"What is it?" Fergus called out before he had even reached his side.

Wills grasped for the horse's muzzle as he slowed. "I must go to Carrickabraghy Castle in all haste." He quickly explained the conversation with Elan.

"You must have a steed," Fergus said, starting to climb down. "You'll never make it otherwise."

"No." Wills stopped him from dismounting. "Look." He pointed in the opposite direction where Tomas and several others were tending to their potato fields. "Round up those men. I need you and Tomas to come with me to Carrickabraghy. Have another alert Captain Stewart; I'll send word after we've seen The O'Doherty. Ask the others to get our sheep in."

"Aye." The word had barely escaped his mouth before Fergus was off. It seemed like an eternity that he waited there but in reality it was only a few minutes before one man left hurriedly for Fort Stewart while Tomas and Fergus returned on horseback leading a third mount.

"And let this be a lesson to you," Tomas said as Wills mounted, "you might like walking and even prefer it but don't allow yourself to be caught without your horse again."

"I have learned that lesson well today," Wills answered before clicking his heels against the steed's side.

Ah, but so much had changed since that day he had become so hopelessly lost in the O'Donnell and O'Doherty forests. The terrain along the Drongawn Lough and Lough Swilly no longer appeared the same. Most was cleared on the old O'Donnell clan property, land that now belonged to William Stewart; and Wills knew his way to Carrickabraghy Castle as he ventured onto O'Doherty land. Should he come in contact with any of his clan, he would request that they accompany him to Cahir himself; he was no longer concerned about an ambush as he once had been.

They remained close to the shore for as long as possible but the terrain was wild with sudden outcroppings of underbrush interspersed with rocks and cliffs. Reluctantly, he determined that the horses would find surer footing if they ventured into the forest. But where once he would have certainly traveled in circles, he found the footpaths more readily, the telltale signs of a bent branch here, a scuff of underbrush there, to guide him.

Their travel took them from the southern edge of O'Doherty land to the northernmost point and yet they did not encounter another human being, though they navigated through several clearings in which a house, a stable or a smithy stood vacant and desolate. Fields were untended, herds left in the care of dogs that watched them with wary eyes but did not bark. Eventually the silence became deafening. Not even the birds were about, though the skies were particularly blue and unusually clear.

Several hours had passed when Wills caught sight of Carrickabraghy Castle. It stood tall and barren, the stone somehow colder than he remembered, and then he realized the women and children that had always been about were nowhere to be seen. He felt as though he was entering an abandoned property but when their horses slowed as they neared the gate, it swung open. Two guards welcomed them; perhaps it was Wills' imagination—certainly it was—that their eyes were more veiled, their greeting more subdued, their attentions more suspicious.

"I have come to see The O'Doherty," Wills announced even before he had dismounted.

The doors to the Great Hall were open wide and as he approached, he detected shadowy movement inside. He felt the cold blade of his sword against his back, a mere movement away, and he was caught between wanting to feel its grip within his hand and wanting, needing, to appear as if he had come in friendship.

It wasn't The O'Doherty that suddenly appeared in the doorway to the Great Hall but The O'Donnell, his broad shoulders nearly reaching from one side to the other.

"Ah, Wills!" he said, moving swiftly to their side. "Fergus. Tomas. What brings you here today?"

"Niall Garbh, how are you today, my good man?" Wills said. But before he could answer, he continued, "We're here to see The O'Doherty."

"Oh, but he is not here," Niall Garbh said smoothly. "Oisin," he called to a man standing near, "get their horses some water and hay." Over Wills' objections, he added, "Come in, the three o' yous. Have some ale and meat, 'ey?"

"Niall Garbh," Wills said, his voice firm as he stood his ground. "Where is Cahir?"

Niall Garbh took a step closer to them. "Cahir and Phelim have gone to Burt Castle. They intend to clear Canmoyre Woods."

"Burt Castle?" Wills felt his heart sink. The castle, another of O'Doherty's strongholds, was less than an hour's walk from where he had spoken to Elan in the woods. It stood at the southern edge of O'Doherty lands to protect it from invasion launched from the south and was a mere stone's throw from Culmore Fort and Derry. Instead, he had crossed to the clan's opposite edge and now stood on the Isle of Doagh, nearly as far to the northwest as was possible without either fins or ship.

"Come," Niall Garbh said. "You have traveled far and you look thirsty."

"How many men did they take with them?"

Niall Garbh chuckled. "Ah, but have you seen Canmoyre Woods? A mess to be sure. They would have taken as many a man as could be spared from his regular duties."

"And how many would that be?" Wills pressed. "A hundred?"

He shrugged. "Perhaps. Maybe more. Maybe less."

The memory of his lunch with Henry Hart, Captain Stewart and Cahir O'Doherty hit him full in the face. Of course. Cahir had spoken of traveling to Burt Castle and Henry had invited him for a visit at Culmore Fort.

"It is a shame you have missed Cahir's wife yet again," Niall Garbh was saying. "Mary Preston would have enjoyed entertaining the three of you—and more so once you have found yourselves some women."

"Mary—she is with Cahir?"

"Aye. She is. Gone to Burt Castle, she has."

"Niall Garbh," Wills said. "Can you spare a few horses? We must get back before nightfall—we left our herds in the field—and ours must rest."

"Of course." He signaled for the man called Oisin. "Get these men fresh mounts." He turned back to Wills. "Have you enough food and drink? I can have the women prepare-"

"Aye, the women. That would be Elan and—?"

At the mention of Elan's name, Niall Garbh's eyes widened for the briefest of moments before they became veiled once more. "I wouldn't know their names, I'm afraid."

"Oh, surely you know Elan. Beautiful red-haired lass, for sure?"

"I wouldn't know who you'd be talking about."

"And you, Niall Garbh?" Wills smiled. "Why didn't you go with Cahir and Phelim?"

His face became hardened and then he chuckled. "I am not the type of lord that fells trees, I'm afraid. But come. Surely you are in need of some cool ale before you take your leave?"

"No. Thank you. That won't be necessary."

A few brief moments later, they were trading horses. As they passed through the gate on their way southward, Wills instructed Tomas and Fergus in a hoarse whisper to keep their horses at a steady walk and to keep their eyes straight ahead. It wasn't until they were out of sight of the castle that Wills signaled for them to stop.

"What the hell was that all about?" Fergus asked.

"Something's not right," Wills said.

"I'll say it isn't," Tomas agreed. "In all my days, I don't recall seeing The O'Donnell at an O'Doherty castle without The O'Doherty himself present."

"Is that so?"

"He is up to something. He was too nice, don't you think?" Fergus prodded. "Oh, let's get you some ale and some food and 'ey, a wench or two could warm your bed and while your willies are being tickled, we'll just go about our business here."

"What would you have us do?" Tomas asked.

Wills glanced behind him. The day was getting on, for sure, the shadows lengthening. The O'Donnell would send a man or two—or several—to observe their movements and see them to Fort Stewart. They most likely would not detect their presence at all but they would be there alright, like the trees had eyes and ears, they would be there.

"We head south," he said. "When we get to the southernmost end of Drongawn Lough, Tomas, you'll head to Fort Stewart. Fergus, you and I will travel on to Culmore Fort."

20

Culmore was the Anglicized name for Cúil Mór, which meant *The Great Corner* in the Irish language, and indeed it not only sat at the mouth of the River Foyle but not far from the point at which two clan lands met: The O'Doherty's and The O'Donnell's. As the English colonized Ireland, the village became the site for Culmore Fort, which housed a garrison of a hundred men strong tasked with protecting Derry, which lay just to its south. In centuries past, it had been the Vikings that had sailed past this point, their ships navigating deep into the island before they were met with formidable resistance; and it was thought another attack on Derry would likely come from the sea again.

It had been a mere twenty years since the Spanish Armada had sunk off Ireland's coast, and as the conversation with Rhiannon's father had implied, it was said the ships had been blown off course during a vicious storm. Whether that was true really didn't matter as their presence so alarmed Queen Elizabeth that she sent a large contingent to Ireland to decimate the Spaniards.

Some had found their way to Derry but had walked through wilderness from Antrim or Donegal, after their ships had sunk to the bottom of the sea; and those that appeared in Derry were the lucky ones, having been taken in by the Bishop of Derry and smuggled out to Scotland.

Now as Wills and Fergus approached from the west, his eyes roamed over the Fort, vainly searching for anything amiss. To call it a fort was rather a stretch, to be quite honest about it; it was a square stone building possibly three stories tall but it was difficult to say, as there might have been four windows in the entire building, if that, by which they could have identified separate floors. It was topped by a heavily armed parapet, however, and as they approached Wills looked upward to find weapons aimed at himself and his friend.

They made their way to the front of the fort where a smaller structure had seemingly been tacked onto the larger building; only one story, it also contained a more modest parapet. Before they could reach the entrance, the doors opened and guards stepped onto the stoop.

"Identify yourselves and your business!" a man with sandy hair bellowed.

"I am William Neely," Wills called out in return. "We have been sent from Captain William Stewart at Fort Stewart, Donegal. We are here to speak with Sir Henry Hart."

"Stay where you're at," the guard returned. While he disappeared inside the structure, Wills was acutely aware of two men watching from the smaller parapet and perhaps a half dozen more from the top of the larger structure.

"How many men do you see?" Wills asked Fergus.

"I have counted eight."

"As have I."

They remained mounted until a few minutes later Henry Hart himself stepped from the landing onto the ground.

"Well, well!" Henry said as he approached. "Come inside, the both of you. To what do I owe this honor?"

"We must speak with you in private," Wills said as they dismounted.

As soldiers moved forward to take their horses and lead them to a nearby stable, Henry ushered them into the fort and down a hallway. "Have you met my wife?" he asked as a woman emerged from one of the rooms.

"I have not had the pleasure," Wills said.

"Then may I introduce Mrs. Hart—the former Miss Frances Bosvile of Eynsford, Kent, England."

As Wills took her hand and bent to kiss it in greeting, a pleasant perfume of wildflowers surrounded them in the close confines of the hall. Her hand was small, even dainty and smooth as a rose petal itself; the hand of a woman unaccustomed to manual labor. As he straightened, he took in her alabaster skin, her cheekbones nearly nonexistent in her plump but pleasant face. Her eyes were dark and set off by heavy brows and her honey-colored hair was teased high on her head and secured with pearls. In contrast to her fleshy face, her shoulders were very narrow, her upper body slim. At her waist, a voluminous skirt billowed outward, hiding the rest of her figure.

As Fergus greeted her in turn, a small boy peeked from behind her skirt.

"And who have we here?" Wills asked.

"Ah, come forward, boy," Henry said. As the shy boy stepped reluctantly from behind his mother, he said, "This is Henry, my son."

"Ah, priming another knight, no doubt," Wills said as he bowed slightly.

"We are dressed rather formally," Henry said as if a bit self-conscious. "We have been invited to dinner. We were just on our way out."

"My apologies for keeping you," Wills answered. "We shall only be a moment."

"Nonsense," Frances said. "Please make yourselves comfortable in the sitting room, and I shall order tea and biscuits." At that, she snapped her fingers and a servant that Wills had not previously noticed stepped forward from the back of the hall, nodded briefly and with a curt "Ma'am" disappeared down another hallway.

"No, really," Wills protested, "we have but a bit of business to discuss and then we shall be on our way."

"Come in, come in," Henry said, ushering them into the sitting room. "Be seated, please."

As the men sat in chairs that seemed a bit too opulent for a garrison headquarters, Frances closed the door demurely behind them.

"Sir Hart," Wills said. "I have a matter of grave importance to discuss with you."

He signaled for him to continue. "Please."

"I have it on good authority that Cahir O'Doherty and Phelim MacDavitt are planning an insurrection."

"Oh, that again. I thought we dispelled with all that in Donegal."

"Aye, sir. I wish we had. However, I have been informed that they are gathering men from across the O'Doherty land holdings, perhaps under the pretext of clearing wood at Canmoyre Woods, but they intend instead to attack Derry."

"I see." He studied them for such a long moment that Wills became doubtful that he understood the importance of his words. "You may be partially correct," he said at last.

The servant girl opened the door and carried a tray of biscuits and tea into the room. They fell silent as she poured their tea. "Is there anything else, sir?" she asked.

"That will be all, Neasa. Thank you."

Henry waited until she left the room before he continued. "Cahir and Phelim were indeed in route here but not for the purpose of clearing wood—or attacking Derry. Cahir relinquished Phelim into my custody earlier today."

Stunned, Wills could think of nothing to say. He could feel his skin growing warm with embarrassment.

"—though I do not anticipate Phelim being—incarcerated, for want of a better term—for more than the evening."

"He is here, sir?"

"He is indeed. However, after we spoke in Donegal, I decided an attempt to terminate these ludicrous allegations was warranted. As we discussed, Baron Howth has a penchant for gossip—unfortunately, much of it malicious—and Sir George Paulet has been a willing recipient of his lies." He scowled. "I do not care for Paulet and none I have ever met has liked the man, but he has the ear of King James, I'm afraid, though some have surmised that he is here in Ireland precisely because the king wished him removed from court." He waved his hand dismissively. "But no matter. I sent word to Lord Chichester in Dublin. There is no evidence that either Phelim or Cahir are planning an insurrection, and in fact, I will be informing Cahir that King James is awarding him additional land—land that should have been afforded him after the Nine Years War. As for Phelim, tomorrow he will be released, cleared of all charges against him."

Wills leaned back and sighed heavily. "I am greatly relieved. I must admit to being somewhat embarrassed at having spread foolish rumors. The person who informed me of such an insurrection was obviously mistaken."

"Does this person have a name?" Henry smiled wanly.

"Elan. I do not yet know her last name, but she works at Carrickabraghy Castle."

"Interesting. I should think someone that close to Cahir and his family would have known the truth."

"To be honest," Fergus said, "we all like Cahir O'Doherty. He has been a pleasant neighbor and other than these charges being floated about, he has given us no reason to doubt his allegiance to the Crown."

"I believe it is in our best interest to put these charges behind us. As I mentioned in Donegal, I have known Cahir since he was just a lad of fifteen and I can tell you that I have the highest respect for him—and for Phelim MacDavitt. In fact," he added, "my son Henry, whom you just met? His godfather is none other than Cahir O'Doherty himself. That is how much I trust and admire the man."

"My deepest apologies," Wills said, rising. "I obviously trusted in a rumor and I can assure you that it will not happen again. Please give my best to Cahir when next you see him."

"Well, you can do that yourself," Henry said as he and Fergus also rose. "You are here now. Why don't you two join us for dinner this eve? We have been invited to Burt Castle by Cahir and his lovely wife, Mary Preston."

The image of Mrs. Hart in her formal evening attire rose in Wills' mind and he felt a fresh wave of embarrassment sweep over him. "I appreciate the invitation, sir, but we must depart for Fort Stewart. I am afraid I sent word to Captain Stewart of a possible rebellion and I must return and admit to my grievous error."

"I suggest I send a soldier to Fort Stewart in your stead. I have fresh soldiers and horses and—begging your pardon for my forthrightness—but you both appear to be in need of food, drink and sleep."

"Thank you, but—"

"I must insist." He picked up a bell from the tea tray and rang it. Instantly, Neasa reappeared. "Arrange accommodations for these gentlemen," he ordered. "Serve them food and drink and whatever else they require. Unless—" he turned back to them "—I can talk you into joining us at Burt Castle?"

"Thank you, sir." Wills glanced at Fergus. "I believe it would be best if we—as you suggested—get a bit of rest and food before returning to Fort Stewart."

"As you wish. I will, however, send a courier to Captain Stewart letting him know the 'insurrection' has been disproved and you will be returning on the morrow."

Frances popped her head into the sitting room. "Henry, dear, if you are finished, we are running quite late."

"Ah, yes. Come." He stopped in the doorway. "Young Henry, Mrs. Hart and myself will be remaining at Burt Castle until the morning. It isn't safe for a woman and child to travel late at night. Wolves, you know. I hope to journey to Fort Stewart soon; I have heard much about all you have done on the old O'Donnell land."

Before they could reply, he was out the door and down the hall, ushering Mrs. Hart and young Henry to a waiting carriage while also directing a soldier to ride to Fort Stewart with news that all was well.

21

Burt Castle rested at the southern edge of the Inishowen Peninsula like a silent sentinel keeping watch over the O'Doherty landholdings. It was fairly new, having been constructed less than a hundred years earlier, and was considered a more contemporary style than earlier Irish castles. Built of the same limestone and rock that was found in abundance throughout Ulster, it rose three stories above the ground and at two of its four corners stood towers that reached another two stories before giving way to parapets that afforded a spectacular view of the Irish countryside—and even Derry, which was a only a few miles away.

Each wall was between four and five feet thick, the towers dotted with perforations for dozens of harkbus, along with larger openings for cannons.

There were two more stories below ground, comprised of dungeons, an armory and soldiers' barracks and offices, eventually giving way to a stone wall that surrounded the castle and grounds, which was in turn encircled by a mote. With Ireland's violent history of invasion ranging from the Vikings and Normans to the Spaniards and English—not to mention battles between clans—it was a formidable fortress built to withstand assault.

Cahir watched from a window on the third floor as the carriage left Culmore Fort. Dusk was already on the horizon but carriage lamps made it easy to follow the Hart party's progress. Truth be told, he was looking forward to seeing his old friend Henry Hart and wished it might have been under different circumstances, but such was his lot.

He felt older than his twenty-three years; indeed, there were days in which he felt as old as his father as he lay dying just eight years' prior. As the English had invaded Ireland, his father had fought bravely but vainly to rid the island of them. Though he formed alliances with other clans, including the O'Neill, MacSweeney, O'Donnell and more, they were, in the end, no match for the English, particularly when Chichester arrived with his strategy to destroy their spirit by killing every man, woman and child that resisted and burning all that lay in his path.

So it was that when John O'Doherty passed away, Cahir, at the tender age of fifteen, made a critical decision: to turn against his fellow Irishmen and side with the English. There really had been no sounder choice and there were some in his own clan that had risen against him, branding him a traitor to his own people. But it was precisely that loyalty to his people that caused him to swallow his pride and march on Derry to defend Sir Henry Docwra from certain annihilation; for the most powerful clan in all of Ulster, The O'Neill, had the English pinned down with the assistance of nearly every other clan in those parts.

But he had seen the future. Oh, one didn't need to be a fortune teller, for sure, to know what was coming, for the English possessed one of the most formidable armies since Roman times; a standing army, one of men bred for the killing. And if Docwra was killed at Derry, he had no doubt that Queen Elizabeth would order the entire island overrun—and the O'Doherty people would fall. Aye, and so it had been that he marched his clan across those miles that he now watched the carriage navigate in the opposite direction, and saved Docwra and the men he had left and became known as The Queen's O'Doherty.

He had tried to remain a loyalist; he really had. He fought against the O'Neills, the Maguires, the O'Donnells and more during nine long years in which he saw countless men die, numerous atrocities committed and too many women and children left starving and homeless. But when that war was over, he still had Inishowen. His people were protected; their way of life, though changed forever, was far better than what had befallen the clans that fought against the English.

Oh, and for certain, he had expected to be awarded much more; he was promised much more. He had been assured of lands that had once belonged to those he had fought against. And to cement his standing in English society, he had courted and married Mary Preston, an Englishwoman of nobility. It had not been easy despite the surface appearance of being quite meteoric: he was knighted for his service to the Queen, was bestowed the title of Lord of Inishowen and would forevermore be known as *Sir* Cahir O'Doherty.

And when Lord Mountjoy himself had traveled with Cahir to meet King James after Elizabeth's passing, he had thrown himself into English society, learning their customs, their manner of speech, their language and their habits. And eventually, he won the hand of Viscount Gormanston's daughter, Mary. A leading member of the Pale, relation to the Viscount should have ensured his status—but it had not. And it was no matter on that account, as his reward had been Mary herself. He'd fallen madly and passionately in love with the woman and she with him, and well, that was that.

If only Sir Docwra had remained in Ireland; all would be different now. But King James was of the opinion that Docwra was too lenient with the Irish, the war to conquer them was taking too long, and he appointed George Paulet in his place. Paulet made it clear that he despised the Irish from the moment he stepped off the ship and onto Irish soil. He was vocal about his preference for ridding the entire island of the people he referred to as devils and monkeys. What transpired then was perhaps the darkest hours the Irish had ever seen; with Sir Arthur Chichester appointed a leading commander, they boasted of killing every living thing they encountered, whether it was man, woman, child, livestock or dog. And for many that survived, their fate was even more cruel than those that had perished, as their farms, their homes, their foodstores— all that kept them alive—was burned to the ground so nothing was left but scorched earth and smoldering embers.

Starvation had set in even as English fortifications were reveling with parties, flowing wine and more food than their nobility could eat. It was said at Dublin Castle, the English had devised a new sport; after they had stuffed themselves full, they ordered the scraps taken beyond the castle gates and tossed onto the ground, where they laughed as starving Irish men, women and children fought over the smallest morsel, eating like dogs in the dirt.

Aye, and it had become increasingly more difficult to ally with the English and there had certainly been countless occasions in which he had questioned his own part in helping make the invaders victorious. Docwra had said himself that without Cahir, he was certain the English could not have prevailed, despite the fact that Spain wavered on coming to the defense of the native Irish.

Cahir watched while his men rode out to meet the carriage as it entered O'Doherty borders. They would escort them into Burt Castle, providing them safe passage.

He sighed. There had been so many injustices since the Queen had passed; lands promised to him had been awarded to Englishmen and Scotsmen instead; he was treated as if he was lacking intelligence; and even portions of his own lands just outside Inishowen—lands that had been in his family for more than a thousand years—were summarily taken from him in English court.

The door opened behind him and he turned to find his wife, Mary, standing there. "They are approaching," she said. She offered a smile; hesitant, nervous but loyal. Ah, but he had done well to marry the woman. Her father's title be damned, the hell with their connections; he loved her. He loved her passionately, with every ounce of blood in his body.

He crossed to the threshold and kissed her gently on her full, soft lips. "Do not worry," he whispered. "No matter what occurs, your safety is assured. I promise you that."

"It is not my safety that concerns me," she answered, kissing him more fully. "It is yours."

22

It was an unusually warm evening for April. Wills lay flat on his back with his hands behind his head as he gazed at the low ceiling. The bed was comfortable enough, he supposed; narrow and lumpy, it was meant for one of the English soldiers stationed there. On the other side of the room lay Fergus in almost the exact posture as Wills, eyes wide while he lay deep in thought. The room was sparsely furnished with a desk, a chair and a trunk for clothes storage, and one tiny window was insufficient for allowing more than a promise of a cool breeze.

"The food was decent enough," Fergus said, breaking the silence that had pervaded them both.

"Venison, I think."

"I didn't much care what it was. I was so hungry I might have eaten anything they put in front of me."

"Aye. Me as well."

They both continued staring at the ceiling as though it held great importance to them.

"I was hoping I would sleep," Fergus said.

"You think it was the dip in the river?" Wills said with a mischievous smile. Ah, the water had been frigid, it had; no doubt about it but a man could be tossed into that water from his deathbed and be revived sure enough.

"I keep thinking about my sheep," Fergus said.

"Your sheep?" Wills chuckled. "Been too long without a woman, 'ey?"

"Ach, you." He stared at the ceiling a moment longer. "I've a few fat ewes ready for lambing, I have. I'm hoping they don't give birth before I get back."

"Aye and for sure you've been in the fields too long."

"And you aren't the same, I suppose?"

"And I am; I admit it. I have a few pregnant ones as well."

They lay there for several minutes, both on their backs, both with their hands under their heads, both staring at the ceiling. Then abruptly they both said, "Are you sleepy then?"

Then as if they were a mirror image, they sat up and threw their legs over the sides of their beds. "No."

"I say let's get on our way back to Fort Stewart."

"Aye, and that's a decent idea. We'll be back before the flock is herded to the meadow in the morn, 'ey?"

23

The Great Hall had an air about it, it did. Cahir had kept the conversation going with Henry and truth be told, his wife Mary hadn't needed encouragement with Frances. Both women were English, both far from home and family; though the Irish had accepted his wife as their own and no doubt they were friendly enough to Frances, they much preferred one another's company. It was just something, he supposed, to do with culture and customs much as it had been for him when he had traveled to London.

In any event, the two women had kept their eyes mainly on each other as they talked, which was quite fortuitous; for other than a few serving wenches, there was not another woman in the Great Hall. As Cahir looked out from the head table that was elevated at the front of the hall, he doubted his decision to exclude the women and particularly the children on this night, as their absence might very well have raised suspicion.

But, he thought as he took another long swig of wine, Henry had not appeared to have noticed. Cahir had made certain to feed them well—all of them, for it was unknown when they would eat so fine again—and Henry had certainly partaken of the variety of meats and breads.

Now as he tilted his tankard, his eyes roamed the hall. Henry had not traveled alone; he never did. Like Englishmen and Irish alike, he journeyed with an entourage of soldiers even for a friendly dinner. The half dozen of them were seated near the rear of the hall, laughing and back-slapping, their bellies filled with both food and drink, as was Cahir's careful instructions. They were surrounded not only by O'Doherty clansmen but representatives from MacSweeney, O'Cahans and O'Hanlons. Even Niall Garbh O'Donnell had sent a contingent, though he stayed away himself; he and Henry knew one another and his presence in the hall that night might have aroused suspicion.

Cahir caught Mary's eye and gave her the briefest of nods.

"Oh, Frances," she said, her voice carrying across the head table, "you simply must see the new sitting room upstairs. We sent for the most beautiful fabric from France and it has only just arrived. You will absolutely adore it."

"Perhaps wee Henry would like to join you?" Cahir asked, pointedly glancing at Henry's son. "It is a bit late for the lad, 'ey?"

"Yes," Frances said, leaning over to place a finger under young Henry's chin. "We'll take you to the room where you'll stay this night."

"Your trunks are already there," Cahir said to Henry. "The men brought them up earlier this eve while we dined."

"Always the most hospitable host," Henry responded. "I must admit, it grows late for me as well. I am expected at Culmore Fort at dawn."

As Mary, Frances and the boy rose, Cahir did as well. "Then allow me to escort you upstairs as well, my friend." He leaned down as if his next words were to be kept private. "Truth be told the best of the liquor is upstairs. Perhaps the four of us can partake in a final nightcap before we adjourn for the evening? Away from all the noise," he added as a rowdy group laughed boisterously.

"A good idea indeed," Henry said, rising as well.

Cahir swept his arm outward in a gesture that allowed Henry, his son and the women to lead the way. As they crossed the front of the hall, he glanced back at his men. They had kept up a good ruse of drinking and talk, he thought, though he knew not a one of them was even a bit in his cups this night. There was too much at stake.

As the others disappeared through a doorway and up the winding stone stairs leading to the bedrooms, he paused and looked back one last time. Ah, but he sorely missed Phelim; but no matter. He would be back soon enough and at a time when his services would be profoundly needed.

⊹≫·≪⊹

The sitting room was dimly lit, the shadows dancing in the corners from flames cast by both candles and the large fireplace. Cahir's instructions had been explicit and now he noted they had been followed with the precision he had expected. Two doors, one on either side of the sitting room, were open, revealing two bedrooms that were carefully prepared for their guests. Young Henry's trunk was open at the foot of the bed in one room while in the opposite bedroom, his parents' trunk was situated at the foot of that bed but still unopened. A platter of food sat on the table in the sitting area, along with several jugs of wine and ale.

The fire was roaring, causing the room to feel a bit too warm, and he crossed to the window to open it more fully. As he did so, he leaned forward to view a number of O'Doherty clansmen outside; some were watching the windows above while others were concerned with events unfolding downstairs. He knew the raucous laughter would quickly give way to shouts and confusion and as he turned back to his guests, he knew that now every second counted.

Four men followed them into the room; two took up places on either side of the door while the others blocked the doorway. Henry turned to look at the men. His face turned ashen but as he opened his mouth to speak, the words froze on his lips.

Before he could sound an alarm, Cahir seized his twin-edged dagger. He came from behind, wrapping his arm around Henry's neck so the blade was against his jugular. As Frances opened her mouth to scream, one of the clansmen rushed to grab her, closing her mouth with his beefy hand while he pulled her arms behind her back with his other hand. The boy was similarly restrained, which was not an easy feat as it turned out.

"I do not wish to harm you," Cahir said, tightening his grip on Henry. "I have no problems with you and my actions are not against the Crown."

"Cahir," Henry managed to croak despite the fact that his throat was uncomfortably mashed with Cahir's forearm, "don't do this, my friend. We can talk."

"The time for talk has passed, I'm afraid. At this very moment, your men are being led into the dungeons where they will remain until this has ended."

"Why? How have I offended you?"

"You have not offended me."

"Let him go!" Frances struggled against the man that held her.

Cahir glanced out the nearby window. A single torch swayed from left to right and back again. "You can scream all you'd like now, Frances. There will be no one to hear you—no one that would care to rescue you, that is."

She began to sob. "Mary—stop this insanity!"

Mary moved away from her friend and tilted her chin upward. "I stand with Cahir," she said simply.

"Let my wife and child go," Henry said. "Whatever your business is, it is with me and me alone."

"I shall tell you what my business is," Cahir said, moving slightly to the side so that one of his men could remove Henry's weapons and belt. "I will take Culmore Fort this night. If you help me, you, your family and your men will be spared."

"Culmore—I can't do that, Cahir."

"You must do it." He pressed the blade against his skin until a trickle of blood began to flow.

"Please don't hurt him!" Frances screamed. "Please! I beg of you!"

The boy was kicking now, his anger mixing with fear as tears flowed down his cheeks.

"Think this through," Henry pleaded. Beads of perspiration broke out across his brow. "To take Culmore Fort is treason. I would be executed if I helped you."

"You can tell them I forced you."

"You think they would believe that?"

"Henry, listen to me. I will kill your wife and your child if you do not cooperate."

Two more men appeared in the doorway. "It is done," one said simply.

"You see, Henry?" Cahir said. "The fate of your family and your men lie with you. Cooperate with me and none will be harmed. Do not cooperate and they will all be killed."

"But why, Cahir? Why?"

"My issue is with George Paulet and Paulet alone. But stand in my way, and I swear to God, I will kill you all."

Henry tried to turn his head to look at his wife and child but Cahir held him immobile. Frances continued to beg, tears streaming down her face. The boy's thrashing limbs had been physically subdued but his cries and shouts reverberated through the room. Mary stood stoically among the O'Doherty clansmen, watching Cahir as if waiting for his orders.

"Mary," Cahir said, "leave us. I do not wish for you to see me slice his throat open." He jerked Henry toward Frances. "But I want the image to remain with her and their child forevermore."

Mary approached the doorway, her shoulders squared.

"No!" Frances begged. "Please don't hurt him! Please!"

"What's it to be, Henry?" Cahir asked. "Do you want your wife and child to be killed as well? Their fate rests with you."

Henry looked imploringly at his son and then his wife. "I cannot help you. I will not help you."

"You would rather have your wife and son killed than Paulet?"

"No. But my duty is to King James. I cannot surrender Culmore Fort to you. I can't."

Cahir tightened his grip on Henry's throat, stretching his neck to the side so his blade had unfettered access to his jugular. "So it's to be then."

"No!" Frances cried out again. "I will help you!"

Cahir's hand froze; the blade still against the vein.

"I give you my word," Frances continued. "I will turn over Culmore Fort to you, even if he will not."

Henry tried to protest but his words were muffled by the pressure on his throat.

"Frances," Cahir said, his voice steady but firm, "are you understanding that if you betray me, both your husband and your child will be murdered here this night?"

The tears cascaded down her face unchecked. "I promise you, Cahir. I promise you."

He watched her for a moment and then looked to Mary, who had remained in the doorway. Mary nodded her head in agreement. "Remove Lady Hart." He kept his grip on Henry until his men had sufficient time to move her down the stairs. Then he nodded to those still remaining in the room. Mary departed first, following Frances' path. The one holding the child released him.

"What's the blood on your arm?" Cahir asked him.

"Ah, the child bit me. It's no matter."

"The child is not harmed?"

"I've been harmed more than he."

Cahir waited until his men were in the hallway before releasing Henry.

"You don't know what you're doing—" Henry sputtered, his hand moving instinctively to his throat.

"On the contrary, I know exactly what I am doing."

"The King will throw all his wrath at you, Cahir. There will be no escape."

"As I said, this is not about the King nor about England. This is about George Paulet."

"Then let me help you. I can petition King James-"

"The time for petitions is over."

"Cahir—" The child raced into his father's arms, cutting off his words.

"The doors to your bedrooms are locked and soon this room will be as well. You have sufficient food and drink. Men will be stationed outside these doors and just below your windows as well. Do not attempt to escape. To do so will mean sure death—not only to you but to your child and Frances as well."

"Please—"

"Your skin is simply scratched, my friend. It will heal."

With that, he moved through the doorway and nodded to the guards. He heard the latch behind him and the key turn in the lock, securing the boy and his father within.

He found Mary in the stairwell awaiting him. "They've taken Frances to the private room just off the Great Hall," she said. Her voice was thick with tension. "Cahir—"

"I would not have harmed him," he interrupted. "Nor Frances nor little Henry. Had none cooperated, they all would have been locked inside until this is over."

"I know." Her eyes met his.

"Mary, do not open their door until you receive word that Culmore Fort and Derry have been taken and Paulet is dead."

24

"We move forward with our plans," Cahir was saying. "We have simply traded Henry's role for Lady Hart's."

The group of men stood in the Great Hall; O'Donnells, O'Dohertys, MacSweeneys, O'Cahans and O'Hanlons all looking to him for leadership.

"Send word to your clans," he said to all but the O'Dohertys, "that tonight we seize Culmore Fort. The others are to join us tomorrow at Derry. Each of your chieftains knows their role."

"And Lady Hart? Will the soldiers at Culmore follow her lead?" one asked.

"They will. They must." With that, he strode into the adjoining room where Frances was waiting. "Frances," he said, his eyes narrowing menacingly, "you must understand that if you do not cooperate fully, my men have orders to torture and kill your child first in front of your husband, and then your husband in a public square. Are you understanding that?"

"I do understand, Cahir. I do."

"Then listen very closely, 'ey? You and I will take your carriage to Culmore Fort. You are disheveled and they must believe you when you tell them that Burt Castle was set upon by another clan, do you hear? You must urge them—nay, order them—to return to Burt Castle immediately to overturn the assault."

"But—if they don't—"

"No, Frances. They must. Otherwise all will die."

+≈≈+

It might have been a fine night for a carriage ride to Culmore Fort. The moon was waning and the cloud cover was intense, but the air was unusually warm. The two traveled in complete silence. They sat at the front, Frances' dainty hands controlling the horses' reins while Cahir sat beside her, his feet propped against the footboard, a knife in either hand. In the carriage behind their elevated seat and behind drawn curtains were four of his best men, their swords and harkbus at the ready. The soldiers that had accompanied the Harts were now wearing ill-fitting tenant farmer clothes while they cooled their heels in Burt Castle's dungeons while the O'Doherty clansmen were dressed in the uniforms of the English soldiers.

Not a cricket chirped nor frog croaked as they traversed the miles between Burt Castle and Culmore. As they passed through thick forest, his keen eyes swept the terrain. The grounds of Burt Castle had been almost emptied when they had climbed aboard the carriage, his men already positioning themselves in these very woods and he had no doubt at'al that they were watching them now. They entered a clearing large enough for a hundred men shoulder to shoulder but it lay vacant and eerie, the shadows long and dark, before giving way to a cow path barely wide enough for the carriage to traverse. The path turned sharply as they made their final ascent toward Culmore.

They stopped just before cresting the last hill. Cahir slipped his knives inside his clothing and with a final warning to Frances, he took the reins from her and startled the horses into a full gallop. The carriage careened over the peak, nearly toppling as it rolled down the hill on the opposite side in the final approach to Culmore Fort, the wheels staggering through ruts in the poorly kept cow path as the horses lurched forward.

He could see the men scrambling at the parapets as they watched their approach. "Now, Frances."

At his command, she began to scream. Mother Mary, how she screamed. She was so convincing that Cahir's mind began racing with the very real possibility that she would double-cross them, but in the next instant he recalled his instructions should that eventuality occur: several clans were joined together now in the woods stretching from Burt Castle to Culmore Fort. The soldiers would encounter unexpected resistance if they attempted to free Henry Hart and his son, and the men stationed at the locked bedrooms and sitting room would no doubt kill them rather than surrender. Events had been placed in motion and whether he lived or died, Ireland had been placed on the path to rebellion.

Soldiers spewed out of Culmore Fort as the carriage pitched to a sudden stop. Mary had stood during the last few yards, barely holding onto the carriage hood behind them with one hand as she waved with her other, intent on ensuring that the soldiers understood that it was she who was hell-bent on reaching the safety of their borders.

"Help!" she screamed as they surrounded the carriage.

Cahir dropped the reins and placed his hands in the air. "Burt Castle has been attacked!" he bellowed. "They have Henry! They have my son!" The high anxiety of the evening's events appeared to crash into Frances' consciousness as tears streamed down her cheeks anew.

Somewhat assured that in the confusion he would not be shot, Cahir jumped from the carriage driver's seat, turned abruptly and wrapped his arms around Mary's waist, helping her to the ground. She grew frantic; so hysterical that no one could understand her words.

A sudden calm began to envelop Cahir like the first vestiges of sunrise that shed their light upon ground previously cast in shadow. He had never thought so clearly. "Frances," he said, "calm yourself."

"But my Henry! My Henry!"

No one quite knew whether she was lamenting the capture of her husband or her son but as a senior officer joined the ranks, Cahir directed his attention to him. "We were set upon at dinner," he stated, holding Frances against him as much to quiet her as well as appear as if he was comforting her and protecting her. "The O'Neills attacked us. They have killed or captured most of my men, along with my devoted friend Henry Hart and his son. It was only by the grace of God that I was able to save dear Frances."

For the briefest of moments, all was silent except for Frances, who had dissolved into sobs. Cahir pulled her into him; she wrapped her arms about his neck and cried with such abandon that his chest grew wet. Though they were shrouded in darkness, many of the soldiers carried lanterns that were held up to illuminate

Cahir's and Frances' faces as well as their senior officer's. He could see the wheels turning in his mind; could see the reasoning his thoughts were mulling in the few seconds he would have before making a decision that would decide all their fates. Cahir was Henry's friend and Mary Preston O'Doherty was Frances' dearest friend in all of Ireland, if not beyond. It was well known that Cahir was the godfather to young Henry. There was no reason to doubt him. He was the Queen's O'Doherty after all, and didn't he fight the O'Neills to save Sir Docwra from certain death?

"Gather the men. Leave a small contingent here at Culmore. We leave immediately for Burt Castle."

As the soldiers hurried to form their lines, Cahir said, "They entered the Great Hall. They have total control over Burt Castle—and my dear Mary. You are likely to encounter them as you leave the forest and enter the clearing outside the moat."

"There are none in the forest?"

"I can speak with certainty that there are none. Had there been, they most certainly would have killed Frances and myself."

"How many were there?"

"Thirty, perhaps."

"Only thirty? And they seized Burt Castle?"

"They had to have known my men left earlier in the day for Canmoyre Woods. I had but a handful of men. It is mostly women and children in the keep."

"So most of your men are at Canmoyre Woods, you say?"

"Aye; on the Inishowen Peninsula."

"Phelim MacDavitt," he said as though the thought had just occurred to him.

"Aye?" Cahir felt the hairs begin to prick along the base of his neck.

"He was to be freed tomorrow, all charges dropped." He motioned for one of the soldiers staying behind.

"Free MacDavitt now. There is no reason for him to spend another night in confinement, though—" he turned toward Cahir with a slight smile, "—Sir Hart made certain he was given a room and the same food and drink afforded to my men. He was not kept in the dungeon nor in shackles."

Cahir nodded. "Thank you." He had a fleeting thought of Henry and his son locked away in Burt Castle; they had done right by each other, it seemed, all the way to the end despite the charade they'd been forced to play.

The officer nodded in return. It occurred to Cahir that he did not know his name, though he had seen him countless times on his visits to Culmore. He was one of many men that rotated through the fort and sent to Derry or Dublin, Donegal or Galway afterward or perhaps before. His speech was English but he was not a Londoner, of that he was certain. Perhaps he was from rural England; perhaps he had joined His Majesty's service to put food on the table or ensure a roof over a young wife's head. He considered asking his name but thought better of it; it was best not to know much about the men who would die this night.

In any event, the officer turned away from him to further direct the flurry of activity that had erupted around them. Cahir counted six men on horseback while the foot soldiers were readying to march. It made perfect sense, as the men could navigate the forest more easily than a hundred horses—if they even had that many at Culmore. He watched as harkbus, swords and ammunition were assembled for each man as he leaned his back against the carriage door with Frances still in his arms.

"I will lead my men," the officer said as the call to arms was silenced, the final soldiers falling into line for the march ahead. "Do you wish to join us?"

"Please," Frances cried out, grasping Cahir even more firmly than before, "please do not leave me! Please!"

The officer raised his hand. "Stay," he said simply. "Stay. You will be safe here."

With that, he mounted a horse and rode to the front of the line.

"Cahir," Frances sobbed against his ear, "you can still stop this. Henry and I will vouch for you; you have my word on it."

"Shh." He made as if he was comforting her as the soldier left in charge of Culmore Fort stepped forward to escort them inside. The truth was, however, that his heart was heavy—weightier than he had envisioned it would be. He had not wished to do this; he had never wished to turn on the Crown or to invite insurrection. But when all hope was gone, the only thing left was to fight or give up. He refused to leave a legacy in which he had curled up like a dog at Paulet's feet, whimpering for a morsel, so that left only one door open for him to walk through.

As he watched the men, perhaps eighty strong, marching off in the direction of Burt Castle, he knew that it was already too late for a change in heart or mind, because waiting in the shadows of the trees surrounding the clearing were more than three hundred men ready to annihilate their English masters.

With the first stage of the rebellion underway, it was time to start the second one in motion: seizing control of Culmore Fort and thereby toppling the defense of

Derry. Cahir knew he was uniquely qualified for the position in which he had found himself; he was both a brilliant strategist and a gifted tactician. Frances' usefulness would soon be nearing its end.

As he entered the structure at the center of the fort, he was met by Phelim, who had just been freed from a locked room on the main floor. His expression was quizzical but a glance at Frances' tear-stained face and the veil over Cahir's eyes forced him into silence.

"You there," Cahir said to the nearest officer, "gather all the soldiers together."

"All, sir?"

"All of them. Even those along the parapets. I have information of great importance to share with you all regarding the defense of Culmore Fort."

The young officer glanced at Frances, his eyes filled with doubt, but at her nod and encouragement, he sent word for all soldiers to gather in the central room on the main floor.

Cahir heard the doors opening behind him and could feel the presence of the men joining him from the carriage. Dressed in stolen English uniforms, he could feel the adrenaline of his men as though it was bouncing off the stone walls, gathering strength until it swirled around them. They were waiting for the soldiers to gather, their backs to the room as if they were in deep discussion, until Cahir began to speak. At that point, they turned to find the final contingent left at Culmore—a mere dozen men—standing toward the middle of the room, all eyes on the chieftain and Mrs. Hart.

Cahir had never relinquished his hold on Frances. They had been close friends, after all; their relationship as open as if it had been announced from the court of London. Now he pulled her tighter against him with her back against his.

The Irishmen fanned out around them, their swords drawn silently.

"My friends," he began, "my issue is not with you; it is with George Paulet of Derry. I will ask you only once to lay down your arms and surrender to my men. If you do so, you have my word that none will be harmed."

The officer left in charge began to step forward, his face reddening, but one of the O'Doherty clan seized him by the forearm. As the officer turned, his eyes raced over him. As he took in the sword at the ready and the others standing prepared for a skirmish, he pursed his lips and turned back to Cahir.

"The others," Cahir continued, "are surrounded as we speak by more than three hundred of the O'Doherty clan and our allies. We can wipe you all off the face of this earth forevermore, or we can merely detain you for two days' time. Which fate is yours is left in your hands and what you choose to do right here, right now."

The doors swung open and all turned. The soldiers began to move for their weapons but as they witnessed dozens of Irish men entering the room, their resolve appeared to deflate in front of Cahir's eyes.

"Give up your weapons," he directed.

As the Irishmen moved to collect the weapons, the soldiers reluctantly parted with harkbus, swords and knives.

"Who has the keys to the armory?" Cahir asked.

All eyes turned to one man, who appeared ready to bolt.

"Do not die needlessly," Cahir admonished. "We will gain entrance with or without your help, whether you live or die."

Phelim reached forward to grab the ring of keys that dangled from the man's belt.

"You, sir," Cahir said, pointing to the officer in charge, "lead your men—all except the locksman—to the room in which Phelim MacDavitt was incarcerated. Two dozen men will escort them. Maintain guards to prevent their escape." As they left the room, he waved his hand at another dozen standing nearby. "Take up positions along the parapet and perimeter."

Next, he turned to Phelim. "Take the rest of the men—but leave me three—open the armory and begin to unload the weapons. Bring them here, to this hall then send reinforcements to the parapets."

"Has it begun then?" Phelim asked.

"Aye," Cahir answered. "It has."

As the Irishmen scattered in the directions of their assignments, Cahir breathed a deep sigh and relinquished his hold on Frances. "You did well," he said.

"Cahir, you promised—"

"Aye. And I am a man of my word." He turned to one of the two men still remaining. "Eóin, bring word to the clan that we have taken Culmore Fort without bloodshed. They may free Henry Hart and his son at first light on the day after the morrow. No harm is to come to them."

"Aye, sir." With that, Eóin rushed from the room en route to the clearing between Culmore and Burt Castle.

"And you, Ranvir, escort Mrs. Hart to her bedchambers. Lock her inside with food and drink. No harm is to come to her—under any circumstances. She is to be freed at first light, the day after the morrow."

"Aye, sir." Ranvir reached out for Frances, but she raised her chin and began to walk from the room. He glanced at Cahir, who nodded.

Frances stopped in the doorway. "Cahir," she said, her voice steady, "remember that Henry and I remained your friends throughout this—this—folly." Cahir began to reply but she continued, "And remember that Henry remained loyal to King James and to England and refused to participate in the overthrow of Culmore Fort. For certainly, what you have done here tonight cannot be undone. You are victorious for now, but how can you possibly anticipate crushing all of the English army? For surely you must know that King James will spare no one in his quest for your head."

With that, she turned from the room and the words that Cahir might have spoken were left waiting at his lips. With Ranvir following Frances to her bedchambers, he was left alone with his thoughts. Aye, what Frances had spoken was true: what was done here tonight could not be undone. But it was only the beginning; for at this very moment, Eóin was on his way with word that they held the fort. It would set in motion the next stage: messengers would fan out across all of Ulster and beyond, carrying with them word of O'Doherty's Rebellion. Even now, he knew the O'Donnells, the MacSweeneys, the O'Cahans and O'Hagans were marching toward Culmore Fort and Derry itself, and soon every clan in Ireland would rise up against their English oppressors.

25

"Do you hear something?" Wills asked, pulling his horse to a stop.

Fergus paused his horse as well. "I do."

They dismounted their steeds in silence, pulling them into a copse. They were, he surmised, somewhere along the southern border of the O'Doherty lands and not far from the property that they had cleared. Once they reached open ground, the travel would be easier and faster. Now that they were headed for home, he had begun to fancy his bed, the warmth of a fireplace and the sensation of a wool bedcover drawn over him in slumber. His belly was full, his thirst quenched and his spirits bolstered knowing that within a few hours, Phelim would be granted his release and cleared of wrongdoing. Perhaps, he thought, all of this unpleasantness would be put to rest and none too soon for his liking, for sure.

Travel at night was not for the faint of heart or feeble of body. There remained large swaths of lawless territory where bands of marauders still roamed, looking for that glint of gold or silver coin in an unwitting traveler's pocket. It wasn't unusual for them to cross into clan territories; it wasn't as if there was a rope outstretched across each border to warn them that they encroached— and even if there were, there was many a thief that would plunge ahead nonetheless.

There were also wolves aplenty on this island; so many that it was said during the Nine Years War, they often devoured the fallen before they could be buried. And now with more land cleared for agriculture and livestock, they hunted further afield and were more aggressive when they found one left unprotected.

Wills watched the horses carefully and determined it was not an animal they heard but a man; the horses tended to be much more skittish around wolves and for good enough reason. A man could confiscate but a wolf would kill.

Leaving the horses in the shadows of the coppice, they inched out, their swords drawn. Wills spotted a movement in the trees a short distance away and signaled Fergus. Together, they moved in a semi-circle around the traveler. He was alone on horseback.

The horse stopped and threw his head backward with a soft neigh before beginning to munch on the berries of a dense bush. Wills moved further to the right while Fergus remained on the left and together, they crept closer, keeping one eye on each other and the other on the animal that seemed oblivious to their approach.

They reached his hindquarters at exactly the same time but as Wills reached upward to drag the rider off its back, he discovered it was bare. A blanket was doubled over and laid across its breadth, the reins hanging loosely at the back of its neck. But before he could reach for the reins, a voice sounded from underbrush close to his ear.

"What the devil are you doing out here?"

Before he could respond, Tomas stepped from

behind the bush. "Wouldn't you be knowing that's a perfect way to get a man killed?"

"Aye, and it could have been your arse with the sharp end of this sword against it," Fergus retorted.

Tomas motioned for him to be quiet. "Lower your voice. We're not alone." He signaled for them to retreat into a thicker part of the woods before continuing, "I've been tracking them for miles now."

"Who?"

"It appears to be the O'Donnell clan; I recognize a few of their men—but the group is too large. They must have neighboring clans joining them as well."

"But why?" Wills asked.

"Why, you say? Did you fall and hit your head, lad? Was it not just yesterday that you sent me to Fort Stewart with news of Cahir's uprising?"

"Aye, aye, but—there is no uprising at'al as it turns out."

"Oh?"

"It was all a misunderstanding. I spoke to Henry Hart himself. Phelim is cleared of all charges and will be released as soon as the sun rises. Why, this very eve he and Mrs. Hart are spending the night at Burt Castle, visiting with Cahir and Mrs. O'Doherty."

"Is that so?" Tomas rubbed his chin. "Well, we've a conundrum on our hands, lads, for sure. Captain Stewart sent me to tell you both that he is gathering forces—the very men we've trained with—to march on Derry at first light. And he's sent a messenger to Dublin and another to Donegal to raise more troops."

"Oh, no." Wills leaned back on his haunches. "This is all my fault; it's a huge misunderstanding. Rumors, 'tis all it was."

"Pardon me gents," Fergus interrupted, "but while you're busy commiserating, there's still the matter of a large force that Tomas has been tracking. Whatever is happening or not with Cahir, certainly something appears to be occurring with the O'Donnells."

"Aye," Tomas said. "He's right."

"Tell me how long you've been tracking them," Wills said.

"I picked them up shortly after crossing into O'Donnell territory; you know that swath o' land at the southern edge of the Inishowen Peninsula? They appear to be traveling from further south."

"Then headed north?"

"If I had a reason to guess, I would say straight for Derry."

"Where are they now?"

"Oh, I would say if we rode our horses in that direction—" he pointed toward the northeast "—we'd be at the tip of their swords in about half a minute."

"Mother Mary," Fergus breathed.

"You're Catholic now, are you?"

"No but I hedge my bets all the same."

"We need to think this through," Wills whispered thoughtfully. The three fell silent for a moment and then he continued, "We remain where we are until they have moved further northward. We won't be doing anybody any favors if we're detected and detained."

"And after they pass? What then?" Fergus asked.

"Then we follow them."

"Should I return to Captain Stewart?" Tomas asked.

"No," Wills said. "If he is already gathering a force and has sent for more, there is nothing else he can do to prepare, with or without the O'Donnells' involvement."

"So do we all three follow them, perhaps all the way to Derry?" Fergus asked.

"Aye, and we determine where their troops are gathered. Then we'll double back, intercept Captain Stewart, and with the movement of the O'Donnells—

or other Irish—known, perhaps the captain can flank them and crush them."

"Remember," Tomas added, "there are perhaps a hundred men at Culmore Fort and a hundred more at Derry."

Wills picked up a stick and drew a triangle in the dirt. "Aye, and this point at the top is Culmore Fort, and the men there will prevent a breach from the north. This point at the lower left is Derry, and the hundred men there will defend it."

"Therefore," Fergus interjected, "if Stewart can swing his men around to the southeast, we can cut them off there as well."

"It will be like three doors swinging shut, 'ey?" Wills added. "They'll be caught in the middle and forced to surrender."

"Well, thank the good Lord for that," Fergus said. "I'm in serious need of sleep and a warm woman and if I must march all the way back to Derry tonight, I plan to get both tomorrow."

26

They peered over a knoll at Derry below. The village lay sleeping in the hours before dawn, unaware of the forces that had begun to surround it. To the south, Wills could see the O'Donnell clan preparing to invade, the distinctive flag bearing St. Patrick's hand holding the cross against the O'Donnell shield flapping in the churning winds.

But it was the activity in the north that seized their attention and held it captive: torches moving steadily from Culmore Fort.

"We must reach Sir Hart," Wills whispered.

"I'd be thinking he knows what's about," Tomas said, nodding toward the torches. "He's gathering his troops against The O'Donnell."

"Then we must fight with him." Wills peered off to the west where the trees captured the ground in long, steady shadows. "We'll make our way around Derry to the west and then northward to join up with Hart's troops."

"It's folly," Fergus countered. "To the west is

O'Doherty territory; we must pass through it to reach Culmore Fort."

"He's right," Tomas said. "We must assume The O'Doherty is joining The O'Donnell; we'd be trapped between the two."

Wills turned to examine the east. "The east could be no better. Even if we circumnavigated The O'Donnell, we would end up on the wrong side of the River Foyle. We've nothing with which to cross it."

"The plan," Tomas said, "was to note their positions. We wait, then, for Captain Stewart's men to approach from behind us and join up with them."

"They're still hours away," Wills said, his voice growing hoarse with tension. "You said they wouldn't be leaving Fort Stewart until dawn, 'ey? The battle for Derry will begin long before."

"Why aren't The O'Donnells readying for battle?" Fergus asked. "Look at them. Surely they see the torches coming from Culmore Fort."

"Aye, but Derry is between them and Hart. My guess is they are waiting for Hart's troops to get closer to the village."

"I say we still wait for Stewart."

Wills was silent. There was merit to what Tomas and Fergus argued, for sure; they could play the part of spies and mentally record the movement of both sides. "How far do you suppose Culmore Fort is from Derry?"

"Six miles, I'd say," Tomas answered.

"Oh, and I see where you're going with this," Fergus said. "How fast can a man march, 'ey?"

"If they march at double step," Wills said thoughtfully, "they could cover six miles in an hour and a half, wouldn't you say?"

Fergus peered at the sky and Wills followed his gaze. It was unusually clear; for a moment he was mesmerized at the brilliance of the stars against the oxford blue skies. He could clearly identify the constellations and the placement of the moon. "It is still two hours until the first rays of dawn," Wills said. "If the captain travels by land, even at a double quick step, he will not reach Derry until afternoon."

"If he travels by sea, he will not be much faster," Tomas said. "He would have to navigate completely around the Inishowen Peninsula."

"You know what this means, gents?" Wills said.

"Aye," Fergus said grudgingly. "It means by the time the captain arrives, the battle could be over."

"Then we haven't much choice in the matter, 'ey?" Wills asked, rolling onto his back for a moment. "We remain here and watch the battle over Derry like three old ladies. Or we get off our arses and join up with Henry Hart."

They looked at one another for a long moment. Then Wills added, "What are we waiting for?" With that, he moved back down the knoll toward the shadows of the trees. Ah, but they say the skies were the darkness just before dawn, but they found their steps easily under the light of the moon and the stars. They made for the thickest of copses, where they would remain sheltered by the trees as if their branches were arms outstretched to protect them; away from the O'Donnell clan and toward the torches traveling from Culmore Fort.

━━◆━━

Less than an hour later, they found themselves close to intersecting with the men traveling southward from the fort. The three had moved quickly, sprinting when the terrain afforded it, while Culmore's contingent had continued to march swiftly toward Derry. Wills kept a wary eye on the O'Donnell clan, but they appeared to be settling in near the south of the village, despite the fact that the others were marching toward them and closing the gap between them. It didn't make sense, Wills thought; he wasn't a military expert, to be sure, but it seemed it would make far better sense for the O'Donnells to ready their men for the onslaught that was certain to occur, wouldn't it now?

As they drew closer to the Culmore group, his anxiety began to heighten until he signaled Fergus and Tomas to duck into the shadows with him.

"What is it?" Fergus asked, peering in all directions.

"Something is not right," Wills answered.

"Aye; I feel it, too," Tomas said. "Why are the O'Donnells waiting there like sitting ducks, 'ey?"

"My thoughts exactly."

"No matter," Fergus said. "We're not far from Hart's men now. We join up with them, give them what we know of the O'Donnells' whereabouts and—"

"But do you see Hart?" Wills prodded. "They are growing close enough now." As they studied the men moving just below them, the hairs began to rise along the back of his neck. These were not men in English uniforms, and they were not being led by Henry Hart. Walking the terrain with his men at the front stood an unusually tall figure wearing a plume upon a Spanish style hat. "Jesus."

"Oh, you'll be calling the Lord's name sure enough," came a voice behind them.

The three turned to find themselves surrounded by men. He recognized more than one as those he had seen at Carrickabraghy Castle.

"On your feet, lads," the man said, prodding Wills with the tip of his sword.

As he slowly rose, he tried to count the number of men but stopped after he'd reached twenty-four. Even if he and each of his friends could take on two or three men at once, they would never be able to fight them all. And—his conscious shouted at him lest he overlook the fact—there were hundreds more behind him being led by none other than Cahir O'Doherty himself. Now it all made sense. Cahir would attack from the north in the first wave and The O'Donnell from the south in the second. The village was doomed even before she had awakened.

27

Cahir O'Doherty halted his men a short distance from the village. "Put them at rest," he told his senior men. "We've not long before the sun rises, and at first light, we attack. Best they quench their thirst and ready themselves."

He watched as his men moved off to the various units. He had fought many a battle during the Nine Years War with these very men and though an uneasy peace had settled in these last few years, he would confidently place his life in the hands of any one of them still. A movement caught his eye and he turned to see three men being marched toward him at the point of swords.

"Well, well," he said as they neared, "I am surprised to see you here, William Neely."

"Cahir," Wills said, "we don't know what is about to transpire here—we were on our way back to Fort Stewart when—"

"We found them just beyond the tree line," one of the O'Doherty men offered. "They were watching you approach Derry. We'd been following them since we discovered them south of Derry."

Fergus swore under his breath.

Cahir's eyes narrowed as he focused on Wills. "Be careful what you say, my friend. You do not strike me as the kind to think that north leads south."

The words froze on Wills' lips. He could feel the men behind him pressing in, the tip of a sword still against his back, tickling at his clothing as if it yearned to punch through to his skin and beyond. His own sword had been taken from him, as had Fergus' and Tomas' weapons. "You are correct," he said at last.

Tomas began to protest but Cahir held up his hand for silence. With his eyes still on Wills, he stated calmly, "Continue."

"We spent the night at Culmore Fort—"

"Did you now?" Cahir said. He smiled in amusement.

"Not the entire night, to be sure," Wills said. "We left shortly after Sir and Lady Hart departed for dinner at Burt Castle." His eyes roamed the men's faces, though he knew that Hart was not among them. "We were on our way to Fort Stewart when—when we spotted your torches. Thinking it was Sir Hart, we returned to offer our assistance."

"If you left shortly after Hart, then you must have slept in the meadow for all the progress you made." Several men behind Cahir began to chuckle but he held up his hand for silence again. For the briefest of moments, he pictured a young, inexperienced William Neely riding in circles on the Inishowen Peninsula; a diplomatic young man arriving at Carrickabraghy Castle to make peace with his neighbors... And now, a more mature man somehow; learned of the ways of the Irish to some extent and willing to respect them. "I have no complaints with you, Wills," he said finally. "Nor any with your friends here nor Captain Stewart. I am afraid you have stumbled upon an event that does not concern you."

"Is Sir Hart—?" he swallowed, unable to say the word.

"I have no grievance with my good friend Henry Hart, either. He is alive and well with his son at Burt Castle."

He breathed a sigh of relief. Then, "Lady Hart?"

"Frances is fine as well. You and your friends will be joining her at Culmore Fort." He signaled and then the man directly behind Wills gave him an order to move.

"Wait," Wills said, turning back to Cahir. "You must know there are civilians living in Derry—women and children that have never wronged you or yours. Is your grievance with them?"

Cahir did not answer but tilted his chin slightly upward until he was peering down on the shorter man.

"If you aim to fight the men of Derry this morn," Wills said, his words rushing now, "at the least, allow me and my friends to escort the women and children to safety."

At this, Cahir chuckled. "And how would you do that, young Wills? Go door to door and alert them to our presence here?"

"Yes." Amid the men's laughter, his voice rose and he pointed to the village. "The villagers do not live with the soldiers; you know that. Allow me to collect them in one place—perhaps the Bishop's home or a church. We will not interfere with your business here." The last sentence rang false, even to himself, and he knew that Cahir detected the poor attempt as well.

Cahir looked first to the village and then to the men behind him. With his contingent alone, they outnumbered the soldiers at least three to one. He had already been notified that those soldiers from Culmore

Fort had laid down their arms as the O'Dohertys had surrounded them, and they were now cooling their heels in the dungeons at Burt Castle. Not a man had died yet—but that would soon change. "Come with me, Wills; your friends as well."

Reluctantly, the sword was withdrawn from against his back and he, Fergus and Tomas followed Cahir to the edge of camp where they could overlook the village below.

"You have been loyal to the English and Scottish settlers," Wills ventured.

Cahir felt a familiar pain shoot through his heart. "Aye. I have at that. But you must know that despite the kindness of Henry Hart, William Stewart and many others like yourselves—a climate of hatred exists that threatens to annihilate my people, and none of you has the power to stop it."

"Perhaps the King's court—"

"I have been to King James' court. I have done everything that could possibly be expected of a man. I have married an English woman to bridge the peace between our cultures. I have remained faithful to the English even when they have broken their word many times over. I have turned against my own countrymen to further England's cause."

"Then why—?"

"This climate of hatred is perpetuated by a weasel of a man sleeping in the comfort of his feather bed at the moment. I am seizing the opportunity to protect myself and my people by removing him from the face of this earth—and in so doing, remove his vitriol before it seeps into everything that is Irish."

"Sir George Paulet."

Cahir nodded.

"Excuse me, sir," Fergus said, stepping forward, "I know you're conversing with Wills here and please forgive the intrusion, but would it not make more sense if you were to—say, ambush George Paulet when he is alone and there's none the wiser?"

"Fergus!" Wills breathed.

"I am only saying that if your business is against him and him alone, then why are you marching on Derry?"

Cahir locked eyes with Fergus MacPherson. Ah, but a mere man would think this way, 'eh? Any man that was not the descendent of Niall of the Nine Hostages, a High Gaelic King one thousand years in the past, might consider slipping into a man's home in the dead of night and slitting his throat and climbing back out the window. Any man that farmed for a living, grew potatoes with his hands, sheared his own sheep or herded his own cattle. But not The O'Doherty; not the descendant of a thousand years of kings and chieftains, not the Gaelic Irish Lord, ruler of the Inishowen Peninsula. No; his wrath might rest with George Paulet but his methods must befit a king.

"I will grant your request, Wills," he said at last. "At first light, we begin our attack against the soldiers of Derry. In those first minutes, you will have the opportunity to save as many women and children on the opposite side of the village as you can. So the choice will be yours: rush to the soldiers and you will fight the force you see behind you here. Rush to the women and children, and you may live to see another dawn." He signaled for the men that had marched them into camp. "Keep these men under guard. When we have entered the village, release them—without their weapons. If they move to the east, they are free. If they move toward the soldiers and the armory at Derry, kill them."

He turned back to Wills. "Take the women and children to Bishop George Montgomery's house and I will spare them."

Cahir had no sooner left the three than his mind raced forward to the task at hand. He found Phelim with his senior officers, a hand-drawn map laid out on a large tree stump, the corners held down by stones as the winds swirled around them.

He knew the village of Derry as well as he knew every inch of the Inishowen Peninsula. He had sat at his mother's knee and listened to the stories passed down through the generations of the monastery that had stood for centuries in that very spot; isolated in the wilds of Eire, it had withstood the darkest of years that had swept over the rest of Europe. He could recall with clarity every road in the village, every footpath, every home that had sprung up under Sir Henry Docwra's leadership. He knew every building the current governor had visited, every whore he had slept with, every man on his payroll.

"Phelim," he directed, "you and your men take the upper fort. I shall take the lower. The O'Donnells will take the marketplace. We must not fail to take the storehouse, the munitions."

"The O'Donnell begs us to burn the village in its entirety."

"Are not the deaths of Paulet and Hamilton enough?"

"He says no. The English will simply send others in their stead."

Cahir nodded. "He is correct. But do not burn the village until you have my order."

"Sir O'Doherty," one of the men offered, "we have reconnoitered and there are no sentries; no night watchmen."

Cahir shook his head. "Unbelievable. It is George Paulet's folly and arrogance that will assist us this day. Make no doubt that we shall be victorious."

"They do not even stir," Phelim said. He also shook his head in disbelief.

"Ludicrous, is it not?" Cahir asked. "Even in the most peaceful of times, were we not always guarded by night sentries, by watchmen along the parapets? The whole village is laid open to us."

"It will not be for long. The sun rises." He nodded toward the distant horizon where the faintest rays of orange could barely be seen.

"Ready your men. We attack within minutes. George Paulet and Sheriff Hamilton are mine. The common soldiers are to be spared if at all possible and sent under guard to Burt Castle."

28

They moved along the narrow roads, the rains of days past preventing the soil from sending dust clouds into the air. As Cahir moved into the lower fort, he knew these paths would be churned into mud this day. Not even the roosters were yet awake, the sun still slumbering along the horizon. They fanned out as they had planned; he knew without looking that Phelim's men were doing the same in the upper fort and the O'Donnells were surrounding the market. A dog barked and then another before silence ensued; a toss of venison upon the ground was enough to satiate them and they cared not by whose hand it was thrown. Now the only sound was the soft steps of the men as they hurried into position.

They were stretched out along the winding paths; roads that had no rhyme nor reason but had simply been cleared as a trail from one structure or point to another. The Bishop's house was easy to spot; it sat adjacent to the Protestant Church. Paulet's home was also easy to recognize, for it was the largest, most opulent residence in all of Derry; a gaudy and wickedly extravagant building that had been erected at a time when all of Ulster's Irish were starving from the manmade famine orchestrated by Paulet and Lord Chichester.

At the very moment when the first rooster began to crow, shouts arose throughout all of Derry. Doors were knocked in and shots rang out as his men raced from building to building, up the stairs to each floor, rounding up the English soldiers.

Overtaking the lower fort was easier than he had anticipated; the soldiers were still in their beds, arrogance and a false sense of security both abundant under Paulet's rule. The surprise attack occurred simultaneously throughout all of Derry, giving no man time enough to gather his weapons or even his breeches before they were gathered up and brought to the edge of the village, where other clansmen were waiting to escort them under guard to Burt Castle.

Still, the shouts rose in a chorus until he was completely surrounded by the din; women were screaming now, children crying, harkbus shots ringing, men shouting. A barrage of gunfire erupted and he turned to face the upper fort, where Phelim and his men were having a tougher time of it. They would prevail; he was certain of it. He had his own mission before him, one that would free Derry and the Irish of Ulster from the tyrannical rule of George Paulet.

✦═══✦

Wills stared at the carnage erupting below, the smoke from gunfire obliterating his view of the upper fort. The attack was pure precision, the act of men that had fought years together and knew their roles. He glanced at their guards, his question stilled on his lips.

"If it were up to me," the leader said, spitting on the ground beside him, "I would slit your throats as soon as look at you. Get up."

Wills, Fergus and Tomas stood, their eyes meeting one another's in the briefest of moments. It was a terrible feeling to be had, for sure, when a man did not know whether his life would be ceased in the next moment and for some strange reason, he found himself thinking of his mother. He could barely remember the details of her face and yet his only thought was that she would never know what had become of her son or the date he had died.

It was ludicrous, he knew; the first throes of battle were below him, men fighting for their lives, fighting for their women and their children, and yet she was there, somehow, in some way, she was there.

"You heard what Lord O'Doherty told you," the guard was saying. "Go for the women and the children and maybe your lives will be spared. Head for the fighting and I will cut you down before you get halfway there."

He didn't remember starting to run. He didn't remember coming off that knoll and rushing down that hill. He didn't remember how he reached the outskirts of Derry without a harkbus or a sword ending his life just beyond the gates. And yet, as though he was only just awakening, he found himself on the dirt paths, banging on cottage doors, scrambling to reach the women and their children, urging them to move to the Bishop's house.

No doors were locked; there had been no need. With soldiers in place, there was no safer place—or so they thought. He tossed open a door, perhaps his third or fourth, yelling for its inhabitants as he had the others. He heard the muffled cries of a child, and he moved throughout the lower floor, calling out to them that he was with the English and he was there to rescue them. Not finding anyone, he thought he was certainly hearing voices that were not there. He raced up the short flight of stairs to a smaller, narrower upper floor, moving from room to room. The beds were disheveled, clothing still on the floor, a pair of bed slippers left untouched. Back down he came and was about to move to the next house when he heard the whimper again. Opening the cellar door, he called down.

"Shh."

The voice was barely audible; the voice of a woman.

"You must get to Bishop Montgomery's house," Wills called into the gloom.

A child burst into tears and he forced himself into the darkness, groping for the people that lay hidden there. He found them behind storage barrels: a young woman heavy with child and two small children clutching at her skirts.

"Come with me," he said.

"I can't. I can't make it."

He reached down to pull her to her feet but his hand came away covered in liquid. Christ, he thought, but the woman was in labor.

"Where is your husband?" he asked. As his eyes became more adjusted to the gloom, he focused on the woman's face. She did not answer his question but her eyes darted quickly to the corner before pain set in again.

Wills looked over his shoulder. Deliberately rising, he crossed to the corner of the room. Tossing half-empty barrels aside, he came upon a man huddled in the corner, his knees to his chest and his fingers interlaced behind his head.

"Good God, man!" he shouted as he jerked the man to his feet. He appeared much older than the woman in labor but at his rough treatment, the children began to cry again. "Is this your family here?"

The man nodded, whimpering.

"Get over there," he ordered. "You'll have to pick up your wife and carry her to the Bishop's house. Children, come along, come to the door. I give you my word no harm will come to you."

"But—but the attack—" stuttered the man.

"They've given permission for every man, woman and child to get to the Bishop's house. No harm will come to you there. You know where it is?"

"I do."

The woman screamed out in pain.

"There will be women there who can help with the labor," Wills said. "Do you have a sword?"

"It's upstairs—in my bedroom."

"Get your wife out of here before she has your child in the cellar!" he bellowed. As the man gathered his wife and children, Wills took two steps at a time to the upper floor. He found the sword propped against the wall beside the bed, and he slipped it into his scabbard as he glanced out the window. Looting had descended on Derry. It was interesting, he thought; when he had first arrived in Ireland, he could not tell one clan from another. But now, as he watched events unfolding, he could clearly identify the O'Donnell clan departing from the residences, their hands filled with items of every description. Further from where he stood, a battle raged in the upper fort between the MacDavitts and Crown soldiers, the gunfire and smoke rising into the air, interspersed with men's shouts. As his eyes scanned toward the lower fort, he spotted Cahir and two men exiting Sheriff Hamilton's home, their clothing spattered in blood.

He raced down the steps. The cellar door was open but the family was not to be seen. Hurrying into the street, he glimpsed the man's back as he disappeared into the crowd, his wife in his arms and two young children trailing behind.

"Wills!"

He turned to find Fergus rushing toward him.

"Where did you find the sword?"

Wills nodded at the house he had just exited. "I borrowed it."

"I must find one as well."

"Where is Tomas?"

"I don't know; I lost sight of him."

The throng was growing around them as more people fled their homes in the wake of the onslaught. Wills found himself shouting to be heard. "Get to the Bishop's house!" he ordered. Then he turned back to Fergus. "I'm on my way to the Governor's home."

"I'll go with you. I'll find a weapon on my way."

Wills turned and abruptly bumped into Rhiannon Ó Dálaigh.

"We really have to stop meeting like this," she said. She smiled as she spoke, but her eyes betrayed her fear and indecision.

"What are you doing in Derry?" Wills asked, incredulous.

"I was staying with my aunt—" She glanced behind her, but in the crowd Wills could not tell which woman she referred to.

The harsh sound of men's shouts rose and he grabbed her elbow. "No matter; there's no time. Get to the Bishop's house. You'll be safe there."

"But you—?"

"I'll join you shortly. Now go! Take as many of these people with you as you can!" With that, he turned and raced back up the street toward Paulet's home. Just beyond, he spotted Lieutenant Gordon at a window in the upper fort, firing on Phelim MacDavitt's men below. As he watched, the man's face quite literally exploded as a ball and black powder found their mark and he toppled forward, his body hanging partly out of the window. Phelim's men then charged the fort and the sound of gunfire grew more sporadic. I'll be needing something more than a sword, he thought frantically. He glanced behind him to find Rhiannon at the end of the road, urging people forward and pointing at the Bishop's house.

Then he took a deep breath and tried to ignore the fact that his lungs were filling with the acrid air of gun smoke as he hurried toward the governor's home.

29

George Paulet's home was massive compared to the other structures at Derry. The foundation, like the castles, was constructed of stone but the floors above ground were timber. As Cahir tossed open the front door and strode into the wide hallway, he felt contempt for everything he saw. The dining table had chairs for twelve and no doubt it had been constructed and delivered at a time in which the Irish people were scrounging in the streets for the smallest of morsels. The rugs were opulent, imported as clans were run from their homes. Trinkets abounded, some of silver and some of gold while fine china was carefully arranged on shelves and tables.

The disgust grew as he moved from room to room. Oh, but if he could take back all those years he had fought for the English. If he could turn back time to the moment he forged the agreement with the English to fight for them in exchange for leaving his lands safe for the O'Doherty clan. If only he could return to that day when Docwra and his men were on the verge of starvation, their munitions run out; he would side with the O'Neills and Red Hugh O'Donnell and others intent on keeping Ireland Irish.

His loyalty ended right now, right here.

He found Lady Paulet sitting up in bed, a bonnet covering her head and the bedcovers pulled up to her neck as if the stout woman's virtue was at stake. He discovered George Paulet hiding underneath the bed in a nightshirt that fell to his knees. A fitting place for the man that had terrorized Derry, he thought, and preyed on those weakened by the power of the English Crown.

He dragged the little weasel from under the bed by his nightshirt. "Get up!" he demanded. "Get up!"

Staring at him now, he wondered at how this puny excuse for a human being could ever have been given the power of life and death over so many. Cahir was at least a full twelve inches taller than he; his shoulders nearly twice as wide and his biceps hard and full. Paulet shifted his weight from one foot to the other; bare feet, he noted, that looked soft and feminine. His stomach poked beneath the thin shirt like a pregnant sow.

He held out both hands now, the palms upward. "Tell me what you want," Paulet said, his voice trembling. "Take anything. Take everything."

Cahir's eyes fell on a sword laid across a writing table. "Pick it up," he said.

"I—I don't want to fight you."

"I said pick it up."

"But I—I—" he inched closer to the sword and lifted it as if it were too heavy for his hands. "I don't—I haven't—not in a long time—"

"Defend yourself."

"No. I can't."

"I refuse to kill an unarmed man, you yellow-bellied bastard."

Paulet tossed the sword to the floor. "Please spare me, I beg of you. Spare my life. I will petition the King on your behalf—I will—"

"Cease your childish chatter. The time for talk has ended. The memory of every man, every woman, every child you caused to die under your governorship will haunt you in Hell."

Paulet dropped to his knees, tears streaming down his face. "Please spare me. I beg of you."

"You sorry excuse for a man; you don't even have the courage to die on your feet!" Cahir's fury broke through as he heard footsteps racing up the stairs. Grabbing Paulet by the throat, he hauled him to his feet and slammed him against the bedroom wall amidst Lady Paulet's screams. Paulet's arms instinctively flew apart, leaving his entire body exposed. Cahir wrenched his sword from its scabbard, the metal clanging. It seemed as if time itself had slowed as he pulled his arm back. He felt the grip as though it was a part of his hand, the sword an extension of his arm, the blade shining, the metal sure. As the steps landed in the doorway behind him, he thrust the sword through Paulet's soft body. He struck in the center of the ribcage, that delicate area that allowed instant access, and once the blade was sinking inside, he heard the thunderous sound of his own voice as he bellowed out the agony, the hatred, the frustration. Stepping even closer, he tilted the sword upward and watched Paulet's eyes widen in horror and shock as the tip pierced those organs between his belly and his throat, sinking it so deep inside that the guard was nearly touching his skin.

Then just as quickly, he pulled the blade back through and as the point cleared the body, Paulet crumpled to the floor, his back against the wall, his legs buckled underneath him, his unseeing eyes staring into Cahir's face.

"Welcome to Hell," Cahir growled.

A sound behind him caused him to whirl about, the adrenaline pumping through his body, his arm begging for another man to pierce. But he found himself looking at three of his men whose eyes were transfixed on Paulet.

Wiping the blade across the bedsheets, he ordered, "Torch this house. Burn everything inside it." He pointed at Lady Paulet who was still screaming. "Drag her into the street if need be." Sliding the blade back into the scabbard, he strode from the room, taking the stairs to the front door, his eyes no longer seeing the spoils of power that had once been seized from the rightful heirs to Ireland.

As he entered the front hall, Wills rushed through the doorway. He stopped for a moment, his sword only a movement away as he took in the sorry excuse for a weapon in Wills' hand. He watched as his eyes took in Cahir's bloodied clothing before roaming to the three men behind him as they dragged Lady Paulet toward the door.

"You will not get past me," Cahir said to Wills, "before my sword and those of my men are rammed through your body."

The man's thoughts were evident on his face as he realized the truth of Cahir's words.

Without waiting for a reply, Cahir brushed past him. As he stepped onto the front stoop, he realized despite his order that all of Derry was burning. The roads were devoid of civilians now and only the O'Donnells, the MacSweeneys, the O'Dohertys and other clans were filling the narrow streets. He watched for a moment as all the discipline of battle evaporated before him, leaving men bashing the glass panes out of windows, others rushing outside with arms laden with silver trays and china figurines; one with a pair of boots in his hands. Thatched roofs were set ablaze, the houses like so many tinderboxes set in a row. The slate roofs of the Derry elite slid off their wood frames as the floors below them collapsed into a growing inferno.

Then his eyes came to rest on the slate rooftop of the Bishop's home.

30

Wills found the villagers huddled together in the library of the Bishop's house as he ushered Lady Paulet inside. It had been a surreal set of circumstances, one he would no doubt ponder for many years to come; clearly outnumbered, Cahir's men had simply brushed past him, shoving George Paulet's wife into his arms before taking to the streets themselves. As he'd hurried her along, she'd recounted George's fate between sobs as their home erupted into a ball of flames behind them.

All eyes turned to him as he entered: wide, incredulous, devastated, alarmed. "Where is Rhiannon?" he demanded. "Rhiannon Ó Dálaigh?"

Indeed, the Bishop's home had become a silent refuge; the children too frightened to cry, the adults too shocked to speak. Sixty people and perhaps more were crowded into a library so large that it housed at least a thousand books.

One of the men pointed to the room across the hall, and he turned abruptly, leaving their questions still in their eyes and on their lips, unanswered. He threw open the double doors to the dining room, allowing them to bang against the walls as they bounced off them, more from his heart pumping and blood coursing than anything he found within the house.

A dozen women gathered around another who lay sprawled across the table, her legs spread as they coaxed out a newborn child.

"You can't be here!" Rhiannon exclaimed, reaching to block the view of the pregnant woman with her body.

Wills advanced into the room, his eyes locked on hers. Grabbing her elbow, he pulled her around to look at him. "All of Derry is lost," he said.

"But—we're safe here—this woman—"

Her face grew pale, her lips still parted, as her eyes locked onto something just beyond his shoulder, and he turned to face Cahir O'Doherty once again.

"I am not here to harm you," Cahir said, his eyes taking in the scene before him. As the woman screamed in agony and the others moved to accept the babe, he crossed to the library.

Wills made his way into the library behind him as the people who had remained huddled on the floor and chairs consoling one another now rose as one, looking to Cahir as though he was their new leader.

"All of you will be escorted to Burt Castle," Cahir announced. As a chorus of objections rose up, he held up his hand to silence them. "All of Derry is burning. You will be safe if you follow my men out of the city."

"But surely, Cahir," an older woman said, "you will not allow them to burn my brother's home."

"Lady Shaw," he bowed slightly, "it is all to be burned, just as George Paulet and Arthur Chichester burned Ulster villages."

"Cahir," a man said, his hands held humbly as he approached him, "the bishop is your friend. He never agreed with Paulet and Chichester; you know this yourself."

"Where is Bishop Montgomery?"

"He is in Clogher," one offered.

Cahir nodded.

"So you will spare this home?" Wills asked.

He shook his head. "I have killed two men this day, Wills: Sheriff Hamilton and Governor Paulet." As a murmur of shock grew around them, he continued, "And I have unleashed hell on this town. All of it will burn to the ground so nothing is left but embers."

"Cahir," an elderly woman said, hobbling toward him with the use of a cane, "look around you. These are priceless books—two thousand or more—from all over Europe. Most are irreplaceable. Certainly, your friendship with Bishop Montgomery will cause you to spare his home and all this knowledge."

He took a few steps into the library and paused to gaze at one shelf. Several of his men remained in the doorway and hall. Outside, his forces were growing as they assembled, covered in soot and blood, wild-eyed and looking for revenge.

Cahir recognized the name on several of the spines: Galileo Galilei. He called himself a Catholic, Cahir thought, and yet he had fathered three children out of wedlock and had become a heretic. And indeed, as he continued his casual walk alongside the massive bookshelves, he discovered titles regarding all manner of science, astronomy, mathematics, geometry—all subjects condemned by the Pope and denounced by any good Christian. Aye, and hadn't he traveled throughout Europe to its finest cities—Paris, Versailles, London, Rome—and he knew these preposterous ideas of planets and nature and so-called scientific 'achievement' to be nothing more than heretical rhetoric meant to undermine the Catholic church.

"Burn it," he said abruptly, returning to the hall. "Burn it all."

A chorus of objections rose. "We'll pay you," one man begged. "Twenty pounds to save the library."

He shook his head.

"Forty pounds!" another offered.

"Sixty!" "Eighty!" "A hundred pounds!"

To each he shook his head as he made his way to the front doors.

"A hundred pounds," a stout man's voice rose above the rest. "It is a king's ransom; a tremendous wealth."

Cahir stopped at the doors and turned back to face them. Smiling wanly, he said, "I am already a wealthy man. What do I want with more?" Glancing outside, his smile quickly faded. "You have only minutes to leave here. Follow my men now and your lives will be spared. Remain behind and you will be burned alive."

"Cahir," Wills said, "what of the woman?" He nodded toward the dining hall. "She cannot walk."

Cahir called to one of his men. "Bring up a carriage or a cart," he instructed. "The woman and her newborn will ride to Burt Castle, as well as the elderly."

Wills followed Cahir out of the Bishop's home. Cahir had been correct; all of Derry was burning. His eyes took in the carnage, even if his mind had trouble processing the images for what they were: the years of work, Docwra's vision of a European city on the River Foyle, the honest people of Derry who had been just as victimized by Paulet as the Irish, all gone. The thick smoke had already filled the air, the flames shooting high and so close to the Bishop's home that at any moment, a wayward ember could catch the wood afire. Even as the thought crossed his mind, he realized the back of the house was already in flames and within mere seconds, it was engulfed, and he turned back to see Rhiannon helping the women fall into line with Cahir's men all the while comforting the children.

"Tell me," Cahir said, bringing Wills' attention back to him, "why did you not fight?"

It was a question he would be called to answer, he knew. Captain Stewart would demand to know, perhaps Lord Chichester and even King James. But as he looked at the flames that were once Derry and beyond it to English soldiers—now prisoners—marching under guard toward Burt Castle, the thoughts came crashing together in his mind like so many pieces of mosaic glass: the village had been left undefended. There had been no sentries; no guards posted. There had been no night watchmen. There had been no one to see the torches as they made their way from Culmore Fort to Derry. Once inside the city, the lower fort had surrendered almost immediately; only the upper fort had engaged in any kind of resistance at all. And now even the building that Lieutenant Gordon had fought to secure had dissolved into nothing more than a bonfire.

"It was futile," Wills said. "All of Derry was lost even before she awakened."

Cahir nodded silently.

"And you, my friend," Wills added, "I fear that you are lost this day as well."

Cahir opened his mouth as if to speak but the roof over the Bishop's house collapsed, sending flames shooting outward like a dragon seeking its prey.

"Allow me to keep Rhiannon with me," he said.

Cahir looked toward a wagon that his men had pulled in front of the bishop's home. "You will have to trust me, Wills, that she will be safer at Burt Castle than with you. When I depart, I know not what the other clans will do."

Wills followed his line of sight to the throngs of people assembling like docile flocks of sheep. When he looked back, Cahir was already gone, making his way to the front of the line where a man stood ready with his horse.

Wills hurried to the wagon where Rhiannon was attending to the woman and her newborn. "Come with us, Wills," she pleaded. Truth be told, there was nothing more he wanted to do. Oh, he didn't relish the thought of wasting away in the castle dungeons, though he was certain that surely the women and children would not suffer that fate. And as God as his witness, he didn't wish to be parted from Rhiannon—not now, not here, not ever. He held out his hand and for the briefest of moments, he thought of yanking her off that wagon and into his arms. He thought of asking her, begging her, pleading with her to remain with him. But there was nothing here, he reminded himself, and Cahir's words had been true enough. There was nothing he could offer her—not water, not food, not shelter. All was lost. Words never surfaced but lay dormant on his lips as the wagon began to move and her hand slipped from his.

He stepped behind the wagon and watched it as it grew smaller. She never turned her face away from him. Despite the fact that she was knelt beside the woman as the wagon bounced and jarred them over the rocky, rough terrain, her eyes remained riveted to his, her plea still on her lips.

He had never seen anything like it, he realized; hundreds of soldiers, men and women and children of all ages, walking steadily away from Derry, their faces occasionally looking back at its burning embers and the soot-filled skies. A silence filled the air now. Children no longer cried; women no longer begged. Those with infirmities still walked on the best they could to a castle a few miles from where he stood and a future filled with uncertainty.

31

They found six men dead: George Paulet, Sheriff Hamilton, Lieutenant Gordon and three more soldiers in the upper fort. Cahir O'Doherty had targeted the two men that had bred his hatred; the others died as Phelim MacDavitt sought to take the upper fort.

The looters were gone by the time Captain Stewart arrived with a hundred men, driven from Derry by the intensity of the flames. Fergus, Tomas and Wills had walked out to meet Stewart, conferring with him in the meadows before finding their horses where they were still tied from the night before. As they rode into the village—or the remains of it, for it was now unrecognizable—he could not believe it had been only the night before that he had arrived at Culmore Fort to inform Henry Hart of O'Doherty's impending rebellion, and now he wondered at the man's fate.

They spent several hours sifting through the rubble looking for survivors or more of the dead and in the end, all they had to show for their efforts were a couple of stray dogs and shards of china. All eighty-five houses had been burned to the ground, along with every business.

Now as they gathered around William Stewart in the field just outside the village, they turned their attention to regaining Culmore Fort and freeing the captives at Burt Castle.

"Last evening," Stewart announced, "I sent a messenger, John Blackstone, to Lord Chichester in Dublin informing him of the imminent revolt. John has not yet returned. However, I can tell you this, though it is not pleasant news to share: the Irish Army in His Majesty's Service is small, very small. Cahir O'Doherty was one of the most loyal Irish chieftains to the English cause, and I daresay that we must be exceptionally careful with whom we trust moving forward. To put down this rebellion I fear will require troops from London, which will undoubtedly take time to collect."

As Stewart continued, Wills looked over the group assembled there: one hundred men that had come from Scotland and England to become farmers. While they focused their attentions on the rebellion, their sheep and their crops were left in the care of what few women there were, along with members of the O'Donnell clan. The irony did not escape him; how were they to know if their sheep were being slaughtered or their crops burned while they were absent?

"Our strategy at present," Stewart continued, "is to march on Culmore Fort. There is a major arsenal there, as you know, and once we have reclaimed the fort and are able to arm ourselves further, we march on Burt Castle to free the hostages there."

+≈•≈+

Culmore Fort appeared deserted as they approached. It was moving on mid-afternoon and though Wills had neither eaten nor slept, he was neither tired nor hungry. He could only think of Rhiannon staring at him from the wagon as they rolled away, and he hoped that Cahir was a man of his word and she would come to no harm. It was one thing to trust Cahir; despite what had occurred here this day, he had been a man of principles. It was quite another, however, to trust in every man in the O'Doherty clan—and those others that had joined the rebellion.

Stewart had divided his small force so that fifty marched toward Culmore Fort; in the event they were attacked before they reached the small outpost, the remaining half could flank the attackers and between the two, they could close in on the O'Doherty clan.

As they drew closer, Fergus asked, "Do you see any movement on the parapets?"

"I do not," Wills answered. "It is as still as I have ever seen it."

"Do they wait until we are within range of their harkbus to pop up and commence firing on us?" Tomas mused.

Wills searched the surrounding terrain. Both Derry and Culmore were surrounded by O'Doherty land. Why, their march from Derry to Culmore had been across clan territory, and how's that for irony? He wondered. And come to think of it, the group that remained behind was now encamped in an O'Doherty meadow.

It seemed completely surreal to him. His instincts called for him to remain in the tree line, to stay to the shadows, and yet here he was, riding his horse beside the River Foyle in the wide open for God and everybody to see. And yet, it was the only course of action they could take; to move into the forest was to move closer to the rebels, men that could appear seemingly out of nowhere, slit their throats or fire their harkbus, and be gone again before they barely knew they'd been attacked. No; Wills was quite accustomed to his throat and aimed to keep it intact.

They reached the doors without incident and moved inside to find it as quiet as a tomb. Wills, Fergus and Tomas dismounted and entered the main building that had served as the barracks for most of the men stationed there, as well as the offices; it had been this building where only last night, Fergus and he had lain on beds staring at the ceiling after a full and satisfying supper.

The halls were empty and for the first few minutes, Wills thought it had been completely deserted. Then he held up his hand, causing his friends to stop and listen. "Do you hear that?" he asked.

"Footsteps, 'ey?" Fergus asked.

Their eyes moved to a heavy door that was bolted shut. Moving to either side of it, Wills called out, "Identify yourself!"

A long moment of silence ensued.

"We are here on behalf of the Army under King James!" Wills shouted.

At that, a sudden cacophony rose up as men clambered for the door.

"It could be a trap," Tomas said.

"With the door bolted shut from the outside?" Fergus asked.

"I've seen worse, I have."

"Who is your senior officer?" Wills shouted.

The voices trailed off until one man answered. "Captain Henry Hart is commander of Culmore, but we were set upon last evening after he departed for Burt Castle."

"Identify yourself!"

"Brice Campbell, Second Lieutenant, sir."

"Scottish lad," Fergus said.

"Help me unlock this door," Wills said, setting his harkbus against the wall. Once the bolt was lifted off the hinges and the heavy door was opened, he found himself staring at perhaps a dozen men. "Where are the others?" he asked incredulously.

"We are all that is left," Brice answered. "Lieutenant Pearce took most of the men to Burt Castle late last evening."

"He did what?"

As Brice filled them in on the details of the prior night, other men joined them in the hall. The grounds were empty, all outbuildings vacant.

"Frances Hart helped Cahir O'Doherty?" Wills asked for the third time in disbelief.

"I heard The O'Doherty order her locked in her bedchambers," one of the men offered.

"Where?" Wills shot back.

With Brice and two soldiers joining them, they made their way up the stairs to the second floor, where they discovered Frances' door locked, a skeleton key laid carefully just outside the door.

"Mrs. Hart?" Wills called.

"Aye," she said. Her voice sounded wary and tired.

"Are you alone?" he asked.

There was a moment's pause. "Aye. Who goes there?"

"William Neely from Fort Stewart." He picked up the skeleton key and turned it in the door. Sliding it open, his hand on his sword, he found Mrs. Hart standing in the middle of the room. Her hair was disheveled, her clothing appearing as if she had slept in it. Just beyond her shoulder, Wills spotted a window; Derry still lay smoldering, blackening the skies.

"Derry has fallen," she stated flatly.

"Aye," Fergus said. "She has."

"My husband is at Burt Castle, along with my son." Her words came faster as she realized the O'Doherty clan was gone and the Volunteer Irish Army had arrived. "They held them as hostages to gain my cooperation."

Something caught Wills' eye and he strode past her to the window. He could see far into the distance from this vantage point but he had to blink several times before he trusted his sight. "Fergus. Tomas."

As they joined him at the window, they watched as a force as great as their own galloped across the rolling hills to the south of Captain Stewart and his men. And as he turned his attention to where the captain waited, he noted the men gathering around one that was in advance of the others.

"Get to the parapet," he ordered Brice. "And wave the Union Jack until they wave their flag in return."

The messengers had gotten through, he thought as he rejoined Mrs. Hart. Oh, and he had never been so pleased to see anyone as much. "Come," he said, taking her hand, "Captain Stewart will want to hear what transpired here."

32

As the pieces of the puzzle were put into place, the consequences of the situation began to sink into Wills' mind with the gravity of a sledgehammer. Had Cahir done as Fergus suggested and murdered George Paulet leaving no evidence and no witness, his fate would have been his alone. But with the set of circumstances they were now forced to confront, it was obvious he not only had changed his own fate but that of Ulster and perhaps all of Ireland.

Lord Arthur Chichester had, to his credit, immediately deployed seventy soldiers from Dublin. It was all he could spare, as the vast numbers of English soldiers had vacated Ireland at the end of the Nine Years War and what was hoped was the dawn of an age of peace. No one had foreseen a subject loyal to the English Crown switching sides so abruptly, even if in hindsight, there had been plenty of clues to follow. Nor could anyone have predicted he would gather an overwhelming force of clans—ones that had been enemies as well as those that had remained his allies throughout the years.

Scouts had been sent ahead of the Dublin troops and by an unbelievable twist of fate had intercepted a note written in Cahir O'Doherty's own hand. As it was read aloud to the men gathered in the open meadow outside Derry, the collective shock was undeniable; for it listed the clans that had already joined with the O'Dohertys and called for every clan throughout all of Ireland to join their forces in what was referred to as a Catholic war. Among the lengthy list were the O'Donnells, MacSweeneys, MacDavitts, O'Cahans — even the O'Hanlons, who were clear across Ulster in the vicinity of the tiny outpost of Belfast. As the list was read off, Wills' mind raced through what he knew of Ulster's geography, realizing that from the east coast to the west, the Irish were mobilizing.

And of course it had little to do with the Catholic faith, if anything at all, he thought, but much more to do with the treatment of the overwhelmingly Catholic Irish by predominantly Protestant settlers loyal to King James. Aye, and Cahir was a crafty one indeed for he must have known his personal tribulations with Paulet and Hamilton — regardless of how hated they were by so many — could not possibly organize a full-scale revolt. But a Holy War — oh, indeed, a Holy War had the strength to roll across the island from east to west and north to south — and perhaps become the tipping point for Catholic Spain to join them.

It was only by this great stroke of fortune in intercepting O'Doherty's note that Lord Chichester knew the extent of the rebellion he was facing even as Derry still lay smoldering. And as the seventy soldiers from Dublin joined with Captain Stewart, the state of their own forces was laid out before them.

In addition to the soldiers sent to the north, Chichester sent couriers to London to appeal to King James for the largest contingent he could possibly spare.

It would take days for the couriers to cross the Irish Sea from Dublin to the tiny port of Holyhead, Wales; more than sixty miles, their speed would be completely at the whim of the winds, whether favorable or no, and the strength and severity of the waves they encountered. Once in Wales, they must then travel from the western shores of that island almost to its eastern edge to reach London—a distance of nearly three hundred miles.

Good God, Wills thought; it could be a week or longer before King James even knew of Derry's burning. Even then, he must amass a force great enough to counter the rebels and his mind threatened to explode when he thought of all the possible routes they might take from England to Scotland to Ireland and finally to Ulster.

In the meantime, all that stood in Cahir O'Doherty's way were the men gathered at Derry and those that had retaken Culmore Fort—less than two hundred in all, if he did not count the Irish clans they had brought with them. Oh, and he noted he was not the only one that eyed those clans with more than a bit of suspicion. These were men from the Dublin area and central Ireland who had forged more favorable relationships with the English forces than those in Ulster had managed. Some would say they rolled over too quickly, gave up too much too readily; others might contend they knew they had little hope against King James' far greater forces. But now, given these dire set of circumstances, they had to be weighing their own odds of victory on one side versus the other; for if it took weeks for troops to arrive from London, O'Doherty's Rebellion might very well have rolled over all of Ireland in a crimson tide and all the men Wills looked at now, including himself, could be slaughtered.

"There will be more that will join us," Captain Stewart was saying, "for couriers have been sent far and wide, calling for troops to join us here. They will come from Donegal and Galway, from each garrison throughout all of Ireland. And let us not forget the hundred soldiers from Culmore Fort and Derry that have been taken by the rebel forces. Our first matter of priority is to free those men that they may fight again."

"I am not to be part of this," one man said. The crowd parted as all eyes turned to Richard Brown. His plot of land bordered Wills' and they often herded one another's sheep into the fields when the other was given competing duties. "I came to Ireland to raise sheep—to provide wool to the English markets. I came neither to butcher the Irish people nor be butchered myself."

"Come forward," Captain Stewart said. The air grew tense as the two men met in the middle of the assembly, standing only a few yards apart. When Stewart continued to speak, his voice was commanding, carrying to every man gathered. "I may remind you that you swore an oath to King James; and on that oath, you were given free passage from Scotland—and some of you from England or Wales. You were given shelter and food. You were given plots of land and though you work that land by crops or livestock, you work not in my employ but as tenant farmers, sharing in the coins from the food or wool provided to the markets. You are tenant farmers precisely because you swore that allegiance to King James, which included fighting—and dying—for him if that is what our fate decrees."

Stewart paused, his eyes sweeping over each man's face. "So let there be no confusion about this point. You will fight for King James now or you will be branded a traitor to England. You will be shackled and imprisoned until such time as a trial can be conducted—which may not occur until this rebellion is put down." He turned back to face Richard. "So think long and hard before you wipe your hands of this. Fight with us now and keep all you have. Do not fight and lose everything you have gained—including your freedom."

A hush fell on the crowd as all eyes moved to Richard. After a moment, he returned to his former post, leaning against a tree. His shoulders were sloped, his face long, leaving no doubt that despite his objections, he understood the consequences of disobeying.

Stewart waited until Richard had settled back in place before continuing. "Dusk is upon us. We make camp here tonight. Lieutenant Archie MacGruder will assign night watchmen. At first dawn, we march on Burt Castle to free the hostages there and regain possession of the armaments taken at Culmore Fort. You are dismissed."

As the men began to disburse, Stewart called out, "William Neely, Fergus MacPherson, Tomas Gallagher. A word with you."

As the three men approached, Stewart waved for them to follow. They strolled a fair distance from the others while he spoke. "Wills, you have made yourself invaluable far beyond that of my aide. Therefore, I will be selecting another to remain by my side."

"But, sir, I—"

Stewart waved down his protest. "I have far more important tasks for you—all three of you." He stopped by a small thicket. Turning toward the northeast, he continued, "I need good scouts with keen eyes, men sharp enough to avoid capture and gather intelligence. Burt Castle, as you know, is roughly three miles from where we stand. But it is through enemy territory—and make no mistake about it, it *is* enemy territory now. I must know how many rebels are between my men and that castle and I must know how heavily fortified it is. At first dawn, we march and men may live or die based on the information you obtain—or fail to obtain."

"I understand, sir," Wills said. "We will leave under cover of darkness, if that is suitable to you."

"It is."

"Captain?" Tomas interjected.

"Yes, Tomas?"

"I want you to know, sir, that despite the fact that I am Irish—"

"Your loyalty is not in question," Stewart interrupted. "You have proven your worth time and again."

"Aye, sir. Thank you, sir."

"If there are no questions, you are dismissed."

As they strolled back toward the encampment, Fergus whispered hoarsely, "It is suicide he's sent us on, for sure. Traipsing through O'Doherty woods in the dark, 'ey? The trees have eyes and ears, they have. We'll not make it to Burt Castle."

"But we must try, my friend," Wills said. "And we must succeed." He thought for a moment. "What day is this? I am afraid I do not even know the date."

The men thought for a moment. "April 19," Tomas said finally. "A Tuesday, it is."

They fell silent then, each with his own thoughts, as the last vestiges of the sun descended beyond the horizon. It was odd in a way, Wills thought; he could not recall a single day in which it had not rained. Even on the most beautiful of mornings with naught a cloud in the sky, there was always rain by afternoon. It was the hide of the beast, being on an island such as this with nothing to stop the clouds as they blew over the Atlantic. And it was the reason, he knew, for the varied shades of green; for the forests that sprang back up even after they had been trampled down or burned out; for the lush vegetation that stubbornly grew amidst the rocks and the limestone. And yet on this date—Tuesday, April 19, 1608—as Derry was torched and burned to the ground, not a single drop of rain had fallen to douse her flames.

33

The mists swirled around them like apparitions, wrapping them in cloaks of frigid night air, circling their throats with an insistence that drove the fog inside them until any warmth their bodies might have contained was extracted from them with morbid precision. As Wills looked upward, the tops of the trees morphed into roiling black clouds so he could no longer tell where the branches ended and the skies began. Aye, and these mists would have been sent from God Himself had they fallen when Derry lay burning but now it was difficult to squelch the persistent notion that perhaps God was on the side of the Irish after all, and these were not mists at all but spirits come to life; departed souls sent to trip them up and impede their journey.

They reached the clearing partway between Culmore Fort and Burt Castle and the first hint of relief began to seep through his bones as they realized it had been the site of a skirmish and yet no bodies were found. The perimeter of evergreens was twisted and mangled, no doubt from scores of men rushing through them. He had to kneel in the clearing itself to study the bare ground, his hands finding more than his eyes could see in the gloom; footprints on top of footprints, the earth churned like butter in a barrel. But as far as they could tell, there was no blood and all led from the clearing in the same direction—toward Burt Castle.

He could not shake the feeling that there were eyes upon them, nor could he escape the memory of his first time lost in the woods. His mind threatened to play tricks upon him until he could not discern whether the sounds he heard were chuckles in the darkness or simply the air twirling through the overhead limbs. The three men moved soundlessly, their horses left in camp so they would create as small a profile as possible and though he frequently checked his companions' location and he knew they did the same, he felt as alone as he ever had.

They had nearly reached the edge of the woods before the land gave way to a pasture where Cahir's livestock frequently roamed on better days, and in the distance lay Burt Castle, a hulking giant of murky stone set against troubled skies. Wills signaled for the three of them to get down and they lay on their stomachs under the last line of trees, watching the castle; not that there was anything at all to watch, he had to admit, as the castle lay as still as death. There were no torches along the parapet, none at the corners as he had seen in the past.

"Can you see anything?" he whispered hoarsely.

"Nothing at all," Fergus answered.

"Aye, and it's as dark as a witch's broom, it is," Tomas said.

He continued to study the structure and its surroundings. It was built for war as much as for living; though he could see only blackness in the round holes scattered along its base, he knew them to be filled with cannons waiting for an attack. Smaller holes not visible from this distance would be large enough for a harkbus and a man to see where he's shooting and nothing more. The walls would be five or six feet thick, they would; and it was only inside those walls that the castle proper was found, safe as a babe in her mother's arms.

The pastures that surrounded it served a dual purpose as well, its grass feeding the sheep and the cattle that grazed there, for sure; but more importantly, it allowed the inhabitants to spot a man from a fair distance away, long before he and his army had the time to mount a proper attack. And somewhere within those cold stone walls were all the inhabitants of Derry, including his beloved Rhiannon, Henry Hart and his son, Mrs. Paulet, Bishop Montgomery's sister as well as the soldiers captured from Culmore Fort and Derry.

Aye, and he proved himself to be both astute and cunning, Cahir O'Doherty did; for without the hostages, they might have bombarded the castle with English cannon fire until its walls crumpled to the ground. But from where Wills lay, his eyes riveted to the imposing fortress, he could not determine how they would ever approach it undetected.

His eyes roamed to its farthest grounds, across the pasture separating the three men from the castle, and into the woods in which they lurked. And there between two trees not ten feet from where they lay, a figure moved.

Startled, he grabbed for his sword, scrambling to his feet so quickly that Fergus and Tomas still lay on the ground, wide-eyed and searching, when they heard the voice.

"Do not be alarmed. It is just I, Elan." She sounded so calm and matter-of-fact that she might have been out for a leisurely stroll on a sunny afternoon.

"Are you alone?" Wills asked as Fergus and Tomas rose, their swords at the ready.

"I am." She moved closer to them, dropping the hood from her head and revealing her red hair as if proving that it was she.

"What are you doing out and about?" Fergus asked.

"Shouldn't I be asking what you are doing?" There was some amusement in her voice. "Surely you must know you cannot be on O'Doherty land without an O'Doherty detecting you."

"Surely you must know," Wills countered, "what transpired here this day."

"I do. And that is why I am here."

"You're a bit far from Carrickabraghy Castle, are you not?" Tomas prodded.

"I journeyed to Burt Castle today with The O'Donnell."

"Niall Garbh O'Donnell?"

"Aye."

"He's at Burt Castle?" Wills asked.

"He is but not for much longer. He is furious with Cahir O'Doherty."

"Why?"

"Their arrangement was to divide the spoils of Derry between the O'Doherty and O'Donnell clans. He expected much in the way of silver and became enraged when he discovered they left most of it to burn."

"Oh and don't we feel quite the sorry ones for him," Fergus said.

"And what of The O'Doherty?" Wills asked. "How did he respond to this?"

"He didn't care about the spoils. For Cahir, this was a vendetta against George Paulet and nothing more."

"I'd say it's a wee bit past that point now," Fergus said.

"What of the hostages then?" Wills asked. "Have you seen them? What's to be their fate?"

"Aye, I have seen them. They have separated the women and children from the men; they are locked into rooms in the towers you see there." She nodded toward the castle at the towers that helped comprise the outermost walls. "Then the men were separated into two groups; the soldiers have been brought to the dungeons and the others are held in locked rooms. I heard The O'Doherty himself say that no one was to be harmed unless they attempted to escape."

Wills looked toward the castle towers and wondered if Rhiannon was looking back at this very moment; not seeing him for sure, but hoping he was there all the same. "Why are you here?" he pressed. "For surely, The O'Doherty and The O'Donnell must know it is dangerous for their clansfolk to be beyond the safety of their walls."

"I bring you an offer."

"And what could you be offering us that we should want, short of surrender?" Fergus asked.

"Niall Garbh O'Donnell."

"Excuse me now?" Wills asked.

She cocked her head as if she was peering at him, but in the gloom he could not see her eyes. When she spoke, her voice had lowered and became more serious. "The O'Donnell wishes to join the English in putting down the rebellion."

"Have you gone completely daft, woman?" Fergus asked.

"Why?" Wills asked. "His men helped to burn Derry; I saw them with my own eyes. He is part of O'Doherty's Rebellion. Why would he give himself over to the English now?"

"Oh, make no mistake about it," Elan answered, "but he is not surrendering. He has merely picked the winning side."

"So he has lost faith in O'Doherty, is what you're telling us."

She shrugged. "I do not presume to know his faith — or lack of it. I simply know that he wishes to join your forces and fight against the O'Dohertys and the clans that have joined him."

"It's a trap," Tomas said, stepping forward. He had been silent to this point, preferring to listen to the exchange between Elan, Fergus and Wills, but now his voice was set. "Do not believe her."

"He is right," Wills said. "I should not believe you. How can we be assured that what you say is true?"

"Two ways. First, at dawn tomorrow the women, children and old men will be escorted to the southern edge of O'Doherty land. If your soldiers remain where they are outside of Derry, they will see them at first light."

"Watch your step, lassie," Tomas said. "If they intend to place the women and children between the two forces of battle, there will be hell to pay, there will."

"The intention is to free them."

"I don't believe you," Fergus said. "I do not believe the O'Donnell will switch sides so readily, nor do I believe the hostages will be given over freely."

"And why would I be here, telling you these things, if they were not true?"

"Perhaps you plan to lead us into an ambush, 'ey?" Fergus said.

At that, her voice became amused and despite the shadows across her face, Wills could have sworn she was smiling. "And second," she said, "I have no need to lead you into an ambush, for you have led yourselves." She nodded and the men turned to look behind them. The trees appeared to come alive as men stepped out from behind them.

Wills made for his sword but Elan stepped forward, her voice serious once more. "They are not here to fight you, and it would be folly for you to attempt to engage them. You are quite outnumbered, as you can clearly see."

"What then?" Wills asked.

"You will be allowed safe passage back to Derry. Bring with you this message: The O'Donnell wishes to fight with the English."

"And how do we find you—or The O'Donnell—to give Captain Stewart's reply?"

"When you leave your encampment, if Captain Stewart is agreeable in discussing The O'Donnell's plans, leave the flagpole in the ground without the flag. If the captain declines his offer, leave the flagpole with your flag still flying."

"And if the captain is agreeable? When should I say they are to meet?"

"The O'Donnell will meet him at Fort Stewart. And there is one more thing: the O'Dohertys are waiting at Burt Castle. To attempt an attack now would be madness."

The three looked at one another as if to gauge each other's reaction but the shadows fell too deeply. When Wills turned back to Elan, she was gone. Quickly looking to the trees where the men had been standing only a moment before, he saw nothing but the trees bending in the wind, the mists dancing around them like apparitions.

34

They could smell the smoke before they had reached the encampment. Wills had assumed as the mists fell upon the dying embers of what once was Derry, the odor that wafted upwards were the last vestiges of wood frame homes or perhaps the Bishop's books. But as they climbed a rise overlooking the encampment, they found Captain Stewart, Archie MacGruder and several others whom he did not recognize conferring as they looked to their south, away from Derry. And as Wills, Fergus and Tomas joined them they too saw the flames rising along the distant horizon in a mosaic of red and orange against a black sky.

"It is Strabane," Captain Stewart stated flatly. "It must be."

Wills had heard of Strabane but only in passing, and now he struggled to recall what he knew about the village. Oh, if it could even be called a village, for sure, for it was not much more than a spot along the road a days' ride from Derry. It was the origin of the River Foyle, a place where the smaller River Mourne met with the Finn.

"What would be its strategic importance?" Archie pondered. "There are no soldiers there; no outpost."

And for certain he was correct, Wills thought as they all stood in place and watched the clouds grow red as the flames' light licked at them. It had been settled by Scots long before the days of The Plantation had been declared, and before them, the O'Neills; from what Wills could remember, the Scots were peaceful folk that raised cattle, sheep and pigs in the valleys and lowlands around Strabane before the terrain gave way to the moors and eventually to the inhospitable Sperrin Mountains.

"It is in retaliation for the Irish villages burned in years past," Stewart said quietly. "Strategic or no, I believe that any settlement of Scots or English is at risk."

"I shall send scouts to Strabane," a man with a cultured London accent announced. "This is preposterous, I might say. While Derry yet smolders to our north, it appears the rebels have circled our encampment and set fire to our south."

"I'd say so," Fergus said under his breath.

Stewart turned as if only just noticing them. "What word have you?"

"Oh, we've word alright," Fergus said before Wills interrupted him.

"We've several matters to discuss with you," he said. "I'm supposing you'll be surprised at what we've discovered."

<hr />

At dawn's first light, the freed hostages began appearing from the forest. First to come were young men with their wives and children, followed by women and children without husbands or fathers and finally, the elderly and infirmed. They arrived in physically good condition and most were emotionally resilient, considering all that had transpired. Most were hungry, having been freed the hour before dawn, though most reported having been offered food and drink the night before at Burt Castle to varying degrees of acceptance.

Wills was frantic to find Rhiannon; he was one of the first to volunteer to meet the people as they emerged from O'Doherty lands. Several times he ventured into the woods on the pretext of helping people find their way, though it was readily apparent they had only to follow the steady stream before them. Fergus and Tomas knew his true intent; their expressions and concern-filled eyes followed his movements and silently questioned his success each time he reemerged. He asked repeatedly if anyone had seen her, but no one knew her by name and her description, unfortunately, fit too many ladies.

On Stewart's orders, they separated the hostages into several groups. While they were offered food and drink, they were questioned extensively. Their plans to march on Burt Castle at first dawn were stymied by the hostages' early release. And now if they were to march on it at all, they needed to know where the hostages had been kept, how many were not freed and how many of the O'Doherty clan and allies were there waiting to do battle.

The sun was beginning to burn off the dew when he spotted Rhiannon. She was carrying the infant babe in her arms, wrapped in the O'Doherty plaid, he noted. The mother walked beside her, thin and feeble, too delicate for her condition to have been caused by one night at the castle, and as they approached, her brow was covered in perspiration despite the cold air, her skin p.m.terrell

too wan. An older woman hobbled next to Rhiannon, alternately relying on a walking stick and Rhiannon's strong shoulder to keep her on her feet.

They were one of the last to emerge and Wills immediately brought them into camp where they were seated around a large fire. The mother was wrapped in wool; as Rhiannon handed her the babe, she pulled her underneath the plaid and began preparations for her to suckle.

"My auntie," Rhiannon said as she helped the older woman sit on a large, flat boulder. "Auntie, this is William Stewart. Wills, Jennyvar Ó Dálaigh, my da's sister."

"Mistress Ó Dálaigh," Wills said, taking her hand.

"Jennyvar," she corrected as he lightly kissed her hand. "I insist."

Wills offered them a cup of tea; the young mother shook her head, her eyes closing as if in sleep but Rhiannon received hers thankfully. Though Jennyvar initially accepted the offer, she quickly declined when she spotted a close friend. Excusing herself, she left the two alone.

"Are you well?" Wills whispered, his brows furrowed.

"I am." She took a long sip of the tea, allowing it to warm her throat before continuing. "But Delaney—the lady who gave birth yesterday—she is not."

"Was she ill-treated?"

"No. On the contrary, Lady O'Doherty herself took an interest in her and the babe. She is weak, Wills; too weak. Did you know she is only sixteen?"

"I did not." He stole a sideways glance at her. "And this is her third child?"

"Aye. Her husband is much older but is no help at'al."

"So I have gathered."

"She will need a wet nurse, I'm afraid. And perhaps a healer for both her and the babe."

Wills nodded. That would be a tall order, indeed, given the circumstances. With Derry gone and Strabane as well, the nearest settlement would be Lifford, he supposed, if it still stood; but it was anyone's guess whether a wet nurse or a healer would be found there.

"Tell me," he asked, "how many people were there of the O'Doherty clan and their allies?"

"I don't know," she said. "As we were brought into the Great Hall, we were immediately separated, rushed into staircases and brought to locked rooms."

"Everyone?"

"Aye. The men were divided by age; women were asked if they traveled alone or with children. They kept the children with their mothers while older sons were kept with their fathers. They asked each of us for our names, our place of birth and our parents' place of birth."

"Why do you suppose they wanted that?"

"I noticed those born in Ireland—such as myself—were sent in one direction while those from Scotland or England went in another."

"And where did they take you?"

"Wait, Wills, there is more—those with high titles received the most attention."

"Such as?"

"Bishop Montgomery's sister was among us. They took her away by herself instead of in groups like the others. Also, Lady Paulet was taken singly as well."

He considered that for a moment. Then, "Were there any others they took by themselves?"

"There were, but I was not close enough to hear their names."

"Do you see any of them here?"

She stood and studied the group that had assembled. "I do not."

"What of Henry Hart and his son? Did you see them?"

"No."

"He has not been freed." His chest tightened at his own statement and he glanced toward Stewart, who was conferring with other officers. As their eyes met, the captain beckoned for him to join them. "Pardon me," he said to Rhiannon. "Please have your fill of food and I'll return directly."

As he joined the men, Stewart said, "Our plans have been adjusted somewhat. Other villages and settlements have been set ablaze; there are reports now that Lifford is afire. Our forces are too small."

"What does that mean exactly, Captain?"

"It means we are outnumbered—apparently, in all directions."

"We do not march on Burt Castle?"

He shook his head.

"I have just learned that high profile hostages were not freed. Henry Hart, Margaret Montgomery Shaw— the Bishop's sister—Mrs. Paulet and others."

"The soldiers from Culmore Fort and Derry also remain hostage," he said. "Some of the men returning said there was a rumor they were taken to the dungeons. We do not know their fate."

"I can return with other scouts," Wills offered. "I can try to get closer, to skirt their perimeter, locate a way inside—"

"Even if you found one, we do not have the numbers to retaliate." He held up a paper that had been carefully folded. "I received this a few minutes ago. Lord Chichester has ordered us to defend our own settlements until he can raise the necessary troops."

"They are not forthcoming from Dublin?"

Again, he shook his head. "They sent us all they could spare." He looked out over the pitifully small group of soldiers. "This—insurrection—took us all by surprise. They did not have sufficient troops in all of Ireland to properly defend it."

"But Galway—Donegal, surely—"

He placed his hand on his shoulder. "No, Wills. We are outnumbered."

Wills glanced over his shoulder at Rhiannon, who had returned to the young mother's side and was assisting her with the babe. Her two small children clung now to her skirts, crying and trembling from the cold and fright as Rhiannon sought to reassure them. Delaney's husband was nowhere to be seen. On the other side of the encampment he spotted Jennyvar with several other elderly ladies huddled in their plaids and warming their hands over the fire.

"I am sending you, Fergus and Tomas ahead of us," Stewart was saying. "We return to Fort Stewart immediately. The others from Derry and Strabane will accompany us. It will be safer there for all of us, until this is sorted in Dublin. We shall put the visitors in the old O'Donnell castle."

"Aye, sir." Wills caught Fergus' eye and motioned for him to join them. "And will you require reconnaissance for safe passage?"

"Precisely." As Fergus and Tomas joined them, he continued, "You are to leave immediately. Send word at each third's distance. Take three more men of your choosing with you."

"Aye, sir."

As they moved away, Fergus said, "I'll ready the horses."

"And I'll get the other men," Tomas offered.

"You've someone to say goodbye to, I'd wager," Fergus added.

Wills nodded, and broke away from them as they prepared for their journey. He hurried to Rhiannon and knelt at her side. "You will be leaving shortly for Fort Stewart," he said.

"But I have family east of Derry—"

He shook his head. "It is not safe. Orders are that you will travel to Fort Stewart." He said this last firmly, his eyes locked onto hers. "I am to travel ahead of the others so I will be awaiting your arrival. You will stay in my home. Your auntie is welcome as well, though she may wish to stay at the O'Donnell castle with her friends." At her objections, he placed a finger gently on her lips. "I will remain with Fergus just a few steps away should you need me. Otherwise, you will have your privacy—and your honor."

She smiled. She appeared tired; her eyes were dark and her lids heavy. "Thank you."

He wanted to say more but he could feel Fergus' presence behind them. He stood. "I will see you in just a few hours."

"And what of Delaney?" she asked.

"She will travel to Fort Stewart as well. Perhaps we can find a woman there to help—" he glanced quickly at the young mother and then back to Rhiannon "—to help," he said again lamely.

She nodded. "I'll try to arrange a horse for her or possibly a cart," she said uncertainly.

"I can ask—"

"No," she said. "You have things to do. Your men await you. I will take care of Delaney and her children." She glanced about. "There are elderly here as well; arrangements will have to be made for all that cannot withstand the walk. I will make that my mission as well."

"Are you sure?"

"Aye. Go." For the briefest of moments, she tilted

her head upward to his as if to kiss him but just as quickly, she turned back to the mother and the children.

He took the reins from Fergus. "Are we ready?"

"Aye. We are."

He mounted his horse and joined the others that were waiting at the edge of camp. They departed at a steady gait as they made their way across the meadow. Just before reaching the first set of trees, he slowed and looked back. He could no longer spot Rhiannon in the crowd, but he noted that Captain Stewart was directing several men to place a flag pole at the opposite edge of camp, nearer to Derry and Burt Castle. As the flag was forced into the ground, he noticed there was no flag flying atop it.

35

All of Ulster was burning.

Colonists flooded the tiny settlement of Fort Stewart in the ensuing days; each questioned regarding their village, its inhabitants and possible identification of clans involved. They came from the east and west, north and south, all with the same tale: surprise attacks, civilians ordered out of their homes before they were torched, and men killed when they fought back. They came in overwhelming forces flying flags of a dozen or more clans and in each instance they were urged to return to their native countries. It appeared as if the Irish were expelling the immigrants and there was nothing and no one to stop them.

Some simply passed through on their way to Donegal and a ship to carry them back to their native country. Others were en route to Dublin, where they believed they would be safer. Outside of Ulster, there was unrest but nothing like the uncertainty of attacks and rebellion they faced here.

Then there were days like today; lazy days that for brief periods of time, Wills could tilt his face upward to feel the mists on his skin, experience the warmth heralding spring, watch the potato farmers at work or the sheep grazing, and try to forget. Then he would remember the harkbus in his hand, see the others guarding the flocks and the crops like never before— farmers turned into soldiers and a new normal emerging—and he had the sensation in the pit of his stomach that nothing would ever be the same again.

From the fields, he could watch the water on Drongawn Lough and his eyes would inevitably wander to the land mass on the other side of it; O'Doherty property, it lay like a silent sentinel, waiting, waiting.

Perhaps that was the worst of it, he thought, the uncertainty of waiting. One day, and he hoped it would be soon, troops would arrive from England and they could claim back the lands lost, drive back the clans... And then what? He wondered.

Half a dozen farmers drove their sheep back to Fort Stewart and the safety behind the gates long before dusk arrived, where once an occasional farmer—himself included—would choose to remain in the fields just a wee bit longer for no other reason than to enjoy the peace and serenity. But today was a special day. Today he was picking up a plaid he had contracted with an Irish lady to sew for him, a plaid that would represent the Neely family.

Her cottage was within sight of the fort, a short meandering walk through the woods. She was waiting for him, sitting on a stump just outside her home; a shriveled crone of a woman she was, her hair so thin that her scalp was clearly visible, her face withered and worn, the delicate skin underneath her eyes drooping so dramatically, it pulled away, leaving the pink exposed. Her eyes were such a pale blue that even the pupil was affected, a sign, Wills thought, of the onset of blindness. He had seen that look in his grandfather's eyes as his visibility waned until at last he could see no more.

"Ah, Lady Penarddun." Wills greeted her as he approached in his native Gaelic, a language she could readily understand, though the Irish Gaelic differed somewhat; for she, like many of their native neighbors, could speak no English at all.

She cackled. "You make me feel special, lad, as if the likes of me could be a lady." She slapped her knee with a blue-veined hand.

"I have brought you some turnips," he said, holding up a bundle for her to see. "It's the first of the season. Would you like for me to carry them inside for you?"

"No, lad. Just set them here at my feet."

He set them next to her feet, noting her shoes were much larger than her feet. She had placed pieces of rags in the backs of her shoes; he supposed so her feet did not slip out.

"And now, lad, have a set on the stump beside me here and I will show you what I have made for you."

He rolled another stump closer to hers and sat. His eyes wandered to the wool she held in her lap. For all her poor eyesight, she somehow had a knack for carding sheep's wool and spinning it into something beautiful.

"Your ancestors, you know," she said with the confidence of a woman who has seen much and knows more, "were in Ireland before they were in Scotland."

"Is that so?"

"Aye and it is. Five hundred years ago, lad, the Neely family lived right here in Ulster. They left in the eleven hundreds for the Scottish Lowlands, so it appears dear boy that you have come full circle."

Wills had been told Penarddun O'Donnell could neither read nor write, nor could any of her ancestors in recent memory. Yet over the centuries the finest of details had been handed down from generation to generation, an intricate tapestry of myths and facts and legends so expertly woven that one could never know where truth ended and fiction began. Her husband had taken the last name of the ruling family, as had his family from centuries ago, though they were not truly related or so it was said; but it was no matter as her husband had passed some forty years earlier, leaving Penarddun childless and alone.

"Aye," she was saying, "so I have sewn you something more than the plaid you requested." She slipped her long fingers under the wool and retrieved a piece of material that had quite obviously been painstakingly constructed. In the center was a castle with three turrets sewn in a grayish-black color, above which was the Red Hand of the O'Neill clan.

"Do you know what this is, lad?" she asked.

"I am afraid I do not, Lady Penarddun, though I have seen the hand."

"Aye, and I am sure you have. It is the Bloody Hand of the Clan O'Neill. It is said that in the days of the Celts, several great chieftains sailed across the waters. They spotted the beautiful Irish coast and as their eyes fell on the magnificent shades of green, they debated who would lay claim to her. Ah, but they were powerful competitors, they were, and after great deliberation they decided they would each row a boat toward the land and whosoever touched her first would lay claim to her."

She placed both hands on her knees, her eyes staring into the forest and yet seeing something miles and centuries apart. "So off they rowed, and it was a fierce competition, it was. The weaker ones dropped back and seeing that all was lost, they watched as two neared the shore. Oh, they were so close that none could tell who would reach it first and as the final stretch was there for the taking, Niall could not bear to lose that beautiful, precious land. So he reached to his axe and he severed his left hand at the wrist and with his right, he tossed it to shore."

"Oh."

She smiled. "Aye, and so Niall won, you see, for it was his hand that touched Eire first. It was in the days before we were told we needed last names… So his descendants called themselves 'uá Niáll' to mark themselves as the children of the champion, and it's since been changed to O'Neill. And there you have it."

As she handed him the material, he said, "You are too kind, Lady Penarddun. But I do not understand what the Bloody Hand of The O'Neill—"

"Your ancestors, dear boy, were descendants of Niall. You are related to the O'Neill clan."

"No. I'm sorry, but I believe you are mistaken."

"And it goes back even further, lad, for Niall was a descendant of another man that had ruled all of Ireland; none other than the prehistoric Irish High King, Niall of Nine Hostages, himself the son of a High King."

"Niall of—"

"Nine Hostages. You see, a High King of Ireland, Eochaid Mugmedón, had five sons. Later as the king grew older, his wife pressured him to name one of his sons his successor. Not knowing which to name, he gave the task over to a druid. The sons were put through one contest after another and with each, Niall was victorious and thus he became the High King upon his father's passing. I have this information, mind you, with good authority, as names have been passed from generation to generation…"

A crow cawed and for a moment, they both looked to the tops of the trees. Then Penarddun continued. "It has been five hundred years since the day your Neely ancestors left Eire. The uá Niáll migrated throughout Eire, you see, changing their name, developing new clans, until the Mac Conghaile clan formed on the western coast. It's a Gaelic name, far newer than the Celts, named after their chieftain, a formidable man known for the strength and tenacity of a hound. And it is there that your name came about, lad. Be proud of it, for you come from a long line of strong and fierce leaders."

Wills looked at the material again with its castle and bloody hand. It couldn't be, he thought. It just simply couldn't be.

"And now for the plaid you came for, lad." With that, she shook out the wool that had lain in her lap. It consisted of the same colors as the crest: interwoven threads of gray and red that might have appeared completely incongruous to anyone else but now—now he knew the gray symbolized the castle and the red, the bloody hand. Interspersed were threads of green— no doubt depicting the color of Ireland.

"It is beautiful," he breathed. "A work of art."

"Take care of it, child. It will last you for generations, it will."

He reached into his pocket and extracted a few coins. It was a large sum and far more than he had a right to spend on a piece of material, for sure, but he was flush with the money from selling his wool in Donegal and he supposed what he was really paying for was the history lesson.

"Oh, no, lad, you are giving me far too much." She tried to push the coins away. "Just some venison when next you have it, and a potato or two should you come by them. I've no need for coin."

"But surely—"

"I've all I need. I live here in peace, child. I sit and listen to the babble of the creek, the song of the birds. I see the sun rise and set with these old eyes and I am alive to watch the cycle of the moon. Each time I cook, I am blessed with a carrot, a turnip or a potato—and sometimes something special like rabbit or venison."

His eyes wandered to the bundle of turnips at her feet. "I will make a point," he said, "to bring you venison and rabbit, m'lady." He rose. Her face tilted upward, a serene smile on her lips, as her thin hands rested in her lap. "But now you have nothing to keep you warm," he noted.

"I've a plaid of my own in the cottage, dear."

"Then I shall get it for you." The door was standing ajar and he stepped inside. It consisted of one room with a fireplace on one side and a lumpy straw bed against the opposite wall. In between were a table that had seen far better days and two plain wood chairs in need of repair. The floor was dirt but brushed so thoroughly that he could see the brush strokes in the soil. He stepped to the bed, retrieved the wool and made for the door. He hesitated briefly, looking back at the fireplace. His eyes wandered to the kindling in a battered metal bin.

Returning to Penarddun, he carefully wrapped the wool across her lap with the extra material available for her to cover her arms as dusk descended. "You've no firewood," he observed.

"I've small branches."

"That is kindling."

She patted his hand. "I cannot lift a piece of wood, dear. Only kindling. But don't you worry. It's a tiny place and it doesn't take much to heat it."

"Then I shall bring you more in the coming days."

"With the venison or rabbit," she said with a shy smile.

"Aye, and potatoes, too, once they're ready to harvest. It won't be long now. I shall repair your chairs when next I come."

"Stay safe, young William Neely," she said, "for there's trouble afoot."

He paused. She closed her eyes and leaned her head against the cottage where the last vestiges of sunlight could find her skin through the tree branches overhead. He wondered what she might have been like as a young lady; how long it might have taken her to become so wise. He said his goodbyes but she did not reply; her smile only grew slightly wider. Then he picked up his plaid and the mysterious crest and turned toward the path leading back to Fort Stewart.

36

ills knocked on the door of his home and hearing no one inside, he slowly opened the door. It took a moment for his eyes to adjust. Rhiannon was not there. He stood in the middle of the home, remembering Penarddun O'Donnell's tiny cottage. His home, in contrast, was larger. It consisted of two rooms, not one. He laid the material across the back of a chair and lit a few candles from the flames in the fireplace. He placed one candle on the table and watched as the shadows were dispelled. Somehow the room felt different than before. Before *her*. It had once been a place he had gone for shelter, a dry place where he could eat his meals, a spot he could lay his head and know that in his slumber neither dew nor frost would form on his face. The fire kept things cozy day and night, the scent of the burning wood permeating everything within; a pleasant aroma, he had to admit, one that reminded him of home though he didn't know why as the Lowlands of Scotland had been deforested for generations and burning wood was tantamount to burning one's own hand.

But, aye, something was different. He inhaled deeply. Was that the perfume of wildflowers he smelled? That was it; it had to be. The cottage had become a home and now it carried the fragrance of an Irish spirit by the name of Rhiannon.

He picked up the wool and carried it into the next room where he carefully laid it across the foot of the bed. She would be pleasantly surprised, he thought, when she discovered it. He was smoothing down the bedcovers when he heard her soft voice behind him.

"Mister Neely," she said with mock indignation, "you should not be here and me without a chaperone."

He turned as he felt his cheeks grow warm. "My apologies," he said with a sly smile. "I knocked and when you did not answer—"

"I've been at the market, trading loaves of bread for meat and vegetables." She adjusted a cloth over the basket she held in her arms. "Would you care to join me for supper?"

"I couldn't—I mean, it isn't proper—"

"We will keep the door open." She smiled. "I've hardly seen you since you moved in next door with Fergus. I'm feeling guilty for taking over your home like this."

She was standing in the doorway to the bedroom. His first thought had been to flee; despite the fact that it was his bed and his bedcovers, it felt like her bedroom now and he had never before stood in a lady's bedchamber. But now as he looked at her, he realized the last thing on earth he wanted to do was leave.

"Your auntie—?"

"You were quite right about her. She appreciates your hospitality, she surely does, but her closest friends are living in the old O'Donnell castle and well, I believe they are pretending to be royalty with their newfound surroundings."

"They have not been traumatized from the burning of Derry?"

She made a sound but whether it was a chuckle or something else, he couldn't determine. "You will find the Irish to be resilient if nothing else."

The light from the candles and fire shone behind her, glinting off her blond hair so it appeared she had a white halo about her. She turned to the side so her back was against the doorframe. As she gazed into the front room, he found himself staring at her profile; she had a petite nose that had the barest upward slope at its tip. Her lashes were impossibly long and curved; her cheekbones high. She looked back at him, her eyes meeting his. The light caught her eyes so they appeared voluminous and such a deep green, a color he wanted to get lost within…

Before he could give himself the opportunity to think, he had crossed the room and taken her in his arms. He didn't remember taking the basket from her; he didn't recall if she had been the one to put it down. All he knew was one moment she was standing in the doorway with the basket over her arm and the next, both her arms were around his neck and he was leaning into her, pressing her against the doorframe with his body.

Her lips were full and soft, yielding as his closed over them. She tasted sweet and as her hands pressed his head deeper toward hers, he wanted to escape into the feel of her fingers through his hair, of her breath against his face, her lips parting to let him in. There was nothing that came close to the feel of a woman's breasts pressed against his chest, rubbing against him as if silently urging him to take them. As he closed one hand around her breast, he felt her inhale sharply and her lips began to tremble.

He started to step back but she pulled him to her before their faces were more than a few inches apart. "Don't stop," she said as she took his mouth in hers.

By God but now a team of wild horses could not drag him away from her. All the reasons why he shouldn't—why they shouldn't—threatened to invade his thoughts but he pushed them away with the strength of a madman; aye, indeed, a man mad for her and what she had to give him.

When at last they disengaged, her hair was streaming about her shoulders, loosened from her braids. "Will you help me?" she asked.

As she reached to free the rest of her tresses, he began to thread his fingers through her long locks, finding the pins while he savored in the silkiness of her hair. It smelled like wildflowers; fresh and airy. He dipped his head to her neck, kissing the soft, smooth skin there and listening to her sighs. Oh, but it was those wee sounds she made that nearly drove him insane with desire. With each breath she took, the rise and fall of her breasts tantalized him and he found himself looking at those mounds as they peeked above the bodice.

His fingers found the ties at the front of her bodice. They hesitated there while he pressed her more closely against him. "Are you certain?" he asked, his mouth against her hair.

"I have never been so sure," she answered, her voice quivering.

His fingers found the end of her tie and he gently pulled it into submission, feeling the long strands separate in his hands. Even before the bodice was off, he had placed his hands inside, feeling her skin, hot and sleek. When it was time to slip the clothing off her arms, he did not know how he could stand being even inches away from her and as quickly as he could, he had taken her in his arms again.

Good Lord, but a woman wore far too many layers, he thought. Though his heart raced and his breath grew ragged, he was forced to slow down, to remove her skirts with another pull of ties, to slide her undergarments away from her, to see her standing before him with the firelight glancing off her skin, glossy with perspiration.

She reached for his shirt, pulling it over his head and discarding it on the floor along with her garments. Her green eyes had grown deeper in color, the pupils so large, so wanting... Her body trembled in his hands and he sought to hold her closer, to assuage her nervousness. He wanted to hear her cry out his name, he wanted her legs wrapped so tightly around his body that he could think of nothing else but her.

He lifted her into his arms and carried her to his bed, laying her down gently. He paused as he leaned over her, tracing the line of her jaw with his finger as she looked back at him. Her breasts were full and as he stood beside the bed, she rolled onto her side to watch him slip out of his breeches and boots.

She was everything he had ever imagined. So yielding, her body accommodated his every move, no matter how slight. He tried to be gentle but as their passions grew, they both abandoned all inhibitions until they were moving together as one. He wanted to explore every last inch of her and he wanted this night to last forever.

37

"Well and so there you'd be!" Fergus exclaimed as Wills stepped outside his home and quietly closed the door behind him.

"You'd wake the dead with that loud voice of yours," he answered.

"Wake the dead or wake your lady?"

"Both, if you want to know the truth of it," Wills said as he strolled toward the livestock enclosures.

Fergus fell in beside him, casting several sideways glances at him. "You bedded her, didn't you now?"

"Ach," he said. "You expect me to spill the details to the likes of you?"

Fergus grinned. "I knew it! I did."

"Say," Wills said, stopping to peer at Captain Stewart's house, "it would appear the captain has some company, 'eh?"

"You won't be changing the subject that easily," he said. But as the door opened and several men stepped outside, he stopped in his tracks.

Niall Garbh O'Donnell himself it was, and oh, but Wills would have recognized the man anywhere. He stood head and shoulders above the others; not as tall as Cahir O'Doherty, to be sure, but then no one he'd ever seen had come close to The O'Doherty's height. Still, he struck a commanding presence much like the men in the Scottish Highlands. His dark auburn hair was long and straight; the cold dawn air caught it but he didn't seem to register the frosty morn as he rolled his fingers through the strands, brushing it back from his face.

Wills began walking toward the group; besides The O'Donnell, his son and three other men chatted with Captain Stewart and Archie.

"What are you doing?" Fergus whispered hoarsely as he followed close behind.

"Good morning to you," Wills said, almost passing them by.

Stewart waved him over. "You remember The O'Donnell?" he asked. His eyes narrowed slightly so the message was clear. "And a few of his clan," he added, introducing the others.

Wills and Fergus shook their hands. "Chilly morning to be about," Wills said.

"Is it now?" Niall Garbh looked to the heavens for a moment. "I had not noticed."

"I appreciate the visit," Stewart said. "I will notify Lord Chichester immediately of your generous offer."

"Anything I can do to serve King James," Niall Garbh answered with the slightest bow. One of his men handed him the reins to his horse and he mounted before continuing. "Cahir O'Doherty is a dangerous man, prone to recklessness. You will need my help to navigate the Inishowen Peninsula. As you're undoubtedly well aware, I know every inch of it—as well as his hiding places." With that, he clicked his heels against the horse's sides and began to move off at a leisurely pace. "Good day," he called over his shoulder.

They watched as the men rode toward the edge of Fort Stewart. They continued slowly, their heads turning in each direction as if they were memorizing details, Wills thought.

"Captain, you aren't—"

"No, Wills."

"He can't be trusted."

"I am well aware of that."

"Then, why—" Fergus began but then caught himself. "Begging your pardon, Captain."

Stewart glanced at one and then the other. "I remember well what you overheard in Donegal, Wills."

"They were plotting, The O'Donnell included."

"I believe the man might have goaded Cahir into attacking Derry."

"Why would he have done that?" Wills mused. "He must have known that King James would not simply allow his settlers to be burned out of Ireland."

"He made me an offer, one that I shall send by courier to Lord Chichester today."

"An offer, sir?"

"He wants O'Doherty lands. And," he added, one brow rising, "he believes if he changes sides and fights with the English, he will be awarded the Inishowen Peninsula as his reward—as well as regaining other lands that once belonged to the O'Donnell clan."

"But his men were there at Derry," Fergus objected. "And the hostages at Burt Castle—as well as our spy, Elan—reported that he was furious there were not more spoils. Surely, you haven't forgotten—"

"No," Stewart said. "I have not. I will make a recommendation to Chichester that he is not to be trusted. However," he added, "it is prudent to give the impression that we are considering his offer. As long as he believes there's a chance he will be rewarded if he remains with us, perhaps it will take him and his men out of the fighting."

Wills noticed Tomas hurrying to catch up with them.

"What of this spy, Elan?" Stewart asked. "Have you determined her identity?"

"Tomas and Fergus both met with a dead end, I'm afraid," Wills answered. "They could not continue their questioning without raising suspicion."

"Find a way," Stewart said. "I want to know her role in all of this—and why she is carrying messages to us. I do not believe she is acting on her own."

"Could she be part of The O'Donnell's plan?" Fergus asked.

"I want proof."

As Tomas joined them, a horse and rider began approaching from the opposite direction from where Niall Garbh had departed.

"Fort Stewart appears much in demand this morning," Archie said.

They waited for the rider to reach them. Dismounting, he saluted Captain Stewart before continuing. "I come from Dublin, Captain, with a message from Lord Chichester."

"Come inside," Stewart said. Glancing at Tomas, Wills and Fergus, he added, "The lot of you."

⁜

The courier, Kendall Potter, finished off the cold meat and leaned back. "So there you have it, Captain. Colonel Richard Wingfield marches toward the Inishowen Peninsula even as we speak with a contingent of seven hundred men. He anticipates arrival later this day and wishes for you to be prepared to march on Burt Castle on the morrow."

"We will be ready," Stewart answered. "I have a hundred men under my command here, and I will send word to the settlers in this region as well. As you know, Doe Castle is also in O'Doherty hands, and there is word that Coleraine is under threat. It has been an uneasy existence in Ulster these past weeks."

"You should know," Potter said, taking a long swig of ale, "that all of Dublin—and London, for that matter—have been told of the atrocities perpetuated against our women at the hands of The O'Doherty."

"Atrocities?" Tomas asked.

Potter looked at Tomas as if he had grown two heads.

"Please elaborate," Stewart said with a slight wave of his hand.

Potter peered at the captain in the same manner. Then he shook his head as if to clear it and said, "It is common knowledge now, Captain, in all of Ireland and England as well, that The O'Doherty ordered all women taken at Derry to be stripped and marched naked to Burt Castle. Once there," he stole a look at the serving wench before lowering his voice, "all the men of the O'Doherty clan as well as those who joined them, were allowed their way with them." He shook his head. "Brutal, it was. Absolutely inhumane treatment; forced into all manner of sexual—"

"I think we understand." Stewart turned to Wills. "You were there when the women were taken to Burt Castle and again as they were released. Each was interviewed, as I recall. Were there reports of such treatment?"

Wills cleared his throat. "No, sir. There was not. The women were clothed as they left Derry and entered O'Doherty territory. They were clothed when they were released. And they reported having been fed under direction of Lady O'Doherty herself and, though they were held against their will without the ability to escape, they reported no ill treatment at all."

Potter made a loud noise as if dismissing this report.

"I wrote Lord Chichester myself," Stewart said, "reporting these details. Where did he hear of these atrocities?"

The courier shrugged. "I do not know the origins, but all of Ireland and England—most likely, Scotland too—are aware of it."

"There is, however," Stewart mused after a moment's reflection, "the matter of the soldiers taken at Culmore Fort and Derry. They are purportedly held in the dungeons at Burt Castle. There are civilians, as well, that continue to be held and we do not know their fate."

"May I trouble you, Captain Stewart, for a warm place to lay my head for a bit?" Potter asked. "I did not stop on the way from Dublin and I fear now that my belly is full, I am in need of a brief respite."

"Of course." Stewart stood and called to one of the Irish servants. "Please show Private Potter to the soldiers' quarters."

The men stood respectfully as the woman escorted Potter out of the room. Once out of earshot, Archie said, "What do you make of this, Captain?"

He shook his head. "Quite obviously, reports of barbarous acts against ladies—whether substantiated or no—will call for a ruthless response. I understand The O'Doherty has around a thousand men at his disposal now. They have run rampant across Ulster while we have awaited the king's men. Well, gentlemen, our wait is nearly over. Tomorrow the real battles begin."

"What can we do for you, sir?" Tomas asked.

"This woman Elan," he answered, "I want to know who she is and what her role is. I do not believe she is nothing more than a serving wench and I do believe she is in the confidence of The O'Donnell."

"I will inquire, sir."

"Dig deep, if you must. But find out." He turned to Wills and Fergus. "I also want to know where Cahir is located and more about Burt Castle."

"Aye, sir."

"Wait until dusk, if you wish, but be back before dawn. We will be prepared to march at first light and I want to provide Colonel Wingfield with as much information as possible."

"Aye, sir." Wills and Fergus took their leave. They stopped at the threshold and studied their surroundings for a moment. "So," Wills said, "it's to be our last day of peace for a bit."

"And you've called these past few weeks peaceful, have you?" Fergus asked.

"Well, The O'Doherty has not burned us out. There's that."

Fergus chuckled. "There is that, indeed." He stepped off the stoop and began to walk away. "I'll tend to your sheep, William Neely," he called over his shoulder. "I think you've someplace you need to be. Just make certain you get some rest in. I'll be at your door before the sun sets."

38

Sir Richard Wingfield had a cherubic face, round and pink, with overly full lips. He had a tendency in repose to look as if he was slightly smiling as though touched from above, and his hair was as fine and shiny as a newborn babe's. This angelic countenance belied his inner nature, however, as Wills was quickly discovering.

He was nearing sixty years of age, a time when most men of the time were handing over the reins to the younger set, but Sir Richard seemed determined to continue a lifetime of military service. His reputation was formidable and fierce; he had first served in Ireland some twenty years earlier before departing for battles in Portugal, France and Flanders. He returned to Ireland during the Nine Years War, was wounded and subsequently knighted for his bravery in battle. After another brief departure to France, he returned yet again, becoming the Marshall of Ireland, which gave him fifty permanent soldiers for all of Ireland.

He returned to Ulster, a place he knew every bit as well if not better than his native England, with more than seven hundred troops now under his command and an order from Lord Chichester to put down the O'Doherty Rebellion, making thick and short work of it.

Captain Stewart had relayed the general plans to Wills and Fergus as they returned from their reconnaissance of Burt Castle: they would attack and seize it and then sweep over all of the Inishowen Peninsula. Wingfield also carried with him a bounty offer of five hundred pound sterling for the head of Cahir O'Doherty once delivered to Dublin Castle. The amount offered was nothing short of a fortune and the entire camp was abuzz with individual braggadocio to capture and kill The O'Doherty.

Unlike the previous night when Wills and Fergus had slipped onto the Inishowen Peninsula with great stealth and secrecy, Sir Richard wanted everyone to witness the British, Scottish and even Irish Gaelic troops serving under his command. And indeed, more than seven hundred men marching toward Burt Castle was a sight to behold, if he said so himself, even if many of them were not quite in formation. It was a time, after all, in which men had competing duties such as his own and set a harkbus or a sword over their shoulders only as needed.

If a man had a horse, he was compelled to ride it and if not, his feet took a pounding over the rough and tumble Irish terrain. What made things particularly interesting for Wills was the introduction of a number of cannons, the rumor being that they would make short work of the castle walls.

As they entered the forest, Sir Richard commanded the troops to cut down any trees that provided an impediment to the army, a task that many took on with relish as if destroying the landscape was part of the retaliatory efforts. The occasional cottage buried deep in the woods was set upon with equal enthusiasm, expelling its residents, ransacking it and then burning it to the ground. By the time the troops had gathered in front of the tree line in full view of Burt Castle, many O'Doherty followers had rushed ahead to warn of their approach.

Wills and Fergus remained with Captain Stewart, who issued an order for his men to remain just behind the tree line and ready to charge the castle when ordered. It was, Wills thought, a memory that would long remain etched into his mind. There was something surreal in the air that day, a charge similar to that experienced during a thunderstorm, though the air was quite still. Not even the birds sang, he realized, as if all manner of flight and hoof had fled before their advance.

Battle could be boring, at least at first, and after the first few minutes most of the men sat upon the cold, hard ground, complaining of hurrying on the march only to wait in the end. Some were quiet and reflective; others debated the best battle strategy and tactics; and still others simply passed the time with cards or marbles.

The castle appeared impenetrable. If it was like others Wills had seen in Ireland, the walls would be four or even five feet thick and constructed of stone and lime. Towers stood five stories tall at each corner of the outer wall and as Wills watched, he could spot O'Doherty defenders along the parapets, readying their harkbus—presumably those stolen from Culmore Fort, he thought—and watching the arriving army with great interest. At one point, he could have sworn he had spotted a woman walking briskly along the parapet and though it was too great a distance to know for certain, he suspected it was Lady O'Doherty herself, perhaps arriving to motivate the defenders.

The cannon had not been arranged yet when those at Burt Castle fired the first shots. The stone cannonballs fell short of the tree line, which didn't prevent many of the men from scrambling backward, prompting their commanders to order them to return to the front. Sir Richard seemed unperturbed by them and used a fancy device the likes of which Wills had never seen before to somehow calculate the O'Doherty cannons' trajectory and distance capable. Then the English cannons were brought into a solid line amidst great fanfare and a single shot was fired off, which landed just short of the outer wall. Then all the cannons were moved forward and another was fired until Sir Richard was confident in their placement.

The bombardment was enough to deafen a man, Wills thought. Smoke filled the air between the English forces and Burt Castle, often so thick the commanders had to space out the shots so they could determine the effectiveness of each shelling. Now the cannons were firing equally in both directions, but unlike the English, the O'Doherty cannons were wedged into place inside the towers, requiring the enemy to move closer to have an effect. Shots occasionally rang out from holes in the towers built for harkbus but the efforts were haphazard, the men apparently concluding that they were only wasting their ammunition at this range.

It was excruciatingly slow. As the morning dragged on, some men took to napping despite the noise while others grew impatient and still others carried on as if there was no battle at'al, pulling out salted meat to chew or continuing with their games of cards. Wills decided one could learn a lot about a man in a situation such as this. Having never witnessed a real battle before, he was eager to learn—albeit from an enforced distance—how the cannons were loaded, the barrel pivoted up or down to achieve greater range and effectiveness, and how smaller arms were kept in reserve until the cannon presumably weakened the opponent.

Several of the commanders, including Captain Stewart, used a curiosity they called a spyglass, which fascinated Wills. Moving closer to the artillery, he determined the funnel was used to see the other side more clearly, a presumption that was made clearer an hour into the bombardment when one of the commanders issued the order to cease fire, which was repeated down the line. All eyes turned to Burt Castle; men that he had assumed were asleep opened their eyes or sat up to watch the next phase unfold, while others stopped their activities to stand and observe.

As the smoke cleared, Wills could barely make out white flags waving from the center of the parapet, directly over the thick wood doors set several stories lower into the outer wall. Three men were selected from the English side, who mounted horses and waited. Then the wood doors were slowly opened inward, until several horsemen could be seen, the center of whom held a white flag.

"Fire the shot now," one Scot mumbled behind Wills, "while the doors are yet open."

"Charge the castle," said another, coming to his feet.

The commanders no doubt heard the growing commotion behind them. Captain Stewart moved to his troops, coming to stand just a few feet from Wills. "Stand your ground, men," he called out. His order was repeated by Archie, whose voice boomed across the lines of men. "We do not continue the attack under a white flag!"

The orders were repeated up and down the ranks while the men on either side rode out to the middle of the meadow. A few words were spoken and it appeared that a note exchanged hands. Then one of the men took the note and galloped back to Colonel Wingfield while the others remained in the meadow.

As luck would have it, the colonel was standing next to Captain Stewart when the note was delivered, and

Wills was not even forced to strain his ears to hear the note read aloud to the commanders.

"It is a communication from 'Lady Mary Preston O'Doherty, daughter of the Viscount Gormanston and wife of Sir Cahir O'Doherty, Lord of Inishowen,'" Wingfield announced. "It reads, 'We hold as our guests at Burt Castle Captain Henry Hart and his young son Henry; Susan Steyning Montgomery, daughter of Lord Philip Steyning of Holnicote, Somerset and wife of Bishop George Montgomery of Derry; and Margaret Montgomery Shaw, sister of Bishop George Montgomery and daughter of Adam John Montgomery, 5th Lord of Braidstone also wife of James Shaw of Greenock, Renfrewshire, Scotland, among others. Should your shelling continue and should it breech our walls, I wish to inform you that we shall plug the holes with the bodies of our guests, beginning with Susan Steyning Montgomery.'"

Wingfield peered over the note at the men in the meadow and Burt Castle beyond. Wills followed his gaze, spotting a woman standing at the parapet above the doors, which were now closed. The commanders then conferred with varying opinions from bombing everyone into oblivion to a ceasefire. Finally, he turned the note over, wrote something on its back, and read it aloud to his commanders:

"'My dearest Lady O'Doherty, it would be my pleasure to cease bombardment of Burt Castle provided you surrender now to Crown forces. Should you surrender, you and your people will receive fair justice under King James' Court of Law for your roles in the rebellion. Should you plug the holes with the bodies of your guests, justice shall still prevail and I fear you shall be dealt with in harsher terms, possibly losing your head or put to death by hanging.'"

He then folded the note and returned it to the rider, who rode back to the center of the meadow and presented it to the Irish men awaiting him. One rode back to the castle, awaited the great gates opening, passed within and the gates closed behind him. After what seemed an extended period of time, the man reemerged, rode to the center, said something so brief that he barely paused his horse, and then all three men returned to Burt Castle. As the English forces returned to Wingfield, one announced, "She said, sir, 'So be it and their deaths shall be on your head.'"

At that point, the cannons were ordered to continue firing.

"Colonel Stewart, sir," Wills said. "May I have a word with you?"

"Aye, Wills," Stewart said, moving away from Wingfield. "What is it?"

"I couldn't help but overhearing, sir, but the thought occurred to me, if Lady O'Doherty is sending the note, then Cahir must have fled Burt Castle."

"Aye, and the thought occurred to me as well."

"Have you heard from Tomas?"

"No, sir."

"We must assume The O'Doherty took some of his forces with him and has moved deeper into Inishowen to the safety of his clan. Once Burt Castle is in our possession, I anticipate our forces sweeping over the entire peninsula."

"Aye, sir."

Colonel Wingfield called to Stewart and he left Wills' side. Wills continued to watch the bombardment or what he could see of it through the smoke. Eventually, the rounds from the castle began to land too close to some of the troops and they were ordered to pull back a few yards.

The afternoon wore on. Scouts spotted livestock not far from the castle and troops were sent to kill or capture the sheep and cattle. It sickened Wills to consider that some of the animals would be put to death for no reason other than their masters were O'Dohertys, even though he understood that if the attack were to continue without effect, it would turn into a siege. Then all food must be destroyed or removed lest a raiding party leave the castle and somehow seize food that could continue to sustain them. It reminded him of his youth in Scotland when neighbors to the north stole their sheep and they stole them back. It seemed so long ago now, as if it had all happened to someone else. He didn't quite know when precisely it had occurred but somewhere along the way, he had left that boy behind.

As dusk began to descend, potato fields to the west and north of Burt Castle were set ablaze. They burned through the night, lighting up the skies over Ireland almost as if it were day. Wills, along with most of the others, attempted to sleep but his thoughts were consumed with Rhiannon. Oh, and for certain she would be safe, as a contingent had been left to defend Fort Stewart in their absence, but still he could think of little else.

The winds off the Atlantic fanned the flames overnight catching much of the forest on fire behind Burt Castle, a circumstance that he was certain was noted in the castle itself. As he drifted off to sleep sometime in the wee hours of the morning, his dreams were a disjointed collection of soldiers in the dungeons, bodies plugging holes, the Inishowen Peninsula ablaze and Rhiannon's gentle face.

39

They surrendered the next day, May 20, 1608. As Crown forces swept through the castle, they freed the hostages, which consisted of a dozen citizens and roughly seventy soldiers. Mary O'Doherty was questioned at length but she provided no information on her husband's whereabouts or intentions. She was then sent under guard to Dublin, where she would be placed into the possession of her father until such time as her trial for treason began.

Cahir O'Doherty read the note hastily written by one of his wife's guards before passing it into Elan's hands, who had then turned northward, traveling deeper into Inishowen until she arrived at Inch Island bearing the news of Burt Castle's capture.

He made his way to the shore, where he sat on a large flat boulder overlooking the Lough Swilly. He watched the waves crash against the rock and listened to the sounds of seabirds for a bit before his thoughts turned to Eire's history and his role within it.

The Gaelic had ruled Ireland for more than a thousand years; the history so intermingled with myth and legend that it was impossible to determine what was real and what was not. But this he did know: there had been four major Gaelic Lords in Ulster and now there was only himself. Oh, and for certain there was no need to rehash in his mind all that had transpired to leave him alone in this fate. He had been a mere boy when The O'Neill, The Maguire and Rory O'Donnell had been at their finest of glories, and it had only been a year since all three had fled Ulster to raise an army in Spain—an army that was taking its time in coming, if in fact it ever intended to help the Irish cause at'al.

He turned to look back at the O'Doherty castle. It rested above him atop a cliff, a lone sentinel that overlooked the ancient burial ground at Grianan Aileach Fort—a ringed fort dating back more than four thousand years—as well as the village of Buncrana to his south; from the beaches along the lough to the rolling hills, the forests to the meadows. It was nearly two centuries old; built on this strategic island precisely because of the extensive views, vistas that would allow them now to spot a retaliatory force should there be one—and he had no doubt there would be.

Inch Castle itself had been constructed by Lord Neachtain O'Donnell, who had owned the land on the opposite side of the Lough Swilly, for his wife's father, Lord Cahir O'Doherty, a man for whom he was named. It was meant to symbolize the alliance between the two clans and now, some two hundred years later, he would depend on Niall Garbh O'Donnell to assist him as he had vowed to do, by defending the lands at the base of the Inishowen Peninsula, lands that belonged to O'Donnell and O'Cahan clans.

His own people had been spread throughout the Inishowen Peninsula from Burt Castle to this castle on the western side to Carrickabraghy Castle at the northern peak as well as others. Now that Burt Castle had fallen, what did that mean for the fate of The O'Donnell and The O'Cahan? There was nothing in the note to reflect their lot so he knew not whether they had been captured or killed. There had been scant information about his own clan; though he understood there had been no fatalities during the attack, he did not know how many might have been arrested and were, at this very moment, perhaps in the dungeons at Burt Castle under English guard or sent to Dublin Castle to await trial.

And Mary—Mary—God bless the woman; she had taken on the Irish cause despite her English ties. How he wished he was with her now, and how his heart ached with the thought of her being handed over to her father to await her trial for treason. No, this was not how this was meant to end.

He heard footsteps approaching and turned to watch Phelim MacDavitt make his way toward him on the meandering path. Directly behind him were three men from the O'Doherty and MacDavitt clans; men that he knew he would call upon to take the rebellion to its very end.

"Cahir," Phelim said as he drew near.

Cahir nodded in greeting.

"I just heard about Mary. She's a feisty one, she is. She'll hold up."

"Aye. I know she will." He hesitated. The weight and the fate of Ulster lay squarely on his shoulders. Eager to move the subject away from his beloved wife lest his heart grow heavier still, he said, "Since the burning of Derry, we've had decent fortune in amassing more than a thousand Irish defenders across Ulster, have we not?"

"We have indeed. You have given the Irish what they had been waiting for; a chance to expel the English and regain our lands." Phelim stroked his beard. "There's a rather large English force, however, wishing to stand in our way of victory. What would your orders be for us?"

"The way I see it, we have no recourse but to march on The Pale." At the mention of it, Phelim's eyes grew wide with a mixture of surprise and eagerness. The Pale was a bastion of English settlers along the eastern edge of Ireland, the opposite side from where they now stood.

"That would mean marching out of Ulster and into the center of the island," Phelim said.

"It would. It would serve two purposes: we would be drawing the English out of Inishowen as we take the fight to their own. And from The Pale, we can take Dublin."

"Take Dublin and soon all of Ireland would be Irish once again," Phelim said.

Cahir nodded. He knew from the look in Phelim's eye it had not escaped his attention that it could save Inishowen from certain devastation. While the English burned the rest of Ulster in recent years, hanging Irish — whether they be man, woman or child — and creating the purely English-made Irish famine of 1603, Inishowen had remained untouched only through his well-publicized alliance with the Crown. Now that the partnership had been terminated in spectacular fashion, there would be hell to pay unless he overcame Crown forces swiftly and completely. "If only I knew whether the Spaniards were coming."

"That would tip the scales in our favor for certain," Phelim said. "But there has been no word from the Earls. And now that Burt Castle has fallen, we cannot afford to wait."

"True indeed. We must strike them now with all we've got." He began the climb toward Inch Castle. As the others fell into step, he said, "We shall leave a contingent here at Inch Castle to defend it."

"And the others?"

He stopped when he came upon a stick. Picking it up, he began to draw a line in the soil. "We must move out of the Inishowen Peninsula altogether. It is too far and would take too long to travel by land toward Burt Castle."

"The enemy is there. We could attack them on our lands."

"Aye, but there is no advantageous terrain on which to make a stand. And I would rather draw them away from our people, our livestock and our food stuffs."

"What do you propose?"

As the men gathered around, he drew a rough outline of Ireland. "We send word into all of Ireland, to all our allies and friends that we are marching south. We must gather more men and munitions."

"We can send the couriers out immediately."

"The main force leaves by boat tonight." He drew a line from Inch Island across the Lough Swilly. "Under cover of darkness, we row to MacSweeney territory."

"What of Fort Stewart? How do we depart Inch Island without their sentries seeing us?"

"Aye, it is here." He drew an 'x' along the southeastern shore of the Lough Swilly. "We leave to our north and land here, in the vicinity of Magherawarden's beaches. From there, we march on Donegal."

"Donegal."

"If we can seize Donegal—and of that I have no doubt—we can cut a clear path to The Pale and on to Dublin. The English will be forced to withdraw from Ulster to combat our threat. And by moving through other clan territories, we leave each clan in defense of their own restored lands once the battle is won."

Phelim studied the rudimentary drawing. "I say we burn Fort Stewart."

"Why?"

He peered at him as if he was mad. "They're Scottish settlers, same as those at Strabane—hell, same as half the villages we've burned throughout Ulster these past weeks. We will not have control of all of Ireland until we have expelled every blasted one of them and burned down their settlements so they won't come back."

"Niall Garbh O'Donnell has been to see Captain Stewart."

"I am aware of that."

"He says he's a peaceful man; more like Docwra was."

"Do not forget it was under Docwra that much of Ulster burned," Phelim growled.

Cahir cupped his chin in his hand. "I wish to move quickly," he said at last. "I do not wish to get bogged down close to Inishowen. I say we send word to The O'Donnell once we have reached Magherawarden that he should move on Fort Stewart. While he is engaged there, we travel to Rosnakill and down the coast to Kerrykeel, then onward to Baile na nGallóglach."

Phelim picked up a second stick and drew an 'x' southwest of Baile na nGallóglach. "Then say this is Donegal here, we would have a clear path overland to it through MacSweeney and O'Donnell lands."

"Aye. So if The O'Donnell moves to capture and burn Fort Stewart, he would be in position to join our forces at Baile na nGallóglach."

"Do not forget Crown forces are in the vicinity of Burt Castle."

"Are you daft, man? How could I forget? It's where my Mary was taken."

"I am only saying that their forces would not be far from Baile na nGallóglach."

"Then if we are engaged, we take a stand there. If not, we continue on a straight path to Donegal. It's of far more strategic importance."

314

p.m.terrell

"It is. And we shall need all the reinforcements we can muster."

"I've no doubt we can. It's our independence we are talking about. The restoration of our Gaelic lands!"

"McMonagle and Maguire lands are close by; we'll send couriers to each. Perhaps as word travels back to The Maguire, he will return with the Spanish troops…" As he spoke, his voice trailed off. Ah, but if only that could happen, Cahir thought. But it would take weeks for word to reach Spain—presumably The Maguire's present location—and weeks more for the Spanish army to arrive. By then, they must have gained control of all of Eire.

"Once we seize Donegal," Cahir continued, "We cross almost due east to The Pale."

"By then, we should have the full force of The O'Donnell, Maguire, O'Neill and McMahon clans."

"Aye, as well as many others. We take the fight straight to The Pale and then on to Dublin." He stopped abruptly. Once in Dublin, he would free Mary. Would she be held in a dungeon at Dublin Castle? He wondered. Or would they relinquish her indefinitely to the custody of her father? He forced his thoughts back to his strategy. "With the capital city fallen to Irish forces, we shall drive the settlers off the island once and for all."

"And you, Lord Cahir O'Doherty," Phelim said with a smile, "You, the remaining Gaelic King, will have orchestrated the entire campaign. You shall be the first High King of Ireland in modern times."

Cahir took a deep breath. "Are we clear on our plans then?"

"Oh, I'd say we are. I will send couriers out immediately so all clans from here to Donegal and from Donegal to The Pale and Dublin shall expect us at their doorsteps."

Cahir nodded. "It's set then." He scrubbed through the rudimentary drawing with his stick to obliterate it, though there was scant chance an enemy would find it there on Inch Island. Then he began the trek up to the castle. "We leave tonight."

40

How hot must a fire become to destroy a stone castle? Wills thought as he watched O'Doherty's Keep at Buncrana burn. It had been said the keep was built in the 14th century in anticipation of the Spaniards landing on Ireland's shores as needed allies to fight the English. The Spanish soldiers never arrived; the English did. And for nearly two centuries, the stone structure had sat just north of the fork around Inch Island, guarding the southern portion of the Inishowen Peninsula.

With an edict from Lord Chichester at Dublin, Colonel Wingfield had ordered it set on fire, which turned out not to be an easy task at all. Wills and Fergus had been ordered inside along with a number of other soldiers, to set fire to the furnishings room by room. Oh, and they went up in blazes, they did—stunning draperies, overstuffed chairs and imported rugs. He coughed now as though reminded of the smoke he had inhaled. His eyes burned as well and rubbing them did no good as his hands were as soot blackened as his face and clothing.

It was a dicey thing, it was, to get two dozen men into a castle of that size, sweep through it room by room with torches, and not burn themselves down in the process. They had barely made it off the stoop when flames began to leap so far out of the windows that all were forced to retreat to avoid embers dropping on their heads. Now there was nothing to do but watch it burn.

And to be sure, they had not been the first to arrive at O'Doherty's Keep. The place had been ransacked and he suspected none other than The O'Donnell himself. Aye, and Elan's words ran in his head still; did the man think he would get the spoils he'd expected from Derry from The O'Doherty instead?

Even a stone castle contained wood, something he discovered as he set the draperies and bedding ablaze; it would be the wood beams that kept the stone walls from falling inward on themselves or outward to the elements. Now that the wood was aflame, weakening those structural supports and burning through to the floor, the walls were in danger of imminent collapse.

He caught a glimpse of Tomas emerging from the forest and waved him over.

"Aye, and I wouldn't have known your mug at'al," Tomas said in greeting. "It looks as if you've painted yourselves for battle."

"The soot painted it," Fergus grumbled. "Such a bloody shame."

"Aye, and it is," Wills agreed. "When you consider all the work that went into building such a magnificent structure and then in a fit of rage, it's all gone in an instant."

"A fit of rage, you say? Or a power struggle that's been boiling over for centuries, more like it."

"I remember seeing that castle as a young boy," Tomas said. "Never went inside it; it wasn't to be for my family, you see. But I remember the tales of it, I do."

"Have you news?" Wills asked.

"And I do. It turns out that Elan is none other than Elan O'Donnell O'Doherty—aye, and you heard me right."

"She's both an O'Doherty and an O'Donnell?"

"Indeed she is. She's a cousin to Niall Garbh O'Donnell and from what I understand she's had his confidence since they were both wee ones. She married an O'Doherty and during the Nine Years War, he was killed at the Battle of Moyry Pass. Cahir O'Doherty took her into his keep, he did, vowing to support her for life in payment of the bravery of his kin."

"So she is more than just a serving wench," Wills said.

"Oh, and that she is. They rarely are lowly servants, you know," Tomas added thoughtfully. "To be in the direct employ of a chieftain, most especially one such as The O'Doherty, she would have had to have family connections."

"That makes sense, I suppose," Wills said. "It's much the same in England and Scotland. A man's—or a woman's—lot in life is determined by who their parents were and their parents before them."

"So, let me get this straight," Fergus said, wiping his face so it made the lines of soot even worse. "The O'Doherty swears to support her for life and yet she seeks out Wills here and the ear of Captain Stewart to tell them that same O'Doherty plans an attack on Derry?"

"And then she informs us of The O'Donnell's wish to meet with Captain Stewart," Wills continued, "to pledge his allegiance to the English forces."

"Duplicitous clan, aren't they now?" Tomas said with a wry smile.

"The problem with one that is duplicitous is you never truly know where their loyalties lie."

"Oh, I believe it's quite simple. Their loyalties always lie within themselves and whatever way the wind blows they have an instinct for survival; it allows them to move freely between factions so there honestly is no allegiance to anyone or anything other than their own welfare."

"So what does that mean for The O'Donnell?"

"Oh, and I can tell you what it means," Tomas said. "His forces have been all over the Inishowen Peninsula. I do not know how he manages it, but he has convinced the O'Doherty clan his men are there to fight alongside them and he has convinced the Crown he is there to burn out the rebels."

"So which is it?"

He shrugged. "As far as I can tell the latter. But they're cagey about it, they are. And I would not bet my supper that he won't change sides yet. It all depends on which way the wind blows, as I said..."

"We must find Captain Stewart," Wills said, "and inform him of Elan's identity—and also of what you know of The O'Donnell."

"It's tough to know friend from foe," Tomas said as they made their way toward the commanding officers. "Under the English, you would think this island was one country. But indeed, it is not. Each clan's lands is a country unto itself. And sure, fighting has occurred between them for centuries and so have alliances, and they change faster than the seasons."

"Have you news of which clans are with The O'Doherty?"

"No one seems to know where The O'Doherty is," Tomas said with a roll of his eyes. "There's some talk he is at Carrickabraghy."

"That would be too obvious, wouldn't you think now?"

"Perhaps. But it's said to be the most fortified castle in all of Ireland."

"One thing's for sure," Fergus said, "there are only two ways to attack it. By land, we'll be rolling over all of the Inishowen Peninsula. There's no doubt about it but they would know we were coming days in advance and they'd be waiting for us, they would. By sea, their cannons will have our boats at the bottom of the sea before we're in position."

"There's Captain Stewart," Wills said, pointing. "We'll provide this information and we'll wait for his orders. It's all we can do."

A collective exclaim rose up and they turned to watch a portion of one stone wall collapse. "Well, that's that for O'Doherty's Keep, 'ey?" Fergus said.

"I wouldn't count it out just yet," Tomas said. "Or The O'Doherty, either. Castles have been burned before, only to rise up bigger and stronger than they were in the beginning."

41

The clouds over the Inishowen Peninsula have been swept in from their journey across the ocean through time immemorial; fat with moisture, they churn and roil as they dot the skies with shades of tumbling gray. They have always created a dance with the moon, swirling around it, dipping, alternately disappearing and reemerging. As the row boats were lowered into the water of the Lough Swilly, Cahir felt as though they were calling to him now, not as puffs of moisture but as the spirits of all those that had gone before him, from his father John O'Doherty to all the lords and chieftains and kings in a lineage stretching back countless centuries.

There were a dozen boats or more sweeping into the current of the lough and surely a sailing vessel would have taken them all much more swiftly into MacSweeney territory but it would have created a higher profile, something that was now necessary to avoid. Cahir stepped into the last one, helping to push it off from shore with his oar but he hesitated for a moment while he took one last look at his castle sitting high atop Inch Island.

Oh, and for certain it was not the first time he left the Inishowen Peninsula to participate in battle. Hadn't he done it for nine long years before the agreement between the Irish and the English that granted these past few years of uneasy peace? And hadn't he left his beloved Mary countless times before as he rode off to battle, seeing her brave face as she waved goodbye, knowing she held her tears until he could no longer see her because she never wanted him to worry about her or her fate?

And yet this time felt different. This time he did not ride out in front of his clansmen on his shining stallion, sitting proud and tall as he rallied them all. This time he did not march forward in full sight because he was fighting alongside the English Crown. This time it was not Mary standing before him waving her farewells but only a memory of her. And this time he was worried about her, knowing she had been forcibly taken from Burt Castle and was even now riding forward under guard to Dublin.

Would she look up at the moon this night, he wondered, and feel him miles away staring at the same? Would she understand that he would come for her; despite all the battles that might lie before him, all the men he may have to slay, he would appear one day to whisk her back to their beloved Inishowen?

He wanted to memorize the way the castle looked atop that formidable cliff; the way the stone appeared blue as it rose against the night skies. He wanted to remember the way the clouds had rolled in from the sea, how they mingled with the mists rising from the lough to enshroud them in their embrace. Too swiftly, the mists grew heavy and thick and too quickly he lost sight of Inch Island.

He turned his back to the peninsula and focused on moving upstream away from Fort Stewart and toward the northern edge of The MacSweeney's territory. The others sat silently as well, and only the occasional lap of water told him there were other boats through the heavy fog, all rowing in the same direction. He had been explicit in his instructions: there was to be no talk until they reached Magherawarden and it would be minimal until they were safely inside one of The MacSweeney's keeps.

One boat had left hours earlier containing only three men. It had been their mission to reach their ally before the others had departed in order to alert them to their approach. It was never prudent to wander into another clan's territory under cover of darkness and certainly all one's senses would be on high alert with the burning in Ulster and the taking of Burt Castle.

As the mists continued to swirl and they steadily progressed northward, the skies began to turn a vibrant shade of pink. At first he thought it was caused by bonfires and his heart nearly skipped a beat as he considered it could be the northwestern edge of the Inishowen Peninsula but as he strained to see, he realized it was the Aurora Borealis. Aye, and it was unusual to see it in April, he thought, and more often than not, it was green and blue. He could not help but wonder if it was a sign from those spirits he had felt earlier, and a foreboding began to grow deep within him. He shook it off; he had never been one to shrink from battle and the higher the odds, the greater the victory. As he turned his thoughts toward triumph, the pink spectral disappeared as suddenly as it had arrived.

The MacSweeneys were originally Gallowglass, an Irish term for foreign warriors. They had arrived in Ireland perhaps three hundred years earlier. They had been a Scottish clan of the Highlands, or so he'd been told, but they had mixed so thoroughly with Norsemen that they became a breed unto their own. Some were as tall as Cahir O'Doherty; broad shouldered and muscular, they embodied the fierce independence of both the Vikings and the Scottish Highlanders—a clan one wouldn't want as enemies. They spoke a slightly different dialect from the Irish Gaelic, even though they had been in Ireland for centuries. Their lands were purported to be among the wildest in all of Ireland.

The clan had been divided into three branches: the Fanad, the Doe and the Banagh. All had, to some extent, made an uneasy peace with the English just as Cahir had, though the MacSweeneys had never truly trusted the English and made it known they were simply biding their time. As a result, the English had never trusted them and most especially Lord Chichester, whose prejudice against anyone with "Mc" or "Mac" preceding their name was well-known. Speculation abounded that his distrust originated with the MacSweeneys. Their lands were nearly surrounded by the O'Donnell territory and the O'Doherty's Inishowen and if he could count on anyone at all, he knew the MacSweeney branches would rally to the support of the Irish cause.

To be sure, there was not much of anything at Magherawarden, which was precisely why Cahir had selected it. The beaches were wide here, the sand nearly bleached white, and unlike most of his own lands, the terrain was fairly flat, giving way to rolling hills and meadows. They steered their boats toward craggy black rocks that seemed a poor match for the gleaming beaches and there they found the entrance to a cave where they had arranged to hide their boats.

As Cahir entered it, he felt transported to another day and another time for there had been many a day in which he had played with the MacSweeney and O'Donnell lads in those caves that dotted northwest Ireland. They were filled with strange symbols, many of them also found near Carrickabraghy, purportedly etched into the stone thousands of years in the distant past. He used to wonder about the people that had walked the shores then; wondered at the reasoning behind their peculiar symbols. Now as he pulled his boat alongside the others, he was struck again by the course of history and the peoples that had come and gone.

"All are accounted for," Phelim whispered. His voice echoed in the confines of the cave, his whisper growing into a chorus of hissing spirits.

Cahir motioned for them to follow him onto the beach. Once there, he said quietly, "Then we are ready to begin our march to Rosnakill."

"It is nine, perhaps ten miles," Phelim said.

"Aye, and as we discussed, if our scouts have not yet secured the necessary horses, we may need to walk the distance." He peered at the skies. Their skin and clothing were already glistening with the fine mist that had fallen upon them on the lough and there was no sign it would let up anytime soon. Ah, but that was Ireland for you, and the gentle water would keep them well hydrated on their trek.

They would travel nearly due west until they reached a crossroads marked by several small dwellings. Then they would turn south before heading west once more.

If luck was with them, they would reach the village long
before dawn's earliest light. They would catch a few short
hours of sleep before mounting MacSweeney horses.
Then they would turn south to follow the Broad Water
to Kerrykeel.

42

Rhiannon awakened with a start. Though the embers had died and Wills' home was cold, she found her hair and skin soaked through. Sitting up, she pulled her knees against her body and rested her chin on them.

She knew what had awakened her; it had been the dream again. It was a strange dream, she had to admit, a dream in which she found herself walking through the heavy fog that rolled in from the sea. It was always so thick in her dreams that she could not see the ground beneath her feet and yet she knew she had to get somewhere. Where, she didn't know, but it was an urgent feeling as if her life depended upon it. Her arms were outstretched, her fingers feeling through the fog but never quite touching that which she sought. She was always alone and as she stumbled deeper and deeper into the thick mists, they began to encircle her like phantoms of giant, deadly snakes. They coiled around her body and grew tighter, constricting her until she could no longer breathe. It was then that she always awakened, gasping for breath and drenched in perspiration.

Gazing around the room in an attempt to fully awaken and shake off the nightmare, she found the shadows in the bedroom were long and dark. Rising, she made her way into the next room where she stoked the embers and laid more wood upon them. After quite a while, she was able to coax it into flames worthy of cooking, though it was still several hours away from morn. To be quite honest with herself, she hadn't wanted the fire for warmth but rather for light. It had been days since she had seen Wills and she longed for his presence so intensely that her chest was pained with the effort.

She wrapped a plaid about her shoulders and opened the door. Stepping onto the stoop, she took a deep, cleansing breath. Ah, but there was nothing quite like the Irish night, she thought. She strained to see the skies through the thickening clouds. She loved star gazing. There was something about looking into the skies that reminded her how very insignificant she really was and how enormous the universe was in comparison. It often made her problems feel miniscule, an advantage to be sure when worries threatened to overcome her.

Something caught her eye and she instinctively recoiled. She grasped the door's handle behind her and quietly closed it, cutting off the light from the fireplace. Once in the shadows, she struggled to catch the movement again. A moment later, she was rewarded with the silhouette of a man rushing from tree to tree. He stopped at the first door down the path from where she stood, banging on it until a dog began to howl and the door was opened. There was a brief exchange and then he was off, banging on the next door. And so it went until half the inhabitants were already awake by the time he reached their homes.

Wills, she thought with a sudden panic. Oh, dear God, please don't tell me Wills and the others were attacked!

She nearly jumped off the stoop and rushed into the path along with half her neighbors. It was a scrawny group for sure, as all the men between the ages of eighteen and sixty-five were away with William Stewart, presumably in the area of Inishowen, leaving only women and a few small children behind.

"The O'Doherty and his men are on their way to Fort Stewart," the young man said as he encountered them.

"How do you know this?" Rhiannon pressed.

"Our sentries along the Lough Swilly coast spotted a number of boats—several dozen of them—leaving Inch Island and heading straight for us. Well, not straight for us, as they'd have run into our men straightaway if they had, but heading northward." The man continued to walk the block, pounding on doors as he answered the ladies' questions. "Gather in the center of the path there and I'll make an announcement just as quickly as I have everyone together," he said finally.

The flush that Rhiannon had felt inside Wills' bedroom wore off with the suddenness of a thunderclap and she was left standing in the middle of the path, switching from one bare foot to another as she tried to remain warm under the thin plaid. Everyone, it seemed, was dressed identically, their bedding undergarments inadequate for the night air and the plaids woefully inept.

When the young man returned, he did not appear to notice their various stages of undress. Instead, he rolled a stump into the center of the path and scrambled atop it to be heard.

"The O'Doherty clan is invading the Stewart lands," he announced. As a chorus of astonishment and panic began to rise, he waved his hands to tamp down the outcry. "Quiet, everyone, quiet. We believe The O'Doherty himself will attack Fort Stewart at dawn and your homes, we fear, are between the Fort and the enemy."

"We should run to Fort Stewart!" one woman cried out.

"No," he answered frantically. "You will not be safe there."

"Why not?" Rhiannon asked. She moved toward the front so she was only a few feet from him. "The fort is surrounded by a high stone wall. Certainly we will be safer there than here?"

"Normally you would be," he answered. He brushed perspiration from his brow. "But most of the men are north of Burt Castle, taking the fighting onto the Inishowen Peninsula. We have sent for them but they will be several hours—possibly even a day—behind The O'Doherty. We believe he will attack at dawn and we are vastly outnumbered. We cannot hold the fort."

"What are you suggesting we do then?" a stout woman bellowed. "Cook a stew and open our doors?"

Again, he waved his arms in an attempt to quiet them. "You'll all be escorted to Baile na nGallóglach."

"Baile na nGallóglach?" a young woman round with child exclaimed. "I have never even heard of this place."

"Baile na nGallóglach is further to the west. It is firmly inside O'Donnell territory and The O'Donnell himself has vowed to help Crown forces. Or maybe it's within MacSweeney lands," he hastened to add, "but The O'Donnell will help us, nonetheless."

"You don't even know where it is!" the stout woman argued.

"I know we have soldiers on their way from Fort Stewart right now, as I speak, to escort you there. And I know it will be safer for you to remain in the keep at

Baile na nGallóglach than on the shores of the Lough Swilly. And just as soon as our men arrive from Inishowen, we shall put down the rebellion and you can return to your homes."

Rhiannon no longer felt the cold ground under her naked feet. She no longer felt the frigid north winds raking across her bare cheeks, causing her eyes to water and her lips to become dry and parched. She only knew the fear that was rising from deep within her, bringing with it a sense of dread of what was to come and the memory of Derry burning all around her. Her eyes dashed across the crowd around her. Many of these women were in these houses in what should have been the relative safety of Fort Stewart precisely because their own homes were gone; whether they were at Derry or Strabane or any number of villages that were torched by the rebels, they already knew the horrors of seeing the enemy rain down upon them.

"When will the soldiers be here to escort us?" she asked, interrupting the others.

"Take only what you can carry," he said, her eyes locking onto hers. "And begin walking toward the fort. Those of you with horses should ride. You leave straightaway."

"What of those in the old O'Donnell castle?" one woman asked.

"They are leaving now as well," the soldier answered.

"How far is it?" another woman asked.

"Perhaps six miles," he answered.

Rhiannon was already making her way through the crowd before his reply fell on her ears. Six miles, she thought. It wasn't far, she told herself. Wills had taken his horse but certainly the soldiers at Fort Stewart would not force women and children to walk. My God, she thought as she remembered her aunt; there were many elderly that would have to ride. Six miles, she thought again as she entered Wills' house and scrambled for her clothes. Six miles could be two hours of walking or less than one by horse if it was relatively smooth terrain. But given the island's propensity for bogs and brambles, six miles often meant an entire day if it was measured by the route a crow flies versus the very real and dangerous detours one often was forced to make.

She slipped into her clothing and shoes, wrapping several plaids about her before making her way back to the door. With her palm on the handle, she stopped to look back. She had come here with nothing, she thought, as her possessions were either burned in Derry or waiting for her in Donegal. But was there anything Wills would save if he knew his home would be burned?

She rushed back to the fire and lit a candle from the flames before making her way around the room once more. Just outside, she heard women's and children's voices along with the occasional male. They weren't leaving yet, she told herself although she didn't quite believe her own words. He had taken his only pair of boots and his few pair of breeches and shirts, and there didn't appear to be anything else of importance. She had moved from the front room to the bedroom and was nearly done there when her eyes fell on the coat of arms. Rushing forward, she grasped the material and bundled it into one of the plaids she carried. Then she left the candle burning on the nightstand as she hurried back through the front room and to the door. Her hand was shaking as she grasped the handle. With one final look back, she opened the door and rushed through as the line of women and children began their journey to Baile na nGallóglach in the dead of night.

43

Wills was asleep in the very home he had helped torch the day before. The stench of smoke pervaded everything but that was true whether one was within the charred stone remains or without; the difference being that charred or no, the part of the structure that managed to remain provided shelter against the driving winds and cold drizzle. The rainfall had a particular effect on the icy embers, strengthening its odor until he had dreamed of setting it afire all over again. Even the shouts from men both inside and out morphed into those that had occurred as they moved swiftly from room to room, setting the furniture and draperies ablaze in a frantic race to destroy everything before they were destroyed themselves.

It was Fergus' voice that finally began to rouse him from his fitful slumber, a voice that began in an opposite corner and somehow seemed to fly directly into his face. Then he was shaking him by his shoulders, shoulders that were already shivering from the cold and lack of proper blankets.

"Wills," Fergus was saying, "Wills, wake up."

He might have cursed him under his breath; he heard himself muttering but didn't understand his own words. The days and nights all melded together; Derry was burning, then most of Ulster and now Inishowen. The inferno was coming around to form a complete circle. The jury was in. This was indeed Hell.

"Wills."

The one word was definitive, authoritative, and the voice had the power to bolt him completely awake. As he sat up, Captain Stewart swam into view.

"Wills," he said, bending to one knee in front of him, "you, Tomas and Fergus must leave immediately for Fort Stewart. We've just received word Cahir O'Doherty may have attacked at dawn."

He scrambled to his feet. "Attacked Fort Stewart, sir? The O'Doherty?"

"Aye," Stewart answered. "A courier has just arrived. The O'Doherty and a hundred or more of his men were seen leaving Inch Island. They believe they have landed just north of Fort Stewart with the intent to attack at dawn."

Still half-groggy, he peered beyond the ruins to the skies outside. They were gray, the cloud cover thick; but it was well past dawn. "Dawn tomorrow?"

"No; dawn today. A few hours ago. The courier left in the middle of the night before the attack."

Realization began to set in. "What are our orders, sir?"

"You three are to scout ahead. I need to know where they are and how many. Bring three more men with you to report back at intervals as usual. Archie is gathering our men and several hundred will march toward Fort Stewart within minutes of your departure."

"Aye, sir."

"I've fresh horses," Tomas said, "standing just outside."

Rhiannon's face swam before him as he quickly gathered his things. "Is there any word on the homes outside the fort, sir?"

"None. I shall require a full report of what stands and what has been destroyed." Despite his professionalism, Stewart's voice caught. "And who perished."

He didn't remember anything after that. He didn't remember rushing through the ruins to the horses. He couldn't recall packing his things into the saddlebags or mounting the horse. He didn't recollect selecting three more men but through the fog he heard his own voice, seemingly disembodied and distant. And it was several moments before the fog in his brain began to clear as the weak sunshine simultaneously burned off the haze, and he discovered he was well out of sight of their encampment.

The hours dragged on no matter how he urged his steed onward. Somehow through the image of Rhiannon's face floating in front of his eyes, he was able to determine that none of the enemy had arrived in force along the Inishowen Peninsula. In fact, it felt more like a land that all had abandoned; all but the phantoms of men, women and children forced to flee their homes as Colonel Wingfield carried out Lord Chichester's scorched earth orders. Gone was the thick underbrush in which the Irish could disappear and reappear at will; gone were the meandering, senseless trails that stopped abruptly well short of any goal; gone were the thick forests that held the chill and blocked the sun. In their stead were scores of trees toppled like piles of charred kindling, the leaves burned completely off so only the trunks remained like torsos of the dead. Smoldering embers that managed to survive the night's drizzle rose like apparitions until they blended into the mists, only to have the sun scorch them anew, sending their ethereal forms weaving and bobbing in their wake.

Occasionally, a person would appear that would cause Wills' eyes to pivot toward them, his senses now hyper alert, only to discover it was an old man or a young woman with a child clinging to her skirts. They walked like the living dead; even the children did not cry but looked up at him with enormous eyes whose souls seemed to have fled in the face of their onslaught, leaving only shells to move forward as if their bodies could do nothing else but place one foot in front of the other, destination unknown.

The history books would show the battles, he thought as he moved past them. They would record that Derry was burned, Strabane and others; but would they remember the nameless, faceless people he passed now? For surely not one of these women or children would have known what plans had been forming in Cahir O'Doherty's mind and had they known, there was naught they could do to stop him. Yet here they were, their lives shattered; their homes and livestock gone, their foodstuffs burned. Here they were to find a way to survive the day and then the morrow and then the next and some would not survive at all.

As they moved out of the burned forests and into the meadows, not even a bird seemed to fly overhead, as if all wildlife had been decimated. And still he urged his steed onward, registering in some recess of his mind that the others did the same and yet feeling completely, utterly alone.

They reached the outskirts of the Stewart lands and at the sight of the first homes, he pulled his horse up. He wandered, as did the others, around the scattered cottages, mentally surveying the crops in the field and the chickens still in their coups. He slipped off his horse and knocked loudly on the door, opening it before anyone inside might have the chance to answer, but he found no one. The embers were still smoldering in the fireplace as if someone would appear at any moment and stoke them alive. The bedcovers were thrown back, the imprint of a body still on the straw-filled mattress, as though someone had only just arisen.

He left quickly, mounting his horse as the others were doing. "We continue on," he said simply.

Their progress slowed as they drew closer to Fort Stewart. Several times Wills or one of the others stopped and tilted their faces upward, perhaps testing the air for the distinct pungent odor of burned wood. They found none but the familiar aroma of fireplaces that beckoned with their warmth instead of threatening with destruction. The paths were well worn here for the livestock that was customarily driven out to pasture but there were none in the fallow nor were the men they had left behind to tend to the crops and the herds.

Fort Stewart's stone walls were in view when they came across their own homes. They were connected in rows of six or seven, the front stoops only a few yards apart from one another, the backs separated by twining hedges only six inches tall at present, tiny courtyards with tinier gardens. He descended on his home as Fergus was entering his.

He registered nothing until he had entered the bedroom to find her gone. The emptiness flooded him and drained him, the hours upon his horse colliding with his emotions into a jumble of confused weariness. It was only then that he stood in the doorway between the front room and the bedroom and forced himself to register the facts so he could confront his next moves.

The fire still burned as if someone had brought it to life earlier that day, then left it to subside while they were gone only momentarily. A candle sat on the nightstand, the wax burned to its base, the light extinguished. The plaids were gone including the one Penarddun had sewn for him. It wasn't difficult to determine that his crest was gone as well; there was only a table and two chairs in the front room, a small bed and stand in the bedroom. Like other young men only beginning their odyssey, he didn't have many possessions but as he remained there in the doorway between the rooms, he felt far older than his years.

He arrived outside to find the others gathering in the middle of the path awaiting his orders.

"They are all gone," Tomas said.

"Is there no one about? Not one?" Wills asked.

"Not one."

He turned to peer at Fort Stewart. It appeared untouched as well; the gate closed. The one structure that rose higher than the wall—Captain Stewart's home—still stood, the windows intact, the darkened casements seeming to watch them like weary, guarded eyes.

"Aengus and Bhaltair," he said at last, "you two will scout to our north. Enlist any settlers you find to assist. See if you can find their boats; I want to know how many there are and how many likely fit in each. At any sight of the enemy, determine their numbers and locations and report back to me immediately. I will be somewhere between Fort Stewart and Broad Water."

As the two men hurried toward their horses, Wills continued, "Gregory, you will return to Captain Stewart after we enter the fort; we'll look for fresh horses there. Tell him we saw no sign of the enemy all the way to Fort Stewart and the homes still stand, and you'll report the fort's condition as well."

"Aye, sir."

"Tomas, Fergus." His eyes moved to the lookout towers. "If the fort has been deserted, we shall continue to our west toward Broad Water. If it has not, we shall discover the events of this past day and night for Gregory to report, and we will discuss our next moves."

No sooner had he finished speaking than all eyes turned toward a lone figure making his way toward them. It was a young man with golden hair and large blue eyes, made even wider by his expression, which seemed to be a mixture of surprise and apprehension. Wills immediately strode toward him.

"You're a soldier from Fort Stewart," Wills announced as he recognized him.

"Aye, Mister Neely. I am."

"Ian, is it not?"

"Aye, sir. Ian MacKenrick."

"What has transpired here?" Wills asked as he took his horse's reins and began the short walk toward the fort.

As the others fell in beside him, Ian answered, "There are six of us at Fort Stewart, sir. We spotted your horses from the tower. In the dead of night, one of our lookouts along the Lough Swilly sent word that The O'Doherty himself had left Inch Island and was moving toward our land just north of the fort. An attack seemed imminent, sir."

As they neared the gates, they were opened by another young man who appeared greatly relieved to see them.

"But an attack did not occur," Wills said, studying the ground inside the walls. He had hoped to see the settlers gathered there; had longed to see Rhiannon's face welcoming him back with a smile that said she was unharmed, but the grounds were as empty and silent as the meadows they had passed to reach it.

"No, sir. It did not."

"Where are the women and children from the homes outside the fort?"

"We moved them west, sir, to the village of Baile na nGallóglach."

"Why there?"

"We thought they would be safer there, sir, as it was further from Inishowen."

"You did not believe this fort was safer than MacSweeney territory?"

He shook his head. "The sentry that spotted their forces thought them capable of overwhelming the meager forces left here. We wished to remove the women and children from harm's way."

"Are you quite aware that Baile na nGallóglach is on MacSweeney land?"

"No, sir." His face grew pale. "We were not aware."

"How long have you been here, lad?"

"Four months, sir. But I was told Sir Richard Winkel was just north of Baile na nGallóglach near Cean-Maghair. Niall Garbh O'Donnell himself is with him, as is Henry O'Neill and Malmurray MacSweeney of Doe."

"You say a MacSweeney is with Sir Winkel?"

"Aye, sir. They have joined the English forces."

Wills hesitated. He did not trust Niall Garbh O'Donnell, of that he was sure. And if The O'Donnell, The MacSweeney and Henry O'Neill had sided with the English, why did Cahir O'Doherty cross from Inishowen to MacSweeney land? Unless, he thought, the others had arranged to turn on Winkel as The O'Doherty joined them. "And what do you know of their movements—The O'Dohertys?"

"We've sent scouts to our north—a group of ten—and we've heard back from them twice. They have seen no sign of O'Doherty or where he might have come ashore."

"How far north were they to go?"

"Well, it's MacSweeney territory," Ian said sheepishly.

"So, in other words, they are remaining on Stewart land."

He nodded.

"The irony is farcical," he breathed. "Did you not just tell me The MacSweeney had joined forces with the English? And you've sent the women and children onto MacSweeney land? You are to find those scouts and inform them that they are to spread out and move into MacSweeney territory. This is not the time to play it safe, man! We must know where they are and what their numbers would be. When the captain returns with forces, it is best we take the fight to them."

"Aye, sir." Though the young man's hands shook, he hurried to ready a horse.

"Gregory," Wills continued, calling the man forward, "Return to Captain Stewart and let him know what we have found here—and that scouts are still in search to our north." Turning back to the others, he asked, "Where are the other forces that had been stationed here?"

"Escorts," the soldier that opened the gates answered. "For the women and children to reach Baile na nGallóglach, sir."

"What of those at the O'Donnell castle?"

"They all left together."

"And they left in the dead of night? Before dawn?"

"Aye, sir."

"And how far is Baile na nGallóglach? Did they say?"

"Six miles, sir. More or less."

"Then they should have arrived there by now. Tomas, Fergus." As the two moved closer, he said, "We will obtain fresh horses here and set out for Baile na nGallóglach straightaway. We will gather as many forces along the way as practical. We must find Sir Winkel. With the captain's forces approaching from the east, we will gather a contingent along with Sir Winkel's men to form a flank on the west and surround The O'Doherty."

"And if we discover rebels at Baile na nGallóglach?" Fergus pressed.

"Then we fight them there. Tomas, should that occur, you will send word back to Captain Stewart so he knows of our situation."

"Aye, sir." He watched as Tomas and Fergus joined other men in swapping their gear from their spent horses to fresh ones. Without so much of a break to do more than fill their flasks with ale, they set out again. Dusk would soon be upon them and he aimed to reach Baile na nGallóglach by nightfall.

44

It was a tiny cottage with walls that seemed too close and windows that were much too small. It was a far cry from the castles Cahir O'Doherty had become accustomed to, and yet he had become all too familiar with these impromptu offices. These last few years had changed his life as relative peace had settled into Ireland yet he was amazed at how quickly his strategic and tactical prowess returned. He had grown from a boy to a man during the Nine Years War; had seen too much blood, too many atrocities, too much pain. And only a year earlier, he would not have believed it had someone told him he would turn against his long-time allies and yet here he was, plotting against them.

Niall Garbh O'Donnell stood across the table from him, pointing at the rudimentary hand-drawn map laid out on the table's surface. "Richard Winkel is here," he was saying, "on my clan lands at Cean-Maghair."

"Has he driven your people out then?" Cahir asked.

He chuckled. "Hardly. I have convinced them that I am on the side of The Crown forces."

Cahir chuckled briefly as he studied Niall Garbh. They had been both friends and enemies over the years, foes and allies; they fought together at times, nearly shoulder to shoulder, and at other times they had faced off across a battlefield from one another. He could change with the wind, which made him far more powerful at some times and quite vulnerable at others. Pragmatic, ambitious, he had seen his clan lands reduced in size yet he had remained responsive enough to English forces that he had avoided the fate of the Earls.

"So your people are encamped there with Winkel?"

"Some of my forces, aye. Others are on the Inishowen Peninsula, defending it against Wingfield's men there."

"I thank you, my old friend, for your aid."

"You would do the same for me, no doubt."

"No doubt." Cahir stroked his beard for a moment. "Who else is with you?"

"Malmurry MacSweeney is there."

"The MacSweeney Fanad of Doe Castle?"

"Aye."

"Has he sided with The Crown then?"

Niall Garbh shrugged. "You know The MacSweeney. They are a fierce bunch, the Gallowglass. They will play both sides to the middle, aligning themselves with the victor before the day is done."

"His clansmen have fought alongside me in this rebellion."

"He is well aware of that."

"What can I expect of him this night?"

"Hard to tell."

Cahir nodded as he considered his options. Cean-Maghair was a heavily wooded area, normally considered too wild for strangers to enter them. As such, it was the perfect spot for The O'Donnell to defend. They knew it, as they had known most of Ulster, like the back of their hands, able to disappear when needed only to reappear when one least expected it. The trails there were hidden from all but the most astute and a man's internal compass was of no use to him there at'al. And on this night, the clouds were thick and black and gray, the moon not much more than a sliver; the kind of night in which a man could easily get turned around and confused. Aye; it was the perfect night for an attack indeed.

"Henry O'Neill has joined The Crown forces as well."

"Henry O'Neill?" Cahir asked, surprised.

"Strategic move on his part," Niall Garbh said. "Hugh O'Neill showed him the devastation that could occur when one opposed the English. You remember his lands were nearly completely destroyed and his people almost annihilated, whether by war or English-induced famine."

"I remember it well." It had been the darkest period of Cahir's life; the blackest time for any Ulsterman.

"So Henry O'Neill," Niall Garbh was saying, "has chosen the other side for his people now that Hugh has fled Ireland. He hopes by siding with the English, some of the clan lands will be restored."

"So he is likely to remain true to the English this night?"

"Hard to tell."

"How many men in all?"

"A hundred and fifty, perhaps two hundred," Niall Garbh answered. "They have night watchmen positioned here—" he pointed to the map "—here and here."

"And we can count on your men this night?"

"You can." Their eyes locked.

"Then we encircle the camp and kill the night watchmen in silence before overrunning the camp."

"When?"

Cahir glanced at Phelim, who had been observing the exchange in silence. "We leave immediately."

"Spare me the time to return to camp," Niall Garbh said, "lest I raise suspicion by my absence."

Cahir nodded. "Leave one of your men with us. When we kill the sentries, he will notify you that the attack is imminent."

Niall Garbh signaled to one of the men behind him. "Quinlan, remain with The O'Doherty."

"Aye, sir."

Niall Garbh began to roll up the map but Cahir placed his hand atop his. "Leave it," he said.

They looked at one another for a long moment of silence and then Niall Garbh nodded. "I shall see you there." With that, he made his way out the door and into the night.

"Quinlan," Cahir said, "wait for me outside."

Quinlan nodded. Once he was outside and the door was closed behind him, Cahir turned to Phelim and their men. "What say you?" he asked.

Phelim shook his head. "We do not know which way The MacSweeney or The O'Neill will fight."

"It has not been lost on me that The O'Donnell could be setting an ambush for us."

"It would not be the first time."

"Aye." He met Phelim's eyes. "Take your men directly behind The O'Donnell. If he meets with anyone along the way—"

"I will send word to you."

"If practical, spread your men to an outer perimeter."

"If practical."

"Aye." Cahir knew the meaning was not lost on his friend and ally. "Slit the throats of the sentries. There is to be no sound until we overrun the camp. We will form several battle lines behind yours so we attack them in waves. Here shall be the code for the staghorns: one long blast heralds each wave of attack; two short blasts indicates The O'Donnell clansmen are with the enemy; three short blasts, the MacSweeney; four short blasts, the O'Neill. Otherwise, all Irish are to be considered allies."

Phelim nodded. "I will notify the men immediately."

Cahir slapped his friend on the shoulder. "I shall see you there."

"May God keep you safe."

"He always does, Phelim; He always does. And may He do the same for you."

<hr />

Cahir recalled a particular Gaelic dance he enjoyed. In times past, the tables and chairs in the Great Hall were removed so the floor was open and the dancers were arranged in a square with each person's partner facing them from across the room. As the music began, they moved toward each other with precisely timed movements before moving back then forward again. It reminded him somewhat of the tidal waves, swelling forward, retreating slightly, swelling again. And now as he waited in sight of the camp, he felt that same expectation.

He knew on the other side of camp facing him but hidden by the darkness, his troops waited to move inward just as they did, to meet in the middle like the couples in the dance. To his right and to his left, more lines waited that would also move to the center. He could feel the excitement in the air, the energy and expectations of his men, the urge to swell like the tidal wave and overcome the enemy swiftly before pulling back into the night.

The O'Donnell had not sent word back to him, which meant he should have reentered the camp without mishap or suspicion. Phelim's men had left immediately afterward and were now surrounding the camp slightly ahead of Cahir.

From his vantage point, he could plainly see a stone bridge. It arched gently over a narrow body of water, the ivy already multiplying from the warmer weather, cascading over its side as if it longed to reach the water. It was wide enough for a decently sized carriage, which meant it was quite adequate for the horses to charge across it; horses that were provided by the MacSweeney and O'Donnell clans. Whether Malmurry MacSweeney himself knew of his own clansmen's aid, Cahir would not be certain of his loyalties until they had routed the camp and they observed whether he rallied his men against them or with them.

Mists rose from the water beneath the bridge; mists that met the fog descending from above to create swirling eddies that effectively hid Phelim's men as they inched forward. A lone sentry stood on the opposite bank, his harkbus supported by one palm as it rested against his torso. His head dropped forward nearly to his chest, only to be jerked back with sudden attention. Then as the night owls performed their nocturnal song, his head descended once more.

Cahir could see two of Phelim's men as they made their way from the safety of the overgrown woods into the water, their hands reaching to the stone to steady themselves as they made their way across. Only one man appeared on the other side. The other dipped below the bridge to emerge on the opposite side outside of Cahir's view.

As the sentry's head slumped once more, Phelim's man rose from the water and rushed up the bank toward him. The sudden movement awakened the sentry and instinctively he rotated the harkbus into position to fire. But before he could get the shot off, the other man emerged from behind, wrapping his hand around his throat to slit it from ear to ear. The man collapsed and they dragged his body away from the bridge and onto the bank to clear the way for the coming onslaught.

The seconds passed. Beside Cahir stood a young man perhaps all of sixteen years old, his fingers nervously cupping the staghorn. The horn itself might have been a hundred years old and used countless times in battle; it would have passed from one generation to the next, the family proud of their role in defending their clansmen. This one was rounded into an almost perfect *o*, the diameter so large that it had been a fine buck indeed that had supplied it.

They waited. Behind him Cahir knew his men were becoming impatient, eager to make the charge, but there were two other points where sentries stood and only when the third was removed would the horns begin.

Phelim's line moved forward so they were only a few short yards from the bridge. When the first horn sounded, it came from a distance toward the south; one long blast. Then the second horn sounded to the west and with Cahir's nod, the young man beside him blew into his own horn, emitting one long blast.

Phelim's men rushed the bridge on horseback, their yells rising into the air like a demonic chorus. As sounds arose from the camp itself embedded in the woods, Cahir gave the command to sound the horn once more. Then he was off, leading the charge across the bridge with his own men, his cap and plume causing his physique to appear nearly seven feet tall, his outstretched arm holding his sword aloft and creating an even more formidable figure.

An odd thing happened to a man when he entered battle; time slowed down. Once he was clear of the bridge and in the middle of camp, every movement seemed protracted. Men emerging from tents appeared like shadows of themselves. As one raised a harkbus, it seemed to happen gradually though Cahir knew it was lightning fast; his own arm seemed to move more slowly as well so he was almost surprised when his sword found its mark and took off the man's arm before he could fire. His horse was swirling in the midst of the fighting so he felt as though he was fighting in all directions at once and as the men fell around him, he realized he was.

Four short blasts sounded and were picked up by all the horns. Somewhere in the back of Cahir's mind like words emerging from the fog it registered that Henry O'Neill and his clansmen were fighting against them. Then three short blasts sounded and he knew the MacSweeney forces would be fighting against each other as those from the northern reaches had accompanied him into the camp, only to find those under the direction of Malmurry MacSweeney defending it. He waited for the two short blasts that would signify that The O'Donnell himself had led them into a trap but it never sounded.

There was a particular fragrance that emerged during battle; one that was not particularly unpleasant but often fueled the desire to fight, maim and kill. It was a unique blend of musket fire, blood and sweat and on this night, it was all mixed with the distinct odor of soil, wet from the Irish mists.

The horns sounded once more, one long blast each, and the next wave of Cahir's men rushed into the fray.

"Seize the cannons!" Cahir ordered. "Seize the cannons!" Part of his consciousness registered his men descending on the cannons, each movement drawn out as though a second had lengthened to a minute's time. All around him he witnessed hand-to-hand combat as the harkbus rendered themselves useless once they had to be reloaded, as there was no time in which to do so. Clothing turned from tan to red; eyes were wide with unearthly stares; painted faces of some of his men appeared like demons through air that churned with mist and fog and smoke.

Then it seemed as if the other side was disappearing before their eyes. He whirled his horse around, his sword ready once more, but there was no one to fight. As he turned to look behind him, the realization sank in that the English forces were retreating.

"Follow them!" he bellowed, raising his steed onto its hind legs. "Follow them! Rout them!"

How long had it taken? He wondered as the melee died down. He never knew in battle; sometimes it was a matter of minutes and other times, hours. His eyes met Niall Garbh O'Donnell's across the camp, his mind registering with razor-sharp precision that the man was as clean and neat as he had been prior to battle. With one slight nod to Cahir, he disappeared along with his men, seeming to flee into the woods alongside Richard Winkel's troops.

45

The sound of musket fire sliced through the still night air. Wills pulled his horse to a stop and cocked his head to listen. Fergus and Tomas pulled alongside him, the others pausing behind. They had developed into a group of almost twenty men; not nearly as many as he had hoped but perhaps as many as was possible, given the rugged and nearly uninhabitable terrain.

Ireland could be a preternatural place. A horse's hooves could sound as though it belonged to another some distance away and not to the animal directly under a man's backside. The winds could morph into a woman's song or a cat's cry, and the ever present mists could form a dance choreographed by ethereal beings. The clouds could cooperate with a man by blocking the moonlight and hiding his presence or they could hinder a man's progress as they obscured everything more than an arms-length away.

"Do you know where that is?" Fergus asked, his voice barely above a whisper as they listened.

"I believe it's coming from north of Baile na nGalloglach," Wills answered.

"I'd say it's in the vicinity of The O'Donnell's lands," Tomas added. "Somewhere around Cean-Maghair, perhaps?"

Wills turned to look at the others behind them; some were speculating and others simply listening. There was none among them that carried the rank of an officer and now all eyes turned to him for direction. In the blink of an eye, his mind registered that each rider carried a harkbus and a sword. "We go to the fight," he announced, his voice echoing as if they were in a cavern and not in the open ground.

As the men voiced their approval and their willingness, he clicked his heels against his steed and set off toward the sound. The land could be treacherous, the soil steady in some spots and like sponge in others and one never knew if a horse's hooves would land upon slate slick with moisture or nearly tumble into burping bog. At one moment, the hooves sounded thunderous as though dozens more had joined in the charge and at the next, all sound had disappeared, forcing him to look over his shoulder to ensure he was not suddenly alone.

They had nearly reached Cean-Maghair Woods when the first of the men rushed out. Wills' senses sharpened as his eyes took in men in various stages of undress. Some were carrying weapons and some not; many ran blindly forward and others limped with injuries that turned their limbs red with blood. A few were on horseback, their words "Retreat to Baile na nGalloglach!" rising into the cold night air.

His horse thundered into the fray as he sought to determine which man was their commander. He called to one on horseback. "Who is in charge here?"

"Sir Richard," the man answered, pointing into the woods.

"Who has attacked you?"

Fergus and Tomas pulled alongside them and Wills reached out to steady the man's horse so he could hear his answer.

"The O'Doherty!"

"Cahir O'Doherty?"

"Aye, one and the same!"

Wills dropped the other horse's mane and the rider took off toward Baile na nGalloglach, passing the men that had strung out in a disorganized line.

As the others in Wills' contingent joined them, he called out to the others. "How many are there?"

"Two hundred!" yelled one.

"Three hundred, and I'd stake my mother's life on it!" another countered.

"Four and there's more coming!"

As Wills began to form a plan, another rider emerged from the shadows of the woods. He wore an English uniform, though the shirt gaped open to reveal his bare chest.

"Sir Richard?" Wills called out as he approached.

"Aye," the man answered, his eyes roaming over Wills.

"William Neely," he announced. "I've been sent by Captain Stewart."

At that, Richard pulled his horse to an uneasy pause. "Is he with you?"

"He is several hours behind. I've nearly two dozen men on mounts. We can launch a counterattack, sir."

At that, he pulled his steed into a full stop. "There will be no counterattack. We are in full retreat."

"What happened?"

"Not here," he answered. "Come with me to Baile na nGalloglach."

All of Baile na nGalloglach was awake this night. As the men retreated, they joined the English troops stationed there, forming a ring around the village. Word spread like wildfire that The O'Doherty himself was on his way there that night to kill every man, woman and child. The suddenness and viciousness with which the camp was overrun prevented even the most seasoned of soldiers from tamping down the hysterics.

As Sir Richard entered the home of the local governor, Wills was left to witness the village erupting into chaos. Moving into the center of the main dirt road, he called out to everyone to gather around him. His voice was authoritative and deep. He felt a sudden calm engulf him as all eyes looked to him. As he scanned the growing crowd, he spotted Rhiannon—barefoot, a thin nightdress peeking out from under a plaid—his plaid. His lips turned up at the sight of her, despite their grave conditions. Having never seen Baile na nGalloglach before, his eyes drifted up and down the roadway.

"All women and children," he announced, "are to gather in the church at the next corner. You will be safe there."

As an unusually tall woman moved forward, others in the crowd shifted to allow her passage. "Why should we listen to you?" she demanded.

"Your choice, madam," he answered, "is to get to the safety of that church right now, or stay and fight with the men."

At that, the crowd dispersed rapidly, the women rushing their children toward the church where the bishop stood waiting. Even the tall woman joined them, though she muttered under her breath. Only Rhiannon waited, her eyes locked on Wills. He leaned down from his horse as she came alongside him.

"I am greatly relieved to see you," he said, reaching out to squeeze her hand.

"Not nearly as relieved as I am to see you," she answered. Her voice trembled slightly, and he wondered if it was through fear or cold.

"I will come to you soon. Go with the others." Reluctantly, he dropped her hand.

She opened her mouth to speak but then closed it. Nodding silently, she made her way toward the others, assuming charge over a group of unruly children and ushering them into the church. With a final glance back at Wills, she disappeared inside.

The men that were not already arranged around the village stood around Wills in uncomfortable silence. He took a moment to study them; they ranged from boys that were barely into their teen years to old men. He singled out the youngest and the oldest among them. "You men will take up arms outside the church and guard the women and children."

He caught Fergus' quizzical expression. Leaning toward him so none others could hear, he said, "If The O'Doherty gets as far as the church, all is lost. There is no sense in spilling the blood of the elders and the children by placing them on the front lines."

Fergus nodded.

"The rest of you men," he continued, his voice booming to be heard, "those that are not soldiers. Search this village for every weapon you can find and every bit of shot. Bring them to the soldiers surrounding the village." As they began to disperse, he singled out a few of the men to remain where they were.

"Tomas," he called, signaling to him to join them. "You will select three men to ride with you to Captain Stewart. Inform him that The O'Doherty is in the vicinity of The O'Donnell's Cean-Maghair Woods and of our situation here."

"Aye."

As Tomas selected his men and moved off, Wills spoke to the remaining men. "Spread out around the village," he said, "just behind the lines that have formed. As situations change, you are to bring word to Sir Richard and myself in the governor's home there." He nodded toward the house. Then he dismounted and added, "Fergus, you're to come with me."

They made their way to the house, entering without knocking to find Sir Richard standing in the dining room and peering over a map.

"Sir," Wills said as he entered, "I have taken the liberty of moving the women and children to the church and the men to encircle the village."

"I have lost my aides," he answered.

Whether he intended to state that they had been killed or were wandering the countryside, he didn't know but he responded without hesitation, "We are here, sir, to carry out your orders. I have already dispatched several of our men to Captain Stewart to inform him of our situation."

Sir Richard nodded. "You'll find among the English and the Scots, natives of Henry O'Neill and Malmurry MacSweeney clans."

"Aye, sir."

"Niall Garbh O'Donnell…"

"Sir?"

Richard pulled up a chair and sat down heavily. He looked at the worn rug for a long moment before continuing. "The O'Donnell and his clansmen had been with us in our camp. He disappeared. When he reappeared, we were under attack."

Wills waited for him to continue. When he did not, he said, "With all due respect, sir, some of the O'Donnell clansmen are engaged on the Inishowen Peninsula. They are looting O'Doherty lands."

He nodded. "Are you saying he can be trusted?"

"No, sir. I am not."

"I believe Niall Garbh O'Donnell himself left the camp to meet The O'Doherty. When he returned, he did not join the fight—on either side."

"And his men?"

"In the confusion, I confess that I do not know which were his men and which belonged to The O'Neill, The MacSweeney or The O'Doherty. They caught us completely by surprise—not one of the sentries sounded an alarm. I spotted one dead as we were in retreat, his throat slit."

After a pause, Wills said, "What are your orders?"

"With regard to The O'Donnell, he is to be arrested and tried for treason."

Wills turned to Fergus. "Send a man after Tomas with this word."

"Aye."

As Fergus left the room, Richard continued, "We have several hundred men between the English troops and the Irish that have joined us. Unfortunately, being in the woods as we were, I have no idea how many of the enemy there are."

"I understand, sir. If I may, I can discuss with you the disbursement of our troops at present." He moved to the map and began pointing to the village's perimeter, explaining how he had instructed the villagers. When he was finished, he added, "Whatever changes you wish to make, I am at your service."

"You did well, William—"

"William Neely, sir."

"You did well, William Neely. Only two instructions I wish to add at present. Gather two couriers. One is to leave immediately for Donegal and the other to Dublin with word of our circumstances."

"Aye, sir."

"And remain close by. I will no doubt have need of your services this night." Richard waved his hand in a slight dismissal.

He nodded. Returning to the stoop where he found Fergus, he relayed the commander's orders. Then he remained in the doorway, his physique framed by the light behind him as it emanated from the fireplace. The house had grown silent except for the occasional snap of burning wood. The road before him was nearly vacant save for the occasional man rushing to the lines with extra munitions. His eyes drifted from one home to the next until they landed on the church at the corner. It was a tiny structure, perhaps all of one room. Two older men stood on its doorstep, harkbus at the ready, stepping from one foot to the next in an effort to remain warm. He pictured the women and children inside, perhaps the youngest of the men waiting for their shift at the doors to begin. He wanted more than anything to stroll down the road and through those doors and take Rhiannon into his arms.

He caught more movement out of the corner of his eye and he turned to watch men still straggling in from the direction of Cean-Maghair Woods. He sighed. But there was much to do. He needed to form a team of men to interview each man returning from camp so they would know whether the enemy was in pursuit. If he had been in Cahir O'Doherty's boots, he thought, he would not end the fight with defeating the camp; he would pursue them all the way to Baile na nGalloglach and beyond.

He stepped into the road. He also needed to form scout teams to move in all four directions, fanning outward from the village. And he needed the word sent to every man on the line that Niall Garbh O'Donnell was to be arrested on sight and charged with treason.

46

Dawn arrived with brilliant red skies and a racing wind that whistled through the streets, blowing anything that wasn't tied down through the deserted roads of Baile na ngalloglach. It discovered men spread around the village, their heads lolling against their chests in spurts of fitful sleep or trembling from the frost that had descended upon them during the night. Through blurry eyes, they searched the terrain for any signs of the rebels, only to be met with hauntingly silent forests.

Wills made his way from Sir Richard to the church with Fergus at his side. They had each stolen only a few minutes of slumber sometime in the wee hours of the morning, succumbing to mental and physical exhaustion as they waited in straight-back chairs in the governor's home for further instructions. Now as the sun rose in a scarlet blaze, they strode purposefully toward the church to begin their mission.

They found the women and children in various stages of sleep; some were laid across the pews, a plaid or two wrapped around them for warmth while others huddled in corners with small children. A woman breastfed her newborn; Wills realized the woman was the one that had been rescued from Derry and try though he might, he could not remember her name. He tried to shake off the feeling that this would be the fate of the vast majority of those here; the key players — George Paulet, Arthur Chichester, Cahir O'Doherty, Niall Garbh O'Donnell — they would be remembered throughout history; immortalized, perhaps. The rest, including himself, would not even receive a footnote but would remain nameless, faceless ghosts in the annals of history.

His eyes scanned the group for Rhiannon and when he did not see her, his heart sank a bit lower in his chest. He cleared his throat. "May I have your attention please?" His voice came out strong and deep; almost too loud, he realized, for the relative silence of the nave.

The door opened behind him and as he turned, his eyes fell on Rhiannon. She entered with the bishop and he noted that both carried bundles of food wrapped in cloths. They set their packages down on an empty pew and looked at him expectantly. He grasped her emotions in the set of her eyes; inquisitive, trusting, she hoped for good news while steeling herself for the bad. He nodded; the movement slight but she detected it and responded with a hesitant smile.

"You have no doubt noticed," he began, turning his attention to those that were rousing themselves from sleep or gathering around, "that Baile na ngalloglach was not attacked in the night as we feared." A murmur went up and he held out his hands to tamp it down. "We are not out of the woods yet, however. I have come from Sir Richard Winkel with news and instructions. You may return home—" again a chorus of voices arose and again, he quelled it "—or wherever you have been staying here. But you will not be permitted to leave Baile na ngalloglach. We fear the danger is still imminent."

As more rose from the pews, he moved toward the high altar, which was elevated by two steps. From this vantage point, he could easily look from one to the other. "If an attack occurs," he said in the most no-nonsense voice he could muster, "you are to return here immediately." He stressed the final word and studied the faces to make certain they understood. "Therefore, those of you living or staying at the edges of the village, it is recommended that you find refuge closer to the center here."

The bishop stepped forward. "All who wish to remain here," he offered, "are welcome to do so."

"Thank you, Father." Wills allowed the offer to settle in before continuing. "Those who have food to share, the soldiers along the lines protecting this village are hungry. If you can organize in groups to bring food and drink to them, it would be much appreciated."

Several of the women began conferring among themselves before turning back to Wills and nodding in agreement.

"Those who have guarded this church during the night—" His eyes landed on an elderly man and two lads in various stages of dozing "—are encouraged to remain close by to resume your duties when called."

A chorus of questions arose, each person seeking to be heard above the others. He sought to subdue the voices but it was several moments before the air stilled. "I do not have all the answers for you. In fact, I have very few. I do not know how long you will need to remain here. Crown forces have been marching all night to arrive here at Baile na ngalloglach and in a few short hours, the village will have hundreds more to feed. We are also actively searching for the whereabouts of Cahir O'Doherty and the rebels and when we discover them, we will seek to bring the fighting to them—and away from Baile na ngalloglach, which is to say that you will remain safe if you remain here."

With that, he stepped down and made his way through the nave to the doors that beckoned to him now—and Rhiannon. He was stopped several times as both he and Fergus sought to calm the fears of the villagers and refugees. Finally, when he reached her, she was still standing as she had before, her eyes wide and expectant. He reached for her hand as he opened the door with the other. "Come with me," he said simply.

She followed him onto the stoop and as the women and children began to depart as well, he pulled her into the roadway and then in between two buildings.

"Are you alright?" he asked when they were alone.

She nodded but swallowed deeply. "I am. And you?"

"I will be leaving shortly to lead a contingent to Cean-Maghair Woods. We've been ordered to assess the situation there."

"Do you need help? Medical supplies or—"

"The village healer is assembling that for us. I don't know what we will find—the dead, the wounded—on our side or theirs." Several villagers wandered past the opening between the buildings, their eyes passing over them. "I—Rhiannon." The words that had kept him awake through part of the night, the emotions, those things he wanted so badly to express to her, now hesitated on his lips.

"Have you eaten?" she asked.

He blinked. "I—I honestly don't recall."

"Come with me." She took his hand.

As they entered the roadway again, Fergus spotted them from across the way and made his way toward them. "Ah, there you are."

"Will you join us for a bit of food?" she asked, continuing to walk toward one of the homes.

He gave Wills a meaningful look out of the corner of his eye. "I've somewhere I need to be."

"How long do we have?" Wills asked.

"An hour, perhaps more," he answered. "We are waiting until Colonel Wingfield's men arrive; my understanding is they are not far now. Where will you be?"

"Here," Rhiannon said, stopping in front of a tiny home.

Fergus nodded. "I will find you."

⊹≈≈⊹

A block of cheese, a chunk of bread and a slice of salted meat lay untouched on the side table beside a pitcher of ale. The gauzy curtains fluttered slightly; the window opened only enough to allow the tiniest bit of fresh air to penetrate inside. The fireplace crackled with the heat of a fresh log, casting its warmth across the room to find the two lovers intertwined on the small bed. The heat and the chill met there, performing a dance along their exposed skin, alternately prickling them with goosebumps and causing their skin to glisten with perspiration.

There should have been so many things on his mind just now: Derry, Fort Stewart, Cean-Maghair, Baile na ngalloglach; Captain Stewart, Cahir O'Doherty, Niall Garbh O'Donnell, Sir Richard... Yet somehow in her arms all else simply ceased to be. The voices from the house's other rooms faded into oblivion, the occasional greetings on the road just outside their window seeming as if they existed in another world. Or perhaps, he thought as he found her lips once more, he was the one that had crossed a threshold; he was the one now existing on another plane where nothing and no one else mattered except the two of them.

Her lips were full and slightly bruised from their passionate lovemaking, yet she was eager for more. He wanted to memorize every last detail from the curve of her brows to the curve of her hips; from the fullness of her lips to the fullness of her breasts... He wanted to feel every inch of her smooth, long legs wrapped around him, her hands gently and then insistently kneading the cheeks of his ass. He wanted to lose himself in her embrace, in the headiness of her perfume, the swell of her breasts rubbing against his chest, in the sweet taste of her lips and tongue and skin...

He had fallen completely, utterly, deliciously under her spell. He always had been, he realized, from that very first moment he laid eyes on her. He knew then and he knew now that she was his and he was hers until forever ceased to be.

***

The insistent knock came too soon and sounded too harsh.

"I hope you've each had your fill," Fergus' voice rang out, "because it would be time for us to make our departure." Without waiting, he cracked open the door. His eyes seemed to register the food on the table, still untouched, before coming to rest on Rhiannon's bare leg as it rested outside the covers.

"Quiet," Wills said as he pulled on his breeches. "She's sound asleep." He grabbed his boots and sat at the only chair in the room as he jerked them on.

Fergus tore off a piece of the bread as he watched her.

"I'll thank you to keep your eyes in your head," Wills admonished.

He turned so his back was to her. "Colonel Wingfield's forces have arrived."

"Captain Stewart?"

"Aye. Leading the way."

"Tomas reached them?"

"He did."

"Where is he now?"

"Tomas or Stewart?" Without waiting for a reply, he continued, "Tomas is taking a nap—a short one, I'd wager—and Stewart is at the governor's house, going over the lay of the land. We're to leave immediately for Cean-Maghair Woods."

Wills pulled his shirt over his head. As he tucked the tail into his breeches, he leaned down to kiss Rhiannon lightly on the cheek. "I'll be back soon," he whispered.

She murmured something but he couldn't make out her words. Her lashes fluttered for the briefest of moments before she fell back into a deep sleep. It was just as well, he thought. Had she been awake, he would find it far more difficult to leave her side.

47

The camp had clearly been a scene of chaos. They found the sentries dead at each entrance, their throats slit or their bellies split open. Mere boys, they were; likely too young to have had their first taste of love or to have found their purpose in life. It was always the youngest among them assigned as night watchers. They served as the first line of defense in the most dangerous of positions and yet they were always considered the most expendable. Now they stared at him with glazed, unseeing eyes, their last vision on earth that of their killers.

Tents were in disarray; some burned, others trampled, still others leaning on one pole that teetered in the wind. It was hard to determine what damage had occurred during the attack and what had been ransacked afterward, for a string of possessions were found, some half-buried in the mud. Several fires had been started but the damp had prevented them from taking full toll.

They had not seen any of O'Doherty's men as they approached the campsite, and the scouts ahead had reported the woods appeared to be deserted. Still, he could not help but experience that now-familiar sensation as if eyes were boring into them. Images of men just behind the tree trunks seem to flit in and out like the vestiges of their movements only a few hours before.

"Pack up all of Sir Richard's belongings," Wills ordered. As he watched two men head off in the direction of the commander's tent, he turned to the others. "Gather up everything of value. I will need reports of any additional wounded or dead."

Several horse-drawn carts were waiting to be loaded; some had been left the night before and others brought this morning. There were no signs of Sir Richard's horses. Though they had no doubt been tied along the perimeters of camp, he assumed the rebels had freed them or more likely taken them as their own.

"The ground is chewed up a bit," Fergus said, pointing to the soil that had been trampled and turned up. "Hard to tell which was from the skirmish and which was there before."

Wills knelt to view the ground. "Aye. Have men move out in each direction as far as practical; there could be more dead or wounded."

He made his way toward a stone bridge, finding another young man lying across the arched structure as if trying to get away. He had not been shot or knifed but it appeared that his body had been trampled by horses. Wills stared into his face for a moment; his hair was flaxen and his cheeks and chin so smooth, he doubted he had been old enough to experience his first whisker. He was about to turn away when the boy made a sudden sound. Kneeling closer, he placed his thumb upon one eyelid and opened it to find a cornflower blue eye staring back at him. A weak moan escaped from dry, cracked lips.

"Over here," Wills called out. As several men joined him, he said, "The boy's still alive. Load him in a wagon and get him to Baile na ngalloglach."

"The path is wider if we cross this bridge and return to the village from the northwest," one man said.

"You are one of Richard Winkel's troops?" Wills asked.

"I am. I've plenty of experience with these wagons and though we've a bit more woods to traverse in that direction, the paths are wider and more easily navigated with the wagons."

He nodded. "Then inform the rest of the men that is the course we shall take."

Breaking down a camp was easier said than done, especially when fewer men were dismantling it than had originally erected it. Nearly all the weapons and munitions were gone, save for a knife crushed into the soil here or a stray shot there. Wills noted that all the harkbus had been pilfered and he began to mentally tally the number of weapons seized at Derry and Culmore Fort and now here at Cean-Maghair. They had quite an arsenal, they did, and with every weapon seized it was one less for the Crown troops, one more man left searching for a replacement.

The wagon with the injured boy left before the others, the boy still mercifully unconscious as it bounced its way along a path hardly fit for a cattle trail and so narrow the trees seemed to be reaching down to run their branches through the cart like a blind man's fingers searching for gold.

Rain had begun to fall before they were finished; a shower that had begun as a slow and steady drizzle before quickly transforming into a harsh downpour that blew sideways with the wind. It turned the camp into a sea of mud that swiftly buried the items they sought beneath gullies of sludge as though Nature herself wanted to maintain possession of them, perhaps in an attempt to memorialize what had happened here. It made their work arduous and even more uncomfortable than it might have been otherwise as steady rivulets poured off their hats and their clothing soaked through. Wills finally called the men together when even a short walk became an exercise in futility as their boots bogged down in the muck.

"We move out along the west trail," he announced, nodding toward the opening in which the wagon had gone, though it was now completely obscured. "Form a caravan."

In the end, the orderly procession he had envisioned became a haphazard process of moving forward if one could. The wheels bogged down repeatedly as the storm intensified but Wills did not order them to halt. The Cean-Maghair Woods were still too dangerous and he had a driving sense that he must return to the safety of the village before nightfall.

He moved on horseback beside Fergus, picking their way along the route so they could best guide the wagons behind them. The path angled to the east before turning south, the only glimpses through the trees revealing bogs that would further impede the wagons.

The rainfall was gray and cold and it fell in sheets around him, so heavy that the leaves often bent as he passed by to pour their frigid contents upon his head and shoulders. Then the murkiness of the forest began to give way as he realized they were nearing a meadow and a clear path to the village.

When he spotted the wagon up ahead, he had to blink twice to register that it was truly there. And when he realized it was stopped just inside the final line of trees, he held up his hand and pulled back on his horse's reins. "Tell them to stop where they are," Wills whispered hoarsely to Fergus. "Total silence."

Fergus relayed the message to the men following them. Wills felt the men move off behind them as he kept his eyes on the wagon.

"That's the one with the boy in it, 'ey?" Fergus said.

"I believe it is."

"Where is the driver?"

Wills shook his head in response. Then turning, he spotted a soldier and motioned him to move forward. "Dismount," he said, "and move to that wagon. Bring back word of the driver and the boy."

"Sir." The man slipped off his horse. Stooping low, he made his way to the wagon. After a moment, the driver's head poked up above the side. Seeing Wills and Fergus in the path behind him, he glanced nervously over his shoulder before climbing out of the wagon and making his way back with the soldier.

"Sir," he said in greeting to Wills.

"What is your situation?" Wills asked.

"They're through the woods, sir. To the west of us."

"Who?"

"The O'Doherty."

"What?"

"It's The O'Doherty, sir, and his men."

Wills quickly dismounted. Glancing to Fergus and the two soldiers, he said, "Come with me."

They crouched as they made their way laboriously through the mud to the wagon. Using the cart as cover, Wills raised his head just enough to peer through the woods in the direction the lad pointed.

The woods extended further south in that direction; so far that Wills could not see the end of them. At first, he did not see anyone at all. But as he forced his eyes to ignore the steady gray rainfall, he caught a glimpse of movement. Thinking his eyes were playing tricks on him, he scoured the area behind the movement and then back until he could barely make out a procession of men and horses weaving in and out of the trees.

He glanced sideways at the soldier that had driven the wagon.

"How long have you been waiting here?"

"Several hours."

"Are you certain it's The O'Doherty?"

"He's the one I spotted first. Tall fellow, he is; he wore a strange cap, reminded me of the Spaniards, it did, and even through the rain, I could swear I saw a colorful feather protruding out of it."

Wills caught Fergus' eye. His expression mirrored his own: no one else could possibly fit that description unless the Spaniards themselves had landed on their shores.

"What is in the direction they're heading?"

"If they stay to the woods, it would bring them fairly close to Lough Keel."

"Where could the lough take them?"

"It can't take them anywhere, sir. It's surrounded by land with no outlet."

"What is it near?"

The soldier thought for a moment. "Just south of the lough is Inniskill and the Tawney Upper. To the east would be the Kilmacrenan Road."

"Where would the road lead?"

"Baile na ngalloglach to the north and Kilmacrenan to the south."

Wills continued to observe the men in silence. "They are not headed toward Baile na ngalloglach," he said thoughtfully.

"How do you know this?" Fergus asked.

"Look at them heading south like they are. If they wanted to attack Baile na ngalloglach, they would be marching right through the spot that we now sit."

He nodded. "Would not make sense, 'ey? Unless they aim to encircle the village."

"What is at Kilmacrenan?" Wills asked the soldier.

"Shy of a history lesson, sir, there's not much there but a wee village. But if they continue on that road, it will lead them straight to Donegal, though it would take them a good solid day. Two, with weather like we're having."

"That's it, then," Wills said. "They are moving to Donegal." He looked at Fergus. "Donegal has the most strategic importance, does it not?"

"Shall we attack?"

"We're outnumbered," the soldier interjected. "With all due respect, sir, I have been watching them for hours. There have to be hundreds of them."

"Then we hasten to Baile na ngalloglach," Wills said. "We report immediately to Colonel Wingfield. Fergus, take two of the fastest men and turn them to Baile na ngalloglach on a different route, away from The O'Doherty. Have them report of our findings."

"Aye." As Fergus stooped low and made his way through the trees to those waiting some distance behind, Wills turned his attention back to the procession.

"You've no recourse but to remain here with the soldier until they have passed," he said to the young man. "We cannot risk moving the wagon now."

"With all due respect, sir, we can leave the wagon, circle back and take the same route as the courier."

"The wounded—"

"He's dead, sir."

"Are you quite sure?"

He nodded. "I'm sorry, sir. He began to call out for his mother and I was afraid he would give away our position. I only placed my hand upon his mouth," he hastened to add, "only to silence him. It was then, after a few moments, that I realized he had ceased to breathe."

"Alright then. We move back the way we came and head to Baile na ngalloglach." As they returned to their prior position, his mind began to race and for some strange reason the village of Kilmacrenan had begun beating a refrain in his brain.

48

Kilmacrenan was the tiniest of villages set amongst the rolling hills and valleys, the landscape laid out in meandering stripes of green and burgundy, the latter of which were a potpourri of wildflowers that had burst forth from the generous spring rains. Even though Wills rode with hundreds of other soldiers, their horses nearly neck-to-neck, he could yet smell the perfume of the flowers made heady from the ever-moist atmosphere that was Ireland. The Rock of Doon loomed high, a hill of perhaps a hundred and twenty meters but which seemed to be much taller as it rose against the churning clouds.

"And it is there upon that hill," Tomas was saying, "that the chieftains of the O'Donnell clan have been inaugurated for hundreds of years; twenty-five in all, the last being Niall Garbh O'Donnell himself only five years earlier."

Wills could picture the ceremonies now as they rode toward it; standing so tall and so proud, the hilltop would have provided the perfect stage for all the

O'Donnells and fellow clans to witness the crowning of their newest lord.

"It is also there in times gone by where chieftains were put to death," Tomas added.

"Put to death?" Wills asked. "By who?"

"By their own clansmen, aye. When crops were fallow, the soil barren or if disease overtook the plants, it was thought in days of old that the chieftain had lost favor with the gods."

"Is that so?"

"Kill the chieftain, sacrifice him to the gods and elect a new one, and if the gods favored the change, the crops would yet grow again and the people would be spared from a slow and painful starvation." Tomas' voice became a hoarse whisper as he continued, "More often than not, the sacrifices would include leaving the body, bludgeoned, dismembered in the burping, shifting bogs."

"I'll bite," Fergus said. "Why would they do that?"

"Oh, it was borne by a superstition that a body must be dismembered, you see, the parts scattered to prevent the person from rising up again to claim that which he had lost and dooming his people in the process."

"What of a proper burial?"

"Not for the king the gods didn't favor. The flesh was left in the open for the crows and the gods."

"I heard it told," Fergus said, "the bodies were miraculously preserved if they failed to be eaten."

"Aye," Tomas said. "They were turned brown by the tannins left behind."

Wills imagined the bodies from an age long gone, an age in which forests grew before they were swallowed up by the agitated soil, an underground monster rising to devour them.

Now a wood road angled its way across the bogs toward the Rock of Doon, a road that seemed to have no destination but simply stopped in the middle of the marshland leaving the traveler stranded amongst the dead.

The green meadows Wills glimpsed in the distance were dotted with sheep, their bleating carrying across the wind to the men that rode past. And even further along the distant horizon were the ragged, wild slopes of hills lesser in stature and importance than the Rock of Doon.

As he listened to Tomas narrating the history of the area as if he was a professor in one of the greatest universities of Europe, Wills could not help but remember the old woman's declaration of his heritage. Ah, but if only he knew whether Penarddun O'Donnell was truly a wise woman or simply an old woman gone senile, for what would it mean if he, William Neely, was truly a descendant of Niall O'Neill? Would it mean that after hundreds of years and so many generations, he would stand across the battlefield from his own kith and kin, aim his harkbus or swing his sword, to uphold others that had never shared his blood while striking down those that did?

As Tomas' voice droned on, he tried to remember the stories his father had told of their ancestors, for there had always been something in the Neely men that caused them to live as much in the past as in the present. Aye, and he had been told as a wee lad that once his ancestors had roamed Ireland oh and for sure it had been hundreds of years in the past. But what did that mean precisely? He wondered. Did it mean that his ancestors had come from Scotland to Eire just as he had and then returned home? Or could it have meant that they had originally lived in this country and if so, what was it that compelled them to leave?

He thought of all the rumors he had heard of the Irish; of the people only half as tall as any other, of their crouched figures and humpbacks, of the hair that grew upon them as though they were more ape than man. And in the end, none of it had been true for Cahir O'Doherty was taller by far than any Highlander Wills had ever seen and for that matter the Gallowglass MacSweeneys were as well; and he had yet to see a stooped person that was not as old as the hills themselves. They grew no more hair than a Scotsman or an Englishman and though some of their customs were a might peculiar, they were not the rough barbarous creatures he had been told about in his youth. Ah, how accurate his sister Beth had been, despite never having left Wigtownshire; for wasn't it Beth that had pointed out how every culture must choose someone they can declare is lowlier than themselves? And certainly by making them appear subhuman, it is far easier to look down upon them with disgust or disdain?

He thought of Rhiannon, Irish through and through and the most beautiful woman he had ever laid eyes upon, and aye, he intended to marry her, he did, though he had not informed her as yet. And they would have as many children as the woman yearned to have, they would, and he would be happy to participate in as many attempts as she'd fancy, and not a one of their offspring would resemble those Scottish tales.

"We'd be aiming for the Rock of Doon herself," Tomas said, breaking into his thoughts.

"Aye," he answered, "and it isn't hard to understand why, now is it?" He jabbed a finger toward the peak. "For an army encamped upon that highest of hills would have an unequaled position in all of Kilmacrenan, wouldn't they now? And able to observe every movement for miles around, 'ey?"

As they continued their movement with cannon, harkbus, men and horses, a murmur began to spread through the ranks until it caused the entire line to come to a halt.

While they remained in ragged formation wondering why they had been rushed from Baile na nGalloglach only to sit on idle horses in the middle of a meadow far shy of their goal, he felt a chill running up his spine as if the winds had become apparitions and their long, boney fingers were creeping up his torso. He turned as others did and saw what had stopped their progress: Cahir O'Doherty and his army.

Spotting Fergus with a scope, he demanded, "And just where did you get that?"

"I found it in Cean-Maghair," he answered with a shrug of a shoulder. "And it did not appear to be English so I determined it must belong to the enemy, which made it ripe for the picking."

"Let me see it, will you?"

Reluctantly, he handed it over. "Don't you be forgetting where you got it," he chided, "for I'll be wanting it back, I will."

Wills peered through the scope. There was no doubt that The O'Doherty had seen them, as he rode in front of his men in a straight line for the English forces. He struck awe akin to admiration in Wills' soul even though he knew he was watching the enemy. His horse seemed larger than the others and it was white where the others were black or brown. His back was as straight as his musket's ramrod; straighter than any man had a right to be atop a galloping steed. His long red hair fanned out from underneath a morion; the metal, polished helmet contained a crest that stretched from front to back and from that crest waved a single feather of purple, black and white unlike any bird Wills had ever seen. The feather was several inches long if not a foot and made Cahir's six foot seven inch figure strike even more of an imposing presence. The helmet also contained cheek guards and though his vision was a bit blurry from this distance even with the scope, he thought he could make out the man's chiseled, English-style beard.

"You've had time enough with it," Fergus said, grasping the scope before Wills could hold onto it. "I'll thank you to find your own."

As his friend peered through the scope, Wills' eyes skirted the men behind Cahir and he knew without a doubt what had caused the murmur in their ranks. There were not a dozen rebels behind him or even a hundred, but several hundred riding as they were, armed with harkbus and swords and the occasional cart-drawn cannon.

He realized then that couriers were riding the length of their own ranks, swiftly moving from one commander to the next. Then the call came down the ranks: they would fight them where they stood.

The lines in the center began to form under the command of Colonel Richard Wingfield himself. Men dismounted and formed their lines of three, exactly as Wills had been taught in those days that seemed so long ago. Captain Stewart's men and Wills among them had been in the front and now found themselves forming a southern flank. Catching Stewart's eye, Wills took off in his direction, Fergus and Tomas on his heels.

"Captain Stewart," Wills said as he drew abreast of his horse, "would you like for us to take the Rock of Doon?" He nodded toward the commanding hill.

Stewart shook his head. "Have your men take the road."

It was not lost on Wills that Stewart had referred to the men as his. "The road, sir?"

"The road leading to Donegal. They cannot be allowed to pass your ranks, are you understanding me, William? If they breach your lines, they will have a clear shot to Donegal with no one else to stop them."

He spotted Archie then at the far end of the ranks, motioning toward the south. "Aye, sir. I understand. They shall not breach our lines." With that, he galloped back to his former position. Raising his voice so all could hear, he said, "We are to form the southernmost line in defense of the road to Donegal. Ride out, men!"

With Wills in front, they rode to a rugged area that might have been considered a gentle roll that stretched from meadow to hill had it not been for the jagged outcroppings of rock. "Horses to the rear!" he commanded. "Assume your lines!"

Men that had been farmers of potato or herders of sheep and cattle sprang into action as though they were professional soldiers. Those that had been assigned to the rear lines—the ones with the lowest rate of actually striking an object with their musket shot—leapt into their roles, driving the horses into an improvised corral in the adjacent meadow, where they would remain until the order was issued to ride once more.

As the others formed their own lines of three, Wills found himself in the perfect spectator position. Flanking the army as they were, their lines rolled outward like a crescent moon, he watched as hundreds of men under the command of Colonel Wingfield formed three solid lines. They appeared to stretch for more than a mile and were easily more men than he had ever seen in one place. They struck an intimidating portrait but as he turned once more in Cahir's direction, he knew that those under the Irish chieftain's command were not daunted. They rode onto the field and Cahir himself drew up where they would stand their own lines as if he knew instinctively how far their harkbus fire would reach. Like the English, they formed three lines of perhaps three dozen men, a cannon, then three dozen more, until they had three lines and three cannons facing off against their adversary.

"Wills," Archie called, riding along the back of the lines at a full gallop, "take my horse. Get down to Wingfield straightaway!"

He had barely slipped off the horse before Wills was mounting and then thundering toward the center lines.

When he reached Colonel Wingfield, he found a flag bearer and another man awaiting him. "Do not dismount," the colonel ordered as he pulled his horse to a stop. "Take this note into the field. You know Cahir, do you not?"

"Aye, sir. I do."

"Then go."

The three men began a sprint across the open field. After a few steps, Cahir himself accompanied by Phelim and one other began to trot toward the center line. As they met, Wills' eyes locked with Cahir's.

"Cahir, my old friend," Wills said as he handed him the note, "I implore you to put down your arms."

He did not respond but took the note. Opening it with calculated deliberation, he seemed to read it not once but twice. Passing the note to Phelim, he turned back to look Wills in the eye. "William, are you certain you will not join us? For I am confident we will take this field today and all of Ireland tomorrow and I should hate to see a fine man such as yourself cut down in the process."

His words took him aback. He felt the eyes of the flag bearer and the Englishman on him and the heat began to rise in his cheeks. "I ask you once more, my friend: put down your arms for you cannot be victorious against all of King James' army."

His eyes peered beyond his shoulder as if he was assessing the lines. "Perhaps not. But I do not see all of King James' army before me."

"What word do I take Colonel Wingfield?"

"I will not surrender nor will any of my men," Cahir answered with the calmness of one assessing the weather. "And should Colonel Wingfield chose to fight us, we will not accept surrender from any of his."

Wills nodded and backed his horse away. "So be it," he answered before turning toward his own lines. It seemed as though it took forever to gallop back to Colonel Wingfield, the eyes of every man boring into him so acutely that he could feel the field vibrate with the energy of the impending battle. The lines parted to allow the three passage to the colonel and his couriers where Wills relayed their brief exchange.

"So be it indeed," the colonel answered.

Wills waited for additional instruction but when the colonel rode along the back of the lines in the opposite direction, he turned once more for the far southern flank. Archie was exactly where he'd left him. He relayed the exchange once more with Tomas, Fergus and the others listening and then watched as Archie mounted the horse and returned to Captain Stewart.

Wills surveyed the lines. The center was equally matched except for the midpoint; where the English lines ran straight with soldiers, Cahir O'Doherty remained mounted on the opposite side. He marveled at the man's confidence for certainly he must know that every man staring him down saw not a chieftain but five hundred pounds sterling.

He did not know who fired the first shot for it seemed that the cannon on both sides were fired simultaneously. It was a laborious process indeed, for it required several men. One loaded a chamber filled with black powder while two men lifted a heavy stone ball, sliding it down the barrel. The chamber pin was hammered in tight and then priming powder was poured from a flask into the powder chamber. With a single command, all men stepped back from the cannon, covering their ears, while another man stepped forward with a flaming torch. He had but to place the torch over the opening to the powder chamber, igniting the powder and blasting the stone ball across the field. The cannon jerked backward on its wood wheels and all the men jumped forward yet again to begin preparations for another fire. Stone balls were still being stacked behind each cannon even as they were firing.

"At rest, men," Wills ordered. As his command carried down the lines, the flank dissolved into men sitting where they once had stood; their harkbus laid across their laps as they watched.

The first cannon shot on both sides fell short, though Wills noted that the Irish cannon had landed closer to their mark. Both sides moved their cannon up while the lines remained steady. It was an exercise in futility, he thought after a few rounds, for the ranks knew precisely how far a shot could travel and remained clear, leaving the only mark for their efforts a gaping hole in the soft earth. They continued this way for another half an hour. When two balls met each other midway across the field, it caused a chorus of shouts to arise from both sides as if they each had accomplished something spectacular. Wills peered down the lines at Captain Stewart, who was conferring with Archie before sending a courier behind the lines to Colonel Wingfield. At the opposite end of the battlefield, it appeared that Richard Winkel had taken the far northern flank.

The cannon continued until both sides were out of shot. A haze had descended on the field that seemed to mutate from the Irish mists to cannon smoke and back again, cutting off any clear view of the enemy. When musket fire rang out, several men in the English front lines were cut down, their screams filling the air.

Will thought that when each of the men returned to their families and their primary roles as farmers and herders, they would speak of this battle in terms of how many were killed on either side and perhaps how many were wounded. What they would not speak of, to their wives or any others, was the length of time it took a man to die. The harkbus balls more often hit a shoulder, slicing through the bone and sinew that held a man's arm to his body, or they hit a leg, knocking a man off his feet, his dangling leg unable to help him stand again. Occasionally, a harkbus ball would strike a torso, leaving a gaping hole. And more often than not, the one struck would not immediately register it but would look in confusion at the arm or leg unable to respond to his brain's command, or they walked a few yards with their entrails heaving out of their abdomen before falling to the ground. Most men would bleed out, the pain becoming severe and then unbearable as their screams filled the air before they dissolved into incoherent pleas. By the time they were too weak to remain cognizant, it was a blessing as they passed into unconsciousness.

Meanwhile, the first line of soldiers would remain standing, firing at the enemy in return and then dropping to their knees to reload while they tried to ignore their comrades screaming in agony next to them for to stop and remove the wounded meant a waste of precious time. While the first row reloaded, the second row fired and then they dropped, too, reloading while the third row fired. It went on like this minute after minute while Wills and his soldiers watched from their flanked position. Occasionally, their commander could call orders to advance, which meant stepping over the bodies of the dead and the wounded, trying not to look their fellow soldiers in the eye, attempting not to allow their minds to wrap around the horror unfolding around them or the fact that they might be next on the Grim Reaper's list.

Then at an opportune time that appeared to have been precisely timed, the most ungodly chorus rose up. It sounded like a thousand men, their voices echoing through the valleys so that The Crown forces on either flank were peering in all directions. It was neither a shout nor a cry but something completely otherworldly. Though some in the center were able to get off another shot, the battle quickly dissolved into hand-to-hand combat as Cahir O'Doherty and his men rushed the field. They came on horses and they came on foot, a sudden onslaught that took the English by surprise and caused the lines to waver. Then came shouting on the English side, commanders ordering their men back to the front and turning around those that were fleeing.

The battle erupted into a melee, the flanking forces unable to shoot because now the English and the Irish were intertwined, the dust kicking up to meet the smoke and the mists.

"Hold your line!" Archie ordered.

Wills picked up the order, shouting it down his lines, but as he saw others under Captain Stewart begin to stand, he ordered his men to rise and form ranks. Stewart's order now beat like a refrain in his mind: they must hold the line at all costs; should O'Doherty breach their lines, they would have a clear path all the way to Donegal—and Ireland would fall.

Through the haze, he could see Richard Winkel's troops joining the battle. Their ranks dissolved and harkbus fire soon ceased, replaced by the resounding clang of swords and axes. Shouts and screams intermingled until one could no longer decipher the words.

Wills peered again down the lines, spotting Captain Stewart and Archie both with their scopes, following the movement on the field.

"Who has the upper hand?" Tomas asked, reaching for Fergus' scope.

Fergus managed to move the piece out of range while he continued to peer onto the battlefield. "I can't tell," he said. When he handed the scope to Wills, his face was ashen.

Wills took the scope and studied the field as best he could through the shifting brume. It took only a moment to understand why the blood had seemed to drain from his friend's face. They were losing and losing badly. The unthinkable was happening right before their eyes: Cahir O'Doherty's forces were winning.

Stunned, he looked back to Captain Stewart. Even with the distance between them, he could see his pallid face and Archie's dumbfounded expression. But of course, Wills thought. Hadn't the English themselves trained Cahir O'Doherty? Hadn't he grown from a boy to a man in the Nine Years War, memorizing English strategy and tactics? And wasn't he now turning those upon the English themselves to become victorious?

Wills stared at the captain, trying to will him to look at him, to issue orders—any orders. Hold the line, they'd been ordered to do; hold the line.

But as the combat continued and fewer men stood on the field, Captain Stewart finally called out the order: advance and attack. As it was picked up from one line to the next, the men broke their ranks and rushed the field, firing their only shot when they could before casting their harkbus aside or using them for bludgeoning. Others reached for their swords.

There were moments in a man's life in which he knows that every image will be seared into his soul forever. As Wills advanced, it felt as if he had been split in half; while his physical body fought beyond anything he'd thought himself capable of, his spirit seemed to hover over the field as though it had already disengaged. On some level, he believed he would die there on that battlefield and for some strange reason that he could not understand, his first thoughts were of his sister Beth. He could see her as if she hovered there on the battlefield; she held a basket of heather and she was smiling sweetly. Then her lips began to move as if she was talking and yet he could not hear her voice. All that filled his ears now were the screams and shouts of men amalgamating into a single horrific voice.

He fired his harkbus into the torso of a man wielding an axe as he descended upon him and then used the barrel to deflect the weapon as it fell toward him. Dropping his harkbus now that it was spent, he grabbed the axe with one hand while unsheathing his sword with the other. A fellow soldier was split open beside him, his blood spurting onto Wills' shirt and breeches. Before the assailant could recoil in another strike, he sliced his neck through with his sword. He was already moving onto the next man even as he saw the first crumple to the ground, his head hanging on by only a few sinews and bare bone before lolling off his shoulder.

There were no uniforms; though some of the professional English soldiers wore red, most of the men on both sides were not truly regulars and wore the same clothing they might wear shearing sheep or harvesting crops. He saw more than one man blindly attacking anyone in their path, whether they be friend or foe, and somewhere in that disembodied spirit he wondered how many would be killed by their own forces this day. For himself, he stared into each man's face and attacked when he saw malice and passed when he saw none, each assessment taking only a fraction of a second.

Cahir O'Doherty was in the center of the fighting. He had dismounted and was battling two men at once and getting the better of both. His men seemed to know instinctively where their leader stood and as Wills tried to reach him, another popped up in his way, slicing his arm with a sword before Wills ran him through with his own. The stench of blood and sweat became nearly overwhelming. The ground churned beneath their feet, the soil turning to slick mud from the heavy rains of earlier that day.

He spotted an enormous man wielding an axe high above a young boy's head and with a vicious shout, he swung his own axe into the man's back, dropping him to his knees. As he whirled around, he saw another of his own soldiers stumbling as a dismembered shoulder spurted blood.

The enemy came at him from every direction; he had no sooner felled one man than another rose to take his place. And it was there on the battlefield that he realized just how much pain a man could block in the height of battle, for it seemed that every man that fell rose again... and again and again.

Everything seemed to move in slow motion; the swinging of axes and swords, the firing of the occasional harkbus. There was no order; not even the semblance of any. It was every man battling for himself, fighting to live while another died, struggling forward and stumbling backward. Somewhere in the melee, he thought he saw The O'Donnell but with the next attack, he was forced to focus on the fight and when he turned again, the man was gone.

The battlefield was littered with men. Few appeared dead; most were writhing in the mud, struggling to get up or straining to roll out from under other men's boots. Bodies fell atop of bodies and always, always the strange mixture of blood, sweat, urine and men emptying their bowels as they lost final control.

When he heard the shouts of retreat, it did not immediately register. But as he continued the fight, he realized the faces he knew, the men he fought alongside, were becoming fewer. And by the time he understood that Colonel Richard Wingfield was calling a full retreat, he was surrounded.

A man's feet appeared to leave the ground as he sailed through the air toward him, his sword held in both hands, his eyes intent on Wills' neck. Though he knew it was useless, though he believed the man would descend upon him before he could lift his own sword, his arms seemed to work on their own accord. Somehow the axe he held in his other hand was dropped and with both hands, he met his assailant's sword with his own, the clang of metal reverberating through his arms with such force that he knew his bone must have shattered. Yet somehow he found the strength to continue the fight, clash after clash, pushing him back. Now his goal was to rejoin his men and yet something inside himself would not permit him to turn and run and try as he might to fight while moving backward, it was all or nothing. It had always been all or nothing, he realized with a start. It was always to kill or be killed.

Then in the blink of an eye, he came face to face with Cahir O'Doherty. The man towered over him, though Wills was six feet himself. His tall metal cap and taller plume made him appear like a giant. His arms were the longest Wills had ever seen and seemed even longer and more formidable in the heat of battle. He had whirled around, his sword held in both hands, an unearthly yell on his lips when he spotted Wills staring at him.

In an instant, Wills knew he could not deflect the blow even as his arms raised his own sword in defiance. He was nearly completely surrounded. Though his eyes remained locked on Cahir's eyes and grime-caked face, it was as though he had developed vision in all directions at once. He saw those English soldiers that had managed to keep both their legs running off the field in full retreat while others stumbled away, their weapons lost in the mud and muck. He saw Colonel Wingfield's face seeming to stare directly at him, shouting as if at the top of his lungs but he could not be heard over the tumult. He saw Captain Stewart's expression, his arm waving frenetically as he steered his men off the battlefield in a total withdrawal. Captain Winkel was already gone, riding his horse into the distance, his men limping along behind him.

And as Cahir's sword descended toward him, he saw another man seeming to sail through the air, a roar on his lips and an axe extended and at the last moment, Cahir whirled away from Wills and caught the man in mid-flight, slicing through his abdomen. As he crumpled to the ground, Wills turned to find a path lay clear before him like the parting of the Red Sea. He tried to run toward his lines, tried to rejoin his men, and only then did he realize his leg had been sliced open and blood was pouring onto the ground beneath his feet.

He thought the men behind him had moved further away and only when he reached a knoll did he realize that they had remained where they were and it had been he that had managed to disengage from the fight, dragging one leg behind him.

In front of him, the lines had fallen apart. The cannon were all gone, the balls embedded in the earth where they had fallen. Harkbus and swords and axes lay scattered in every direction. Men crawled on their bellies to escape the fighting while others ran and still others, like himself, limped forward. In the meadow only a few riderless horses remained as most of them were far in the distance already, ferreting their riders to safety. The sounds of musket fire and shouting and cannons had rendered his hearing nearly useless.

Somewhere out in front of him he saw through eyes bleary with sweat and blood, Captain Stewart still atop his horse, using his sword to direct the men to the rear — though the rear seemed to be anywhere off the field and the further away the better. And as he dragged his leg forward, he saw a lone soldier seemingly oblivious of the order to retreat, standing where his own lines had once been. The man raised his harkbus and took his time in aligning his sight as if he had all the time in the world. Stumbling forward, Wills glanced over his shoulder to see the center of the field where he had just stood, now nearly empty of Crown troops. Cahir O'Doherty still towered in the middle, his arms still outstretched with a weapon in each but no one left to fight. And as he watched, the harkbus fired.

The ball caught Cahir almost in the middle of his back. As he buckled to his knees, every man that had surrounded him seemed to look at him at precisely the same time. He wavered for a moment as though he was trying to pick himself back up, his sword still outstretched in one hand while he still gripped the axe with the other. The blood gushed out his back in waves, almost appearing to gurgle. Then his axe dropped to the ground beside him, his hand still clutching it. And then his sword tumbled as he doubled over, his metal cap scraping the mud as he collapsed.

Wills knew he should turn away; every ounce of willpower still left inside him was shouting for him to continue the retreat but he could not look away. And as he continued to stare at The O'Doherty, he realized something had shifted on the battlefield. The Irish were falling apart.

The few Englishmen still on the field were gaining the upper hand as the clans began to run from the field. With their leader gone, they panicked.

Wills turned back to find Captain Stewart still directing men in retreat. Somehow he found the voice to shout at the captain until he looked his way. Then Wills pointed frantically at the field. He heard the word shouted over and over, "Attack! Attack!" and did not realize it was his own voice until he was back on the field and the first man he encountered took his breath away with the first clangor of the swords meeting.

Somewhere along the way, he had picked up another man's sword and still another's axe and was fighting his way back to the center even as the O'Doherty clan fell apart.

Then others began to join him, renewing the battle and with their own hellacious shouts, cutting down the clans. The cannons were turning around, the men rushing back to the field, stopping partway to fire at the fleeing Irish. Colonel Wingfield was ordering the men back to form lines, lines of harkbus that would cut down the men from behind as they raced for the safety of the woods.

When at last the fighting was done and the last shout died away, Wills was still at the center. Finding no one else to fight, his legs gave out from under him and he sank to his knees in a pool of mud and blood. The men were stacked around him, bloodied corpses and disembodied limbs. As he wavered there on his knees, he saw Cahir O'Doherty's motionless body lying only a few yards away, his lifeless eyes staring at him.

Then his body was being hauled to his feet by two strong arms, one on either side of him. And as Fergus and Tomas half-walked and half-dragged him off the field, he looked back to find Colonel Wingfield, Captain Winkel and Captain Stewart converging on Cahir's body with the soldier that had felled him with one sure shot.

49

The soldier's name was John Trendor and in the end, he was allowed to behead Cahir O'Doherty. He left under guard for Dublin carrying the chieftain's head in a gunny sack. In the coming days, a variety of rumors found their way back to camp, chief among them that the head was stolen from under John as he used it as a pillow, remaining fast asleep as it was taken. None of them were believable, as it was John Trendor himself that was paid five hundred pounds sterling for delivery of Cahir O'Doherty's head to none other than Lord Arthur Chichester himself.

The body was quartered but none would say whether the English did it out of reprisal or the man's own clan performed the rite in deference to the thousands of years of history that spoke of changing a clan's fate when the king's destiny was met with misfortune. It was doubtful it was the latter, as the clan was on the run, unlikely to return to Kilmacrenan.

Phelim MacDavitt was cornered shortly after leaving the field; as Wingfield's men regrouped, they surrounded

him and his men. Word was that Phelim put up a
ferocious fight as did his men but as the MacDavitt clan
dissolved into chaos they proved no match for the
hundreds of English that descended upon them. Though
he was wounded, they captured him alive and he sat at
this very moment under heavy guard in nearby Lifford
some twenty miles east.

A bounty had been placed on Niall Garbh
O'Donnell's head and though he was believed to be
somewhere deep in the woods of Donegal, his capture
had taken on lesser importance than caring for the dead
and wounded.

Too injured and too weak to move, Wills remained
in a camp erected within clear view of the battlefield,
although most of the time he was completely unaware
of where he was. Most days he lay on his plaid on the
hard ground inside a medical tent, soaked in sweat
though the nights were cold and shivering as the days
grew warm. His leg had been sliced open from knee to
ankle, the muscle and the sinew exposed before an Irish
healer packed it with an herbal poultice that he was
certain would kill him and then the English surgeon
finished the job by sewing him up, poultice and all,
before wrapping his leg in a bandage that felt too tight.

In the days that followed, he often awakened to the
sight of a woman leaning over him with a cool wet cloth
upon his head or wiping down a chest drenched with
perspiration. Sometimes she spoke in a lilting Irish
accent and he found himself calling for Rhiannon before
falling back into an unconscious stupor.

His arm had taken many a blow as well and he
supposed the same poultice that had been packed into
his leg had also been crammed into the cavity that had
been his arm and now a bloody bandage covered him
from his shoulder to just below his elbow.

Sometimes he awakened to find a woman pouring a foul-tasting liquid down his throat, her soft murmurings causing him to cooperate in the faith that what did not kill him would make him stronger, for at this moment he knew if the tent was overrun by rebel forces, he could do no more than watch it unfold and even then only until he succumbed to a dream world that was becoming more real to him than life itself.

It was while he lay in this deepest of slumbers that he saw Rhiannon the clearest. She often lay beside him on the plaid, her leg draped over his, the cool touch of her fingers calming the heat in his body. Her eyes were not filled with worry but with an eerie serenity and despite his confidence that he was slipping into death, her words tried to reassure him that this would pass.

Other times he awakened in a fury, believing the battle was still underway, convinced that he must return to the field and continue the fight. Sometimes he struggled against too many hands pushing him back to the plaid, their voices intermingling with Rhiannon's as they sought to calm him. And when thunder boomed, he heard the cannons' roar until eventually the rain soaked through under the tent, saturating his bed upon the muddy floor and leaving him alone in the puddle.

+≈≈+

"Well, and would you look there," Fergus' voice resounded. "He is finally awake, he is."

"Get me out of here," Wills said. He attempted to sit up but as the room began to spin, he groaned and remained somewhere between lying prone and sitting while he willed his elbows not to collapse under his weight.

"And that's precisely what I plan to do. But first let's get you out of the tent, 'ey? Go sit under a tree somewhere. This place smells like piss and puke, it does." Without waiting for an answer, he slipped his arms underneath Wills' and hauled him to his feet.

A loud groan involuntarily escaped him. As his friend steadied him with one arm around his waist, Wills wrapped a weak arm across Fergus' shoulder. He was astonished at what he saw before him. In his stupor, he had not realized that others shared the tent with him and as he passed by more carried than by his own power, he began to fathom just how fortunate he truly had been. All of the others were missing a foot, a leg, an arm or a hand and one man's head was bandaged so that only his nostrils and mouth were exposed.

"We took a beating, we did," Fergus said as if aware of Wills' thoughts. "But we won the day."

When they emerged from the tent, the sun's brilliance caused him to recoil and it wasn't until they had settled underneath a nearby oak tree's giant branches that he realized the heavens were the stormy, muted skies he had long ago grown accustomed to and the sun was barely making its presence known.

"It took you long enough to come after me," Wills said.

"I was with you almost the entire time, I was," Fergus said. His voice was uncharacteristically soft. "I left only once, and Tomas remained with you then. Did you not hear us as we told you of all that was transpiring? We thought you were lost to us for a while, we did."

"How long have I been—?"

"Nigh on three weeks."

"No."

"Aye, and you're smelling like it, too."

He leaned against the broad tree's trunk. He felt as if someone had pummeled his eyes and his tongue felt like it had been stuffed full of sand and grit. He wasn't wearing his own clothes but someone else's and somewhere along the way he had lost his boots. Peering at his bandaged foot at the end of his bandaged leg, he realized his boots would serve no purpose for him now at any rate.

"Rhiannon," he said.

Fergus cut him a sideways glance. "Aye?"

"Does she know why I have not been to see her? Or—did she visit me here? I seem to recall seeing her more than once..."

When Fergus answered, his voice was low and quiet. "You were dreaming, my friend."

"So she did not come to visit me?" His heart felt heavy at that and at the same time, his head was filled with a mixture of anger and profound sadness.

He turned so he was facing Wills. "I'm afraid she did not."

"Did she know of my circumstances?"

Fergus sighed.

"What is it? Oh, but do not tell me she has found another—"

"No, Wills. She did not find another. I have no doubt of her love for you; no doubt at'al."

"What is it then?"

He took a deep breath. "I do not know how much you remember of that day," he said finally. "But after Cahir O'Doherty was killed, the clans—their organization—it fell apart."

"Aye. I do remember; as if it was yesterday, I remember."

"As you laid there more out than in, I told you of Cahir's demise and of Phelim MacDavitt putting up a final fight, he did, and of the bounty on Niall Garbh O'Donnell's head."

"So that is how I knew," he said. "I thought I was dreaming."

"No. That you were not dreaming. But Rhiannon could not have visited you, I am afraid, my old friend."

"She has fallen ill?" He tried to rise but after a moment's struggle, he collapsed back against the trunk.

"No, Wills. It happened suddenly. She did not suffer."

For a moment, he did not comprehend his friend's words. He waited for him to continue but when he did not, he asked, "What are you saying? Out with it, Fergus."

Fergus sighed again and shook his head. "Before the tides turned in our favor, Captain Winkel's men were in full retreat. Some of them never stopped despite the fact that the blowers sounded the horns to rally them back. Some of them made it all the way to Baile na ngalloglach. They were panicked, Wills. They were panicked."

An icy chill began to seep through his bones as he watched his friend's face.

After a moment, Fergus dabbed at his eye. "They told the villagers they had lost. And they told them that Cahir O'Doherty's men were on their way to rout the village and all of Ulster."

A heavy cloud passed before the remnants of the sun and somehow it felt as though it was passing directly through his heart. Numbness began to creep in and he longed to return to the tent, to close his eyes and to see her there again, for she had been there despite all that his friend had said; she had been there. She had spoken to him, comforted him, slept beside him...

"The women and the children were told to flee but no one knew which direction was safe, for if Cahir was victorious at Kilmacrenan, it meant that the Inishowen Peninsula would also beat back Crown troops, and to the north were the O'Donnell and the MacSweeney..."

"Which way did she choose?" His voice sounded disembodied and so far away that surely the words could not have come from his own lips.

"She was found to the southeast, still on O'Donnell land. She didn't get far."

"What did they do to her?"

"She died suddenly, Wills; that we know."

"What did they do to her?" he repeated.

"As the clans were fleeing—and mind you, we do not know which she encountered—they shot their muskets into the lot of them."

He nodded in silence.

"She was buried, Wills. Her father traveled to Baile na ngalloglach to take possession of her, he did, and she was buried in their family plot. It's a beautiful spot, it is; at the crest of their gardens overlooking Donegal Bay and the sea beyond."

He closed his eyes and pictured the gardens where they had first kissed. "She would have liked that." His voice threatened to crack so he fell silent and as the minutes passed, the silence seemed to fill his soul. He didn't realize that he still sat at the base of the tree until Fergus patted his good knee.

"So for three weeks, you've had nothing but broth and the skin hanging off your sorry bones is proof of it," he said. "And I've been smelling chickens and ducks on the flame, I have. You remain right here—as if you could get up by yourself and walk away—and I'll be back with a plate full of food for you, I will."

"Thank you but I'm not hungry."

"Hungry or not, your services are needed."

Reluctantly, he opened his eyes.

"Aye, and the Captain does not care if half of you is bandaged. We've a rebellion to fight and we need every man."

"What word do you have?"

"Most of the clans have been defeated so you picked a fine time to take your nap, you did. But The O'Donnell is still on the run and Mulmory MacSweeney has taken a large contingent to Tory Island. And I've been sent to take you there."

50

How long had it been since his first night aboard a ship? Wills wondered. He remembered it well, he did; he remembered the sway of the vessel in the mercurial Irish Sea had forced him to the deck where he'd emptied his stomach over the side. It was the very same night he'd first met Fergus and they had both been assigned to the menial tasks of swabbing the decks. But he remembered it now as though it had happened to someone else and he only recalled the telling of it, for much had happened since that first fateful night that had taken him from Wigtownshire.

Now as the ship took the swell of the Atlantic Ocean, he felt his legs move with the rock of the vessel as though they were one and the same. The salt air slapped his face and as he licked the salt from his lips, he realized this was where he wanted to be. The water spoke to him now as it had never spoken to him before, cajoling him, teasing him, begging him to remain.

They joined a fleet of ships some nine miles off the coast of Ireland, completely surrounding the tiny island the Irish called Toraigh and the English referred to as Tory Island. And it was tiny indeed; at only three miles long and about half a mile wide, a castle dominated one end of the rock like a massive home built on too small of an acreage.

"You see that?" Tomas asked, pointing to an even higher structure. "That would be the Tor Mór." Ever the historian, he related the tale of the ancient peoples. "That means The High Tower, but of course you would know that, and it's where the Fomorian King Balor, known as the one with the evil eye, imprisoned Ethniu, his own beautiful daughter."

"And why on earth would he do that?" Wills asked.

"An oracle had prophesied that King Balor's own grandson would kill him and when his daughter married and became pregnant, he imprisoned her here. She gave birth to three sons, or so it's said, and he ordered them drowned at birth. But one survived, he did, and he grew to manhood and indeed, he killed King Balor."

The ship slowed as they approached the others; they sat nearly beside one another, forming a complete ring around the island except for the occasional gap. As they turned to make their way to the far side, Wills supposed their ship and others behind them had been ordered there to complete the circle and ensure that none of the rebels escaped the island.

"I have never heard of the Fomorians," Wills said.

"Haven't you though? Oh, they were a supernatural race, they were. Giants, I believe, and far more powerful than mortal man."

"Ah, so it's a myth then."

"I'll be begging your pardon," Tomas said with a huff. "I'll have you know it certainly is not a myth and it truly did occur. And there's the High Tower to prove it."

Wills glanced at his friend. He had pursed his lips and was staring at the tower. "And what is that over there?" he asked, pointing to another structure.

"Oh, that would be the monastery. You have heard of Colmcille—Saint Columba?"

"You've told me about him before, have you not? Didn't he begin the monastery at Derry as well?"

"I have and he did. And he founded the monastery here in addition to all the others and the monks lived here in peace until 1595."

"What happened then?"

Tomas' voice grew soft. "Then the English came. They destroyed the monastery—what you see there are only ruins."

"Why did they do that?"

He shrugged. "They wanted to destroy all that was Irish."

He allowed that to sink in for a bit. "And the castle is a MacSweeney's?"

"No. I just told you it belonged to the Fomorians. But Mulmory MacSweeney and Shane MacManus O'Donnell are there now; aye, and the last holdouts of the rebel forces. You see that ship over there? That belongs to Sir Henry Folliott, the Governor of Ballyshannon. He was the first to discover their presence and now all the Crown forces that can be spared are here to lend assistance."

Wills glanced at his leg. His breeches were pulled up to his thigh on that leg and the bandage still stretched the length of it, though he was able to move about with a bit more dexterity than he could only a few days before. A walking stick given to him by a kind Irish woman completed his pursuit of independence. "And what are we to do?"

"We're to sit," Fergus said as he came alongside the two men. "And make certain none of the rebels make it past this point. And see there?" He pointed to another ship. "That would be Captain Stewart himself and when we pull alongside, he wants a word with you, he does."

+⇌⇌+

"William Neely," Captain Stewart said by way of introduction as he entered the captain's quarters.

Wills was surprised to discover several men seated around a small table. "Sir," he said simply. He was acutely aware of his bandages, particularly the one on his leg and foot that resulted in a slight limp.

"You remember Colonel Wingfield," the captain was saying as the colonel rose to shake his hand. "And Captain Winkel. And have you yet met Sir Henry Folliott?"

"Colonel, Captain," Wills said in turn. "Pleasure meeting you, Sir Folliott."

"Likewise."

"Sir Folliott has been commissioned to develop a village next to Ballyshannon Castle," Captain Stewart continued.

"Ah," Folliott said, "and it has been five years since I began and I'm afraid I have little to show for it thus far. Things tend to move more slowly here."

The men around the table chuckled. "And it does not help that you've been pulled away to help squash a rebellion, does it now?" Winkel said.

"Have a seat there, Wills," Stewart said, pulling up a chair.

He had barely seated himself before Wingfield spoke. "I wanted to have a word with you myself," he said. "I was in a position to witness your bravery on the field at Kilmacrenan."

"Thank you, sir, but I was no braver than any other man."

"Ah, but I beg to differ," Stewart said. "I saw your actions as well. As we were in full retreat, you remained in the center of the fighting. Do you happen to know how many men you fought that day?"

"No, sir. I was a bit busy to count."

The men chuckled again as Wingfield said, "I lost count as well, William. You were quite impressive."

"I spotted that the day we met. You remember that day, Wills?" Stewart said.

"Aye, sir," Wills said. Though it seemed a lifetime ago, he added, "I remember it well."

"Quite the expert with the sword."

"It is my preferred weapon."

"And where did you learn how to wield an axe as you do?" Winkel asked, leaning forward.

"I am not certain, sir. Instinct, I suppose."

"Instinct." Colonel Wingfield cocked his head. "I think it's a bit more than that, sir."

"I have asked you here," Stewart said, "to tell you that I have recommended that King James grant you a bit of land here in Ireland—once the rebellion is over, of course."

"A bit of land, sir?" Wills blurted the words before he could stop himself. Quickly, he fought to maintain his composure.

"You have a home on my estate and you are always welcome there," Stewart continued. "But you have proven your worth in this rebellion and once it is done, you are released from your commitment to me— though, should another situation arise, The Crown must be able to count on your assistance."

"Of course, sir."

"It is not much land," Wingfield said, "but you can select where you want it to be from the O'Doherty,

O'Donnell or MacSweeney territories—provided, of course, it has not been previously granted to another."

"I don't require much," Wills said. "Just a shelter for my head on a stormy night."

Stewart chuckled. "It will be a bit more than that, Wills. We have asked The Crown to grant you a thousand acres."

"A thousand acres?"

"As I said, it is not much…"

The rest of the words were lost as Wills' mind raced. *A thousand acres* beat a refrain in his head. Now he knew beyond a shadow of a doubt that the lad from Wigtownshire was gone forever, lost in a different life, a different place and time. He realized that a silence had descended on the group and looking up suddenly, he managed to say, "Thank you, sir."

"So," Stewart said, "that is all, Wills."

Realizing he was being dismissed, he came to his feet.

"Are you quite alright?" Winkel asked as he watched his struggle to put weight on his injured leg.

"Aye, sir. 'Tis nothing. Though I doubt," he added, "that I can fight so many just now."

"With any luck at'al, you won't have to," Folliott said. "Your ship carries with it provisions for the others. Our task is to remain in place around Tory Island until we have starved its inhabitants."

"A siege," Wills said.

"Precisely," Stewart said, walking with him to the doorway. "Good day."

Wills nodded again to the others. "Good day. And thank you again, sir." He made his way onto the main deck where Fergus waited for him. As he rejoined his friend, he paused long enough to gaze once more on Tory Island. How many men were contained there on the island, he did not know, nor did he know how many provisions they might have. His eyes wandered to the parapet where several men watched them, their harkbus silent, their shot out of range of the ships. He wondered what they must be discussing at a moment like this as they looked at the circle of English ships surrounding them. He wondered if any of them had seen Cahir O'Doherty as he was felled on the battlefield, or if any had been with Phelim MacDavitt during his final stand.

51

The days turned to weeks. Rotations were scheduled in which one ship left to obtain food and drink from nearby Donegal, affording its men a raucous night before returning the next day to make its rounds disbursing the provisions to the others. Then a few days later, the next ship would leave and so on until all had their turn and a second round was well underway. All the while, the island remained silent. Men still stood upon the parapet and now with the aid of Fergus' found scope, Wills could determine that they served in shifts. But where once a full squad walked the length of the castle parapets, only half that many could be spotted now and where once they walked as a soldier on high alert, they were most often found casually leaning into the embrasures.

Though each ship was outfitted with cannons, none were used; Wills supposed it was determined to be a waste of good shot, as the outcome was inevitable even without it.

An interesting schedule was enacted regarding the cooking of food to ensure that the aroma was constant, day and night. For Wills' ship, they ate at the break of dawn and again in mid-afternoon but for others, it was late morning and again late evening. It meant that at any given time, one could see the smoke from the cooking fires arising from the ship's uppermost deck— not the usual place to cook, to be sure, but one that could catch the ever-present winds, thereby spreading the scent. As they sat on deck and ate their food and drank their ale in the full presence of the men at the parapets, Wills wondered if they, too, could smell the enticing aromas and decided that of course they could and it was a brilliant psychological tactic to spread the scent to starving men.

In the beginning, a high flag flew above Colonel Wingfield's ship, that of the new Union Jack. But as the weeks turned to a month, they began to rotate the flag around the circle. And then Wingfield left altogether, presumably to return to Ulster to finish overseeing the work there.

News traveled with each ship back from port, bringing with it word that the rebellion had been completely put down save for the men on Tory Island. As they received these tidbits, they shouted the news from ship to ship; not because they had to but because it brought more men to the castle embrasures, men who leaned into the wind to catch the news themselves.

"Aye, and there it goes," Fergus said as the Union Jack was raised on their own ship. It would mean for the next twenty-four hours, they would serve as the focal point for the men on the island, though it had become nothing more than listening to it flap in the wind before it was passed on to the next.

"Aye," Wills said, though his attention was focused on the ship returning from Donegal. It, too, flew the flag but it would be lowered in deference to the command ship once it drew nearer.

He walked to starboard where the other would come alongside to report the latest. And, aye, he walked now and it felt good to be rid of the bandages and be afforded full breeches and a boot, though the scar along his leg would take months to heal if ever it did. His shoulder, too, was regaining its mobility, the bandages removed from his arm to reveal yet another nasty gash.

The men appeared more excited than usual as they docked alongside. Stewart himself came aboard, his eyes sparkling. He had barely climbed aboard Wills' ship before he was saying, "He's been captured, Wills."

It took him a moment to determine who it was the captain spoke of. "Niall Garbh O'Donnell?" he said at last.

"Aye, Niall Garbh O'Donnell himself and his son, too."

"Alive?"

"Alive and on their way to London as we speak."

Wills turned to Fergus. "Spread the word," he said.

"Gladly I will." Fergus had barely made it to the stern before the word was traveling like wildfire. It seemed as if the men's voices were louder than usual and with each retelling, whoops and hollers went up until the entire circle was cheering.

"Lend me your scope," Wills said as his friend returned.

"You do not have a scope?" Stewart asked.

A bit embarrassed, Wills said simply, "No, sir." Then he turned his attention to the men along the parapet.

"You shall have one by the end of this day," Stewart declared. "Every man with a ship under him should have his own scope."

He did not respond but continued watching the men. He hadn't really contemplated the fact that he was considered the ship's captain, though he commanded it on the short journey to Donegal and back. He had been there twice thus far and neither time could he manage the courage to call on Rhiannon's family and visit her grave. She still came to him every night without fail as he drifted off to sleep in his hammock, and perhaps, he thought, if he did not actually see that mound of dirt and the tombstone above it, she would remain alive in his mind, forever young and beautiful.

"Keep the noise up," Wills said. Immediately, he heard his command repeated from ship to ship. More men joined those atop the parapet and still more came as the celebration continued. "What must they be thinking?" he mused more to himself than to any of the men surrounding him. He finally lowered the scope and handed it back to Fergus. What must they be thinking?

+⸺⸺+

It was midafternoon when a rowboat left Tory Island. One man carried it out of the rampart in full view of the ships. It was the first time they had seen movement outside the stockade and a silence fell on the ships as men positioned themselves along the decks to watch.

As the boat was placed into the water in front of Wills' ship, he watched the parapets once more before moving back to the lone man. Everything grew deadly silent as he approached.

"Bring him aboard," Wills ordered. He watched as men dropped netting over the side of the ship. One man scurried down to secure the rowboat as their visitor climbed up the netting. He noticed that Stewart, still at anchor in the ship next to his, was preparing to board as well.

"Bring him to the cabin," Wills instructed Fergus and Tomas. As his friends moved out to offer a somber greeting, they ushered him toward the cabin. He noticed the man's clothing was so loose he was having some difficulty keeping his breeches from falling and as he moved past the cooking fire, he almost appeared as if he would bolt directly for it.

When Stewart joined him, they made their way into the cabin where they found the man seated at the table, Fergus and Tomas guarding the door. "Back to work," Wills said to the others gawking. As they cleared out, only Fergus, Tomas, Stewart, Archie and Wills were left in the room with the man.

"I am Captain William Stewart," Stewart said.

"William Neely," Wills added.

"James MacDowell," the man answered. With a trembling hand, he held up a note.

Stewart stepped forward to receive it. He read it silently and then handed it to Wills, who read it through once and then, unable to fathom its contents, read it again. When he was through, he locked eyes with Stewart. Then they both looked at James MacDowell.

"Have you read this note?" Wills asked him.

"I was there when The MacSweeney wrote it."

"That would be Sir Mulmory MacSweeney?"

The man averted his eyes. "Aye."

"Is this true?" Stewart asked. "Has MacSweeney begun killing his own men?"

The man's Adam's apple bobbed as he swallowed hard. "Aye, sir. He is requesting a Pelham's Pardon, sir."

Wills glanced at Stewart. "I am not familiar with this Pelham's Pardon."

"Sir William Pelham," Stewart answered. "Ruthless man; he conquered much of Ireland in the mid fifteen hundreds and became Lord Justice of Ireland. A Pelham's Pardon is the refusal to grant any Irish rebel surrender unless he had killed another rebel of equal or higher rank."

A chorus of voices sounded on the deck and Wills stepped to the portal to peer toward the island. As he watched, three heads were raised on pikes set along the keep's pinnacle. He turned back to MacDowell. "Have you seen this?" he asked, stepping away from the window so the man could view the island.

MacDowell remained seated, however, and did not look toward the portal. "I have seen them already," he answered.

Wills looked at Stewart. Their eyes met for the briefest of time before Stewart said, "How many men are on the island?"

"I do not know, sir." He kept his eyes downcast.

"You *do* know," Wills said, stepping forward.

"I do not know, sir," he repeated. His face took on a blank expression. His eyes were sunken, his lips cracked and his shoulders drooped.

"He will have to do better than that," Stewart said.

"Sir?" MacDowell asked.

"He must ensure that every man there will surrender their arms."

"I don't know—"

"That is my answer. You will take that to him." Stewart motioned for Fergus and Tomas, who came to either side of the man, assisting him to his feet.

As they walked him out of the cabin, Wills followed. MacDowell hesitated just outside, his nose held high as he breathed in deeply. "May I have but a morsel?" he asked.

Stewart had followed them onto the deck as well. "No," he said. "You may not."

Wills glanced at him, catching his eye briefly before turning away.

"Then a swallow of ale," MacDowell begged.

"Take him to his boat," Stewart ordered.

"Please! Please!" he begged as he was led back to the netting.

As he was forced to scramble down to his boat and depart for the island, Wills noticed that he rowed more reluctantly than he had on the voyage over. He hadn't noticed the captain at his elbow until Stewart spoke.

"If we allowed him to eat or drink, we would have a steady stream of rebels bringing news of any kind just for a morsel or two," Stewart said.

"Perhaps that would work," Wills said. "We could put each one in chains until all had surrendered."

"Nice try," Stewart said as he returned to his own ship. "But no."

⊹⟫⟪⊹

Two more weeks passed before another boat rowed out and by this time the pinnacle had a long row of heads upon it. It had become a pastime to watch the sea birds dive upon them, picking the flesh and carrying off the hair, presumably to use for nest building. Like the first boat, a lone man rowed out and as it drew near, Wills peered down from the upper deck to spot a gunny sack in a growing pool of blood in the bottom of the rowboat. This time it came to Henry Folliott's ship, which had the distinction of flying the high Union Jack and this time, Wills was forced to wait with the others as the news was shouted from stern to bow until the entire circle received the perverse news. Sickened, Wills could do nothing but wait as the lone man returned to the island and then a short time later a line of men walked out slowly, placing their harkbus and swords in a heap in full view of the ships.

"Doesn't seem right, does it?" Fergus asked as he came alongside Wills.

He shook his head. "I suppose God will be the judge of that."

Tomas rested his forearms on the railing and watched as rowboats were brought out and the men boarded them four to a boat. "God and the King of England," he said. "You know," he added thoughtfully, "I know many of those men. I knew Mulmory MacSweeney as well. And I know he had to have been a mighty desperate man indeed to have murdered so many of his own men."

"Aye," Fergus said. "But he came to a fitting end, didn't he now?"

The vision of the survivors hacking their own chief to death loomed large in Wills' mind as he watched the men row out, one boat to each ship. "Only twenty-four?" he asked.

"Word has it that once MacSweeney was dead, the survivors turned on each other," Tomas said in a low voice. "I suppose this is all that's left."

"So that's what it's all come to?" Wills mused. "The O'Doherty dead and his wife on trial; Phelim and Niall Garbh in irons. The MacSweeney killed by his own clansmen."

"I suppose so," Fergus said, watching one boat as it came alongside their ship. As the men tossed netting over the side to assist the four men into the ship and into custody, he added, "So this sad group of skeletons are all that's left of O'Doherty's Rebellion."

52

Two Years Later

Wills stepped onto the front stoop and breathed in the morning air as he finished his cup of tea. Behind him the wood crackled and popped in the fireplace and as the smoke from the chimney met the morning mists, the aroma of burning wood intensified. It brought back memories, as it so often did, but Derry was on her way to becoming completely rebuilt though he supposed it would take a good long while. London was footing the bill this time around and there was talk of renaming the village Londonderry and surrounding it with a high stone wall and perhaps a moat.

A new governor had arrived as well and perhaps what was most surprising was the official inquiry into O'Doherty's Rebellion wherein London arrived at the determination that George Paulet's own crass behavior had led to the burning of Derry and the subsequent insurrection. Not that it had helped the Irish cause, Wills thought as he gazed out over the land—his land—of a thousand acres. No; what was originally begun as a resettlement of Scottish and English Protestants that would live side-by-side with the Irish Catholics had been inexorably changed. Now the official Plantation movement was underway bringing in thousands not to live beside the Irish but to supplant them.

He heard the hammers pounding and his attention was diverted to his new home. Oh, and the one behind him was fair enough, as it had three rooms and was quite cozy with its stone walls and thatched roof, but this new one was to be two stories tall with a proper slate roof. John Dowell led the building himself and it was him now atop the tallest wood post as they finished the framing. Aye, and it was *that* John Dowell of Tory Island that dropped the first syllable from his surname to appear more English and it would be the very same that would inhabit this cottage once the new home was finished.

The goal had been for each settler to move at least twenty-four more to every thousand acres he had been granted and transfer the Irish someplace else — where wasn't exactly determined as it was to be off the island completely. But that turned out to be logistically impossible and Wills was content with hiring the Irish for he'd never been one to judge a man by his birth or his religion or, for that matter, his clan.

The same could not be said of Sir Arthur Chichester, who had inherited 170,000 of nearly 219,000 acres of the Inishowen Peninsula, displacing countless members of the O'Doherty clan. He made no bones about it; he did not trust any man with *Mac*, *Mc* or *O* before his name and seemingly overnight half the population had changed their surnames.

For Wills, the location of his land had been a simple choice and though it was at the base of Chichester's estate, it had been granted nonetheless. As he stood on the stoop, he could see Burt Castle rising still through the mists of morning. No longer inhabited by an O'Doherty but by Arthur Chichester himself when he visited his lands from Dublin, and it was doubtful that an Irishman would ever again occupy it. It was said that on the anniversary of Derry's burning, ghosts appeared along the parapet and again on the anniversary of the counterattack, and many an Englishman left the castle in the depths of night, claiming to have been accosted by a ghostly presence nearly seven foot tall.

Only a short ride away from both Burt Castle and the cottage where Wills stood was Derry, the rebuilding causing it to look like an entirely new village and not at all like the one where he had landed on his first trip to Ireland. He took a sip of his tea and noted with pleasure that as the fluffy clouds scurried to the east, he could see straight through to the River Foyle.

He heard a woman's voice calling his name and he stepped off the stoop to watch his sister Beth as she almost danced across the meadow with her basket. He smiled and shook his head. Oh, Beth, he thought. She would return to the cottage with a basket filled with wildflowers and before long the tiny cottage would smell more like the outdoors than the outdoors itself and in another day or two as they began to wilt, she would march off for more. And you know, he wouldn't have it any other way.

After the rebellion, he had purchased the ship he'd been on at Tory Island and officially became its master and commander and now bore the title of Captain William Neely. He'd had his money from the wool he'd sold and Fergus and Tomas had made up the rest, becoming minor owners—which he had to remind them of on more than one occasion when they thought they were the sea captain and not himself. Oh, but truly there was no doubt and better friends he could find nowhere else.

They still had the sheep, combined their herds in fact for he had little interest in them these days. Both men had built cottages on the Neely land, choosing the parcels they preferred and both were but a short distance across the meadow and through the woods— which had been thinned out considerably when all of Ulster had burned. Even Penarddun O'Donnell's cottage was burned to the ground and in the two years since, what had remained of her eyesight had left her completely, though her mind and memory was as sharp as ever. No doubt her Irish neighbors would have cared for her, for that was the Irish way of it, but he'd convinced her to move onto Neely land where she would be safer. She lived now in a cottage built to resemble the one she'd lost to make it easier for her to navigate in her blindness; it was set at the edge of the woods where she preferred the shadows and the comfort of the wildlife there. When she sat on her stoop as she was doing now, she could hear the babble of a creek winding past.

And as for himself, he had turned his sights to the sea and on his first journey back to Wigtownshire he had surprised his family by not only reappearing in their lives but coming with a ship and a crew. He still remembered with pleasure and pride the astonished expressions on each of their faces.

Beth had returned with him on that very trip; she had been his first Plantation settler, he liked to say. He had lost count of how many he sailed here now, though they were duly noted in his captain's logs. He picked them up at various ports in Scotland and Wales and at a tiny inlet called Lyver Pool in England. He brought them all to the port in Derry, which now had a row of hostels and pubs along its riverfront. They had gone off in all directions to find their new place in the world; most he would never see again while a few he would cross paths with quite regularly.

Phelim MacDavitt, to the surprise of no one, had been found guilty of treason and rebellion and had been put to death, despite the prior ruling that Paulet had instigated the uprising himself. Afterward, his head was placed on a pike and erected above Dublin Castle, right beside Cahir O'Doherty. They had remained there for a bit as a warning to others who dared incite rebellion but after a while they began to disintegrate and eventually Phelim's fell off and rolled away, God only knew where, and a local church petitioned Lord Chichester for the return of Cahir's head. It was said the church placed it in a tiny alcove near the entrance where churchgoers saw it on their way to and from worship services; and why it was there and what message could have been intended, Wills could not begin to imagine.

Niall Garbh O'Donnell and his son Neachtain were sentenced to remain in the Tower of London until their natural deaths and sometimes Wills thought that was a punishment worse than death, particularly for the younger man. Despite the years that had passed, he still found himself awakening as though he was still at Fort Stewart and all the chieftains were yet alive. He could still see The O'Donnell in his mind's eye riding tall atop his stallion, proudly surveying the land as if it was still his and to be imprisoned in a room for the rest of his life seemed a fate even worse than caging a wild animal.

Of course, the Spaniards had never come to Ireland's aid and before the end of the year, word traveled back regarding Rory O'Donnell, one of the three earls that had fled Ireland the year before the rebellion. As it turned out, he had not been in Spain at'al but Rome. He had contracted an illness common in the marshlands outside the city, had died and was buried in the Franciscan Church of San Peitro in Montorio, Rome.

Even Henry Hart and his wife Frances were arrested and tried for treason but though many suspected they were complicit in the taking of Culmore Fort, in the end there had been insufficient evidence to convict them as Frances had argued successfully that she had been in fear for her life, her husband's and her young son's. Sir Henry's reputation had been severely damaged, however, and Wills didn't believe he would ever again command a fort such as Culmore. Ironically, despite the scandal, Hart had chosen to remain in Ireland and had even been granted land in the very heart of O'Donnell territory—so close he could look out his windows onto the battlefield at Kilmacrenan.

Wills had finally journeyed to Donegal and to the Ó Dálaigh estate, where he had been welcomed with more fanfare and courtesy than he believed he was entitled. Lady Ó Dálaigh had insisted he remain for tea and biscuits and it being a particularly warm and sunny day, they had taken the refreshments into the gardens and midway through he had asked to see Rhiannon's gravesite. Lord and Lady Ó Dálaigh and Ginny had accompanied him but as he ran his fingers along the stone and his lips had moved in a silent prayer, they had discreetly left him alone with her. He'd spoken to her for quite a while and he could have sworn she had placed her palm upon his shoulder and whispered in his ear.

Later, he would try to convince himself 'twas naught but the wind that blew in from Donegal Bay licking at his flesh and teasing his ear but he knew in his heart that it had been Rhiannon. And he felt her still each night as he closed his eyes, her leg curling over his, her body snuggling against his side and there had been many a morn when he did not wish to awaken for fear of breaking the spell. He even slept under the plaid that had graced her shoulders last, for her parents had kept both the plaid and the crest in Rhiannon's childhood trunk and presented them to him the day he'd come calling. When she'd been found outside of Baile na nGalloglach, she had been grasping both.

So much would have been different had Cahir never attacked Derry, for the day he attacked he was to receive word that he had been approved in the employ of the Prince of Wales and surely with such a position he might have petitioned for the removal of Paulet as Governor of Derry. Certainly, his lands would have been saved and many lives spared. There was no word from Mary Preston O'Doherty; some rumors had her imprisoned in a room in her father's home and she had created quite a stir when she testified that Niall Garbh O'Donnell himself had encouraged Cahir to rebel. Despite her role in O'Doherty's Rebellion, she was granted a pension of £40 per year.

Beth drew closer and he set his cup on the stoop behind him and strolled out to meet her. It was good to have a woman about, even if it was his sister. Beth was convinced he would meet another someday and love her just as much or more than he had Rhiannon. Sometimes he was doubtful of that and other times as he sailed the seas and thought of the ports he would visit, he hoped... he hoped. As he approached Beth, her brilliant smile seemed to carry across the meadow and she was talking even before he could hear the words, and you know, he wouldn't have it any other way.

Next in the Checkmate Series

The land granted to William Neely would come at a high price for in the years following O'Doherty's Rebellion, two Irish societies would emerge. The first would become intertwined with the English and Scottish settlers, adopting their customs, their language and religion.the second, far larger, particularly in Ulster, would give rise to resentment against the immigrants and the English Crown.

The weather became increasingly colder, freezing rivers that were once free-flowing; the winters were longer and the growing season far shorter, resulting in crop failures. Interest rates reached a rate of thirty percent as the Irish economy spiraled downward.

Despite the harsh conditions, Wills would learn to love again. Yet as his new wife bears him children to fill their new home, they were spiraling toward a conflict that would prove far more dangerous and deadly than O'Doherty's Rebellion. Now the owner of a fleet of ships, he would unwittingly add to the mounting animosity against him by delivering more and more English and Scottish settlers to Derry.

Hugh Oge MacMahon, Conor Maguire, Phelim O'Neill, Rory O'Moore and others would rise as leaders in the Irish communities, planning a bloody rebellion that will threaten Wills' future and his very survival as well as his wife and their children. As one quarter of the settlers he delivered to Ulster are massacred, he faces an uncertain future as his family, his land and his livelihood hang in the balance.

A Note from the Author

When I set out to write this book and the *Checkmate* series, my goal was simply to bring history alive through the eyes of my ancestors. Since the time I was a young girl sitting at my father's knee, I was told of our family's exploits and adventures dating back centuries. As an adult, I found scores of genealogy records listing names, dates of births, marriages and deaths and where those names fit into neat charts. But all our ancestors are so much more than a list of names and dates because their stories tell the history of our world and the evolution of its peoples.

As I delved deeper into the lives of William Neely and Sir William Stewart of Wigtownshire, I realized I could not tell their stories without the backdrop of O'Doherty's Rebellion. This sent me on a journey to find out as much as was possible about each of the major characters in this book: Sir Cahir O'Doherty, Niall Garbh O'Donnell, Sir Henry Docwra, Sir Henry Hart, Phelim MacDavitt, Sir George Paulet, Sir Arthur Chichester and many others. In most instances, I used paintings of the characters for their physical descriptions and when no paintings existed, I sought out their descendants to use their likenesses or relied on history's descriptions. I used character traits compiled from extensive research and for those I have portrayed as less than noble, I have only History to blame. Though it is true that the victor writes the history, I attempted to tell this story from both sides of the conflict.

I also attempted at every turn to remain faithful to historical facts and records, including the events leading up to O'Doherty's Rebellion as well as the Rebellion itself from the burning of Derry to the surrender at Tory Island and its aftermath. However, there are no diaries or journals kept by any of these men to my knowledge so I tried to place myself in their shoes in order to tell this story not as a listing of dates and events but rather from the perspective of human beings, most of whom were trying their best with what they had.

With regard to William Neely of Wigtownshire, I found scant information and once I discovered his relationship to Sir William Stewart, I followed that trail. If you are a Neely descendant, I would enjoy hearing from you, particularly if you have information regarding the Neely family in Ireland. Future books in this series will include William's son who was granted land at Ballygawley, County Tyrone and his descendants.

This is actually the third book I have written about the Neely family. *River Passage* covers Mary Neely and her family's journey with John Donelson at the height of the Chickamauga Indian Wars to help found Fort Nashborough (now Nashville, TN). *Songbirds are Free* is the story of Mary Neely's capture by Shawnee warriors at Fort Nashborough, her three years of captivity, her eventual escape and journey home. In all these books, I have attempted to remain faithful to historical records but I have taken creative license with regard to their conversations, their thoughts and their emotions as no records exist of these. I hope the result has been a richer experience for the reader and an appreciation of what our ancestors have endured.

p.m.terrell

www.pmterrell.com

Appendix A – People

Chichester, Sir Arthur (1563-1625), born in May 1563 in North Devon, England; married Lettice Perrot in 1606; he had one son, Arthur, who died when he was only one month old. He died from pleurisy in 1625 in London at the age of 62 but was buried at Carrickfergus, Ireland. He had been instrumental in the founding and development of Belfast.

Docwra, Sir Henry (1564-1631), born at Chamberhouse Castle, Crookham; married Anne Vaughan; had five children (Theodore, Henry, Anne, Frances and Elizabeth); died on April 18, 1631 in Dublin at the age of 67. He was nearly impoverished when he died, despite the fact that he had been granted land at Ranelagh and Donnybrook.

Folliott, Sir Henry (1568-1622), born in 1568 in Worcestershire, England; married Anne Strode; fathered seven children (Thomas, Michael, Arthur, Charles, Anne, Frances and Elizabeth); he acquired more than 3,000 acres in County Donegal, including several salmon fisheries. His residence was Wardtown Castle, Ballymacaward, County Donegal. Died in 1622 in County Donegal at the age of 54.

Hart, Sir Henry (1569-1637), born 1569 in Risby, County Suffolk, England; married Frances Bosvile; fathered 10 children (Henry, Eustace, George, Richard, John, Thomas, Merrick, Anne, Mary, Frances); died September 6, 1637 at the age of 68 and buried at Londonderry/Derry.

MacDavitt, Phelim Reagh (1567?-1608), born around 1567 in County Donegal; he was tried and hanged at Lifford, County Donegal, in 1608. He was decapitated and his head displayed on a pike above Dublin Castle until it fell off in a strong wind. He was also quartered and there is no record of any burial site. Records of any marriage or children have been lost to history.

Neely, William (1590-1664), born in Wigtownshire, Scotland in 1590; married Margaret McKill in 1620; fathered 8 children (William, John, Walter, Robert, Rory, Matthew, Margaret and James); died in 1664 at the age of 74 on his land at the base of the Inishowen Peninsula, Donegal, Ireland.

O'Doherty, Cahir (1587-1608), born on the Inishowen Peninsula, 1587; ascended to become the last Gaelic Irish King in Ireland in 1601; died on July 5, 1608 at the age of 21 at Kilmacrenan, Ireland. He was quartered and beheaded. His head was placed on a pike at Dublin Castle and later removed to a niche at St. Adouan Church, where it remained until 1954 when it rolled away in a strong wind. The O'Doherty (Ó Dochartaigh) Clann Association was formed in the 1980s and operated from Inch Island through 1999 and from Duncrana from 1999 to 2007. It is now based in Michigan. Reunions are hosted every five years (http://odochartaigh.org/).

O'Doherty, Mary Preston, daughter of the 4th Viscount Gormanston; she had one daughter (name unknown). Her dates of birth and death are unknown and I could find nothing more about her life after O'Doherty's Rebellion.

O'Donnell, Niall Garbh (1569-1626), born in 1569 in Tyrconnell; married his cousin Nuala (sister of Hugh Roe O'Donnell and Rory O'Donnell); one daughter, Grania and one, son, Neachtain. His wife left him when he switched sides from the Irish to the English and fled to Spain with their daughter during The Flight of the Earls. Found guilty of treason and for his participation in O'Doherty's Rebellion, he and his son Neachtain were imprisoned in the Tower of London until their deaths. He died in 1626 at the age of 57.

St Lawrence, Christopher, 10th Baron Howth (1568-1619), born 1568 near Meath and grew up at Howth Castle near Dublin; married in 1595 to Elizabeth Wentworth but separated in 1605, for which he was ordered to pay £100 annually in alimony; fathered three children (Nicholas St Lawrence, 11th Baron Howth, Thomas and Margaret); died on October 24, 1619 but was not buried until January 1620.

Stewart, Sir William (1582-1646), born in Wigtownshire, Scotland; married Frances Newcomen in 1610 in Ireland; fathered six children (William, Robert, Catherine, John, Alexander and Thomas) and died in 1646 at the age of 64 in Newtown-Stewart, County Tyrone, Ireland (now Northern Ireland).

Trendor, John was an infantry soldier during O'Doherty's Rebellion and was the soldier credited with killing Cahir O'Doherty. He collected five hundred pound sterling in Dublin after presenting the head to Sir Arthur Chichester.

Wingfield, Sir Richard, 1st Viscount Powerscourt, (1550-1634), born in 1550 in England (possibly

Portsmouth); married Frances Rugge; fathered two daughters (Frances and Anne); died on September 9, 1646 at the age of 64.

Appendix B – Places

Baile na nGalloglach was a Gaelic name. It meant, quite literally, the village of the mercenary warriors—the Gallowglass, that race of men that were part Scottish Highlander and part Norseman. Today it is better known as Milford.

Burt Castle was built during the 16th century on the Inishowen Peninsula near Culmore Fort and Derry. The castle remains as of this writing but is in ruins. It was once surrounded by a moat but that was filled in by one of the subsequent owners.

Canmoyre Woods was a heavily forested area in the vicinity of Burt Castle and Culmore Fort.

Carrickabraghy Castle was built during the 16th century on the Isle of Doagh and was originally one of the largest and finest castles in Ulster, comprised of seven towers as well as rectangular stone walls and a substantial keep. During the 20th century, an English ship on a training mission off the coast of Ireland used it for firing practice and destroyed all but one circular tower and one small rectangular section. It is located in the northwest corner of the Inishowen Peninsula near the entrance of the Lough Swilly.

Culmore Fort was located on the point of Culmore Bay at the entrance to the River Foyle and just north of Derry. It was originally built around 1555; a tower house remains there today and is owned and maintained by the Irish Society.

Derry is an Anglicized version of Daire or Doire, Gaelic for Oak Grove or Oak Woods. It was renamed Londonderry after it was rebuilt in 1613; however, the Catholic population still refers to it as Derry while the Protestant population calls it Londonderry. It is the second largest city in Northern Ireland and the fourth largest in all of Ireland. The rebuilt walled city (fortified after O'Doherty's Rebellion) is a top tourist attraction on the west bank of the River Foyle, while the more modern expansion is on the east side of the river.

Donegal is more commonly known for the town in western Ireland but it also refers to County Donegal. The original name was Dun na nGall, which meant Fort of the Foreigners, and the town served as the center of government for the powerful O'Donnell Clan until O'Doherty's Rebellion. Donegal Castle, one of the O'Donnell's dwellings, exists today as well as Donegal Abby, which dates to the 15th century. County Donegal is in the Ulster province but when the island was divided between the Republic of Ireland and Northern Ireland, County Donegal remained with the Republic. It is the largest county in Ulster and the fourth largest in Ireland.

Drongawn Lough is a body of water at the base of the Lough Swilly, sandwiched between the Inishowen Peninsula to the east, the old O'Donnell territories to the west and Inch Island to the north.

Fort Stewart was named for Sir William Stewart. It is situated along the western coast of Drongawn Lough in County Donegal, southwest from Inch Island. Its construction was completed in 1611.

Inishowen Peninsula was Anglicized from Inis Eoghain, which means The Island of Owen. Eoghain was Eoghain mac Neill, a son of Niall of the Nine Hostages, a High King of Ireland, who gifted him with the peninsula. Prehistoric monuments, rings and symbols exist throughout. It is the largest peninsula in Ireland, comprising 218,523 acres, of which 170,000 were granted to Sir Arthur Chichester after O'Doherty's Rebellion. Many of O'Doherty's descendants remain on the peninsula. The Inishowen 100 Tourist Route is a popular 100-mile scenic drive around the island that takes in many of its monuments, castles and points of interest. It is considered by many to be the most beautiful region of the island. The largest town, Buncrana, has a population of less than 4,000 (2006 census) and the center of the island consists of a bog, much of which can only be navigated by experts.

Isle of Doagh is a peninsula in the northwest corner of County Donegal just off the coast of the Inishowen Peninsula. It is the location of Carrickabraghy Castle and was strategically positioned to protect the Lough Swilly from sea invasion.

Tory Island (Oilean Thorai in Gaelic, later shortened to Toraigh) is an island nine miles off the western coast of Ireland's County Donegal. The main language on the island is Irish Gaelic; however, most inhabitants (96 at last count) speak English as the island has become a main tourist attraction. According to local legend, the island was originally founded by the Fomorians, a giant race of people. In the 6th century, Colmcille founded a monastery there. Most of the monastery and other buildings were destroyed by the English in 1595 as retaliation against the Irish chieftains. The island elects the King of Tory, who speaks on behalf of the people there and welcomes visitors. The island is a tourist attraction with many prehistoric, historical and

mythological sites of interest. It is only three miles long
and just over half a mile wide.

Wigtownshire, Scotland today does not resemble the
Wigtownshire depicted in this book. In the year 1608,
the region had been so deforested that King James made
it a crime to cut down or prune a tree or burn wood in
a fireplace. It is located in southwest Scotland close to
the English border and is situated on the Irish Sea. Many
of the names in this region are of Norse and Gaelic-
Norse origin. Artifacts have been discovered there dating
to 2300 BC. A massive henge (980 feet in diameter) and
six times the size of Stonehenge has been discovered
here dating to 2500 BC.

BIBIOGRAPHY

A History of Ireland in 250 Episodes by Jonathan Bardon, Published by Gill & Macmillan, Dublin, 2012

Donegal Annual: Journal of the County Donegal Historical Society, 2007

Fadó Fadó: More Tales of Lesser-Known Irish History by Rónán Gearóid Ó Domhnaill, Published by Troubador Publishing Ltd, United Kingdom, 2015

Roots of a Man, Video Documentary, Pat O'Dougherty, Jeff Campagna, 2005

The Clan Territories of Ireland (map), Tyrone Bowes, Ph.D., Galway, Ireland, www.irishorigenes.com

The Family History of Hart of Donegal, various contributors, published 1907, Mitchell Hughes & Clarke, copyright expired

The Scotch Irish A Social History by James G. Leyburn